The Wild West

The Mythical Cowboy and Social Theory

WILL WRIGHT

SAGE Publications
London • Thousand Oaks • New Delhi

SAGE Publications Ltd
6 Bonhill Street
London EC2A 4PU

SAGE Publications Inc
2455 Teller Road
Thousand Oaks, California 91320

SAGE Publications India Pvt Ltd
32, M-Block Market
Greater Kailash - I
New Delhi 110 048

British Library Cataloguing in Publication data

A catalogue record for this book is available from
the British Library

ISBN 0 7619 5232 2
　　0 7619 5233 0 (pbk)

Library of Congress catalog card number 2001131837

Typeset by SIVA Math Setters, Chennai, India
Printed and bound in Great Britain by Athenaeum Press, Gateshead

CONTENTS

ACKNOWLEDGMENTS

As part of a series on cultural icons and social theory, this book was encouraged by George Ritzer, the academic editor of the series, and Chris Rojek, the series editor at Sage Ltd. I am particularly indebted to Chris Rojek, who as a friend, a sociologist, and an editor has given me valuable support and comments. Many friends read various stages of this book and provided careful criticisms: Vine Deloria, Jr, Ian Gomme, Steven Kaplan, Jane Eblen Keller, Boyd Littrell, Carl Pletsch, William Sheidley, Ron Thorn, Alexandra Todd. The book has also benefited from many recurring discussions concerning myth, society, and theory with these and other friends: Stanley Aronowitz, Carrie Baldwin, Carol Clover, Gary Means, Brian O'Brien. Finally, I am most indebted to Dianne Brooks for her insights, intelligence, and endurance. She read and improved many versions, and the support of her and many others helped the following book to take shape.

INTRODUCTION

The Individualist Cowboy

The cowboy myth

A lone cowboy emerges from a vast wilderness. He rides a horse and wears a gun, and he represents freedom and equality. The wilderness is dangerous but beautiful – forests, mountains, deserts, prairies. It offers the hope of a new social order built on an open frontier. This is the famous and familiar image of the American Wild West. This image evokes many familiar characters and events – ranchers, gunfighters, Indians, settlers, sheriffs, wagon trains, cattle drives, mining camps, violence. This Wild West imagery always tells a cultural story, a story that portrays a theory. The story is about building a new society, a new society in America, and this new society rests on the theory of market individualism. Individualism justifies market institutions, particularly American institutions, and Wild West imagery reflects individualism at the level of cultural entertainment, providing popular, painless understanding.

As the cowboy rides the wild frontier, he symbolizes individualist ideas. The Westerns that tell his story comprise a myth of social origin, the myth of the Wild West. As he fights for truth and justice, to save the decent citizens, he endorses individualist values. He fights for a new society, a civil society based on market relations. The cowboy myth explains market relations, the relations of individualism, using cultural imagery. It explains these relations for daily social life, for ordinary inter-actions. In an entertaining way it suggests to people in market society what values they should have, what attitudes bring success, what actions they should take. All social myths explain social relations through dramatic cultural images, and the cowboy myth explains market society as its social myth of origin.

The myth reflects explicit individualist commitments, commitments the theorists articulated and discussed – freedom, equality, rationality, autonomy, opportunity, private property. It also reflects implicit market commitments, commitments equally important to the market but usually tacit in the theory. These implicit commitments include the need for an open frontier, violence as a civil necessity, white male superiority, and an endlessly productive environment. As the cowboy tells us about market society, he uses cultural images, not theoretical concepts. As a result, he often tells us things the theory does not, things the theory only assumes. The cowboy can serve as a cultural guide to the assumptions and concepts of individualism, to what individualist theory asserts as well as to what it hides. As he rides across the wild frontier, he defends the individualist promise, and his myth can be used to illuminate this promise as well as its hidden assumptions.

The Wild West is probably the most popular myth of our time. It is celebrated in movies, television, novels, and advertising, as well as in clothes, furniture, art, music, rodeos, vacations, and games. In advertising, for example, the image of the western wilderness is used to sell many products – cars, cigarettes, brokerages, computers, telephones – by identifying these products with freedom and opportunity. Political candidates in America often try to suggest honesty and integrity by wearing cowboy clothes. Two recent American Presidents, Richard Nixon and Ronald Reagan, have suggested that Westerns are good models for values and behavior, and another, George Bush, has recommended country-western music as an inspirational source of important ideals. Americans often revel in Wild West imagery, from Monument Valley to the Marlboro Man, but cowboy images are also popular in many countries of the world, countries in Europe, Asia, Africa, and South America.

The Wild West images that support individualism derive from American history. America was built on individualist ideas, more than any other country. America, therefore, developed the institutions and culture of individualism in their most complete form. The cowboy myth is specifically American, but America represents a theory, the theory of market society. The cowboy, then, is a market character, a symbol of individualism, not just an American character. As the market has spread around the world, the cowboy has become a global character, expressing the values of individualism. The American Wild West is the home of the cowboy, but the cowboy represents the American *idea*, not just American history. The cowboy rides through a market myth of origin, and the market requires individualism wherever it occurs.

Myths always offer instructive, entertaining models of appropriate social actions, actions that are compatible with dominant institutions. The cowboy myth offers instruction about market institutions, and market institutions are based on the idea of rational individuals. The central assumption of individualism is that individuals are 'naturally' rational. Rational individuals can understand and shape their world with no need for faith or tradition. All societies before the market were based on sacred traditions, traditions supported by faith and religion. In these societies people could only accept and obey traditional social rules, including the rules of class inequality. People in a rational society, however, can criticize their social order using their 'natural' rationality.

Members of a rational society can have rational interests, but members of a religious society can only have sacred duties. While a religious society can never be changed without offending the gods, a rational society can always be changed to serve rational interests.

If individuals are rational, they can live in a *civil* society as opposed to a sacred society. In a civil society, all social relations – all institutions, laws, and government – are based on rational agreements, not on sacred authority. A civil social order can only be arranged by rational citizens to serve their private interests. It cannot be imposed by a dominant class in the name of divine truth. A civil society, then, must be committed to individual equality, in the sense of equal opportunity. All individuals are equally rational, and none would accept a social order that denied them equal opportunity. This vision of civil society legitimated market ideas, the ideas of freedom and equality, the idea of private property. Rational individuals will generate social relations based on market competition, and market competition in turn will generate a civil society.

According to individualist theory, this new civil society must emerge from the realm of Nature. Only in uncorrupted Nature – the original State of Nature, the unspoiled wilderness – are individuals truly equal. Nature must generate a free and equal society, and America was seen by the early individualists as exactly this realm of Nature. America was the State of Nature, an unspoiled wilderness of freedom and equality. America was innocent of European corruption, a corruption that included class structure. Its wilderness would enable a new beginning, changing Europeans into 'natural' individuals. This was the image contained in the theory, and it became the frontier myth. The frontier hero (the market hero) emerged from the wilderness to build a civil society. He symbolized freedom and equality, the end of class privilege, the end of sacred duties. He first appeared in early America as a scout in the eastern forests, knowing the Indians and blazing trails. He became most culturally resonant, however, and most mythically famous, when he changed to the lonesome cowboy wandering the Wild West.

The individual and the market

The cowboy defined the individualist myth, and the myth reflected individualist ideas. These ideas were developed, most importantly, first in England by Thomas Hobbes (1588–1679) and John Locke (1632–1704), then in Scotland by Adam Smith (1723–1790) and in America by Thomas Jefferson (1743–1826). Hobbes influenced Locke, and Locke influenced Smith. Locke influenced both the American and the French Revolutions, and Smith also greatly influenced the creation of American market society. Thomas Jefferson, in particular, was influenced by Locke and Smith when he helped to write the American Constitution and when he was President of the United States. In the England of Hobbes and Locke and the Scotland of Smith many feudal institutions remained. Jefferson in America helped fight those institutions and build the new market institutions, the institutions of individualism.

All these men embraced the idea of the rational individual. More exactly, they all embraced the new idea of a rational, mathematical universe, the new idea of scientific knowledge. If the universe is sacred then it can only be understood by God, and people must accept a sacred social order. If the universe is rational, however, then it can be understood by rational individuals, and those individuals can create a rational social order. This was the social implication of the new idea of science, the implication developed by the early individualists. Hobbes based his social ideas directly on the physics of Galileo Galilei (1564–1642), and Locke and Smith based their social ideas directly on the physics of Isaac Newton (1642–1727). Galileo and Newton proposed a rational universe, a universe that would run by itself just like a rational machine. This is the idea of rational Nature, where Nature (the universe) can be understood rationally and scientifically. If Nature is rational and individuals can understand it, then God, faith, and sacred duties become far less important. If individuals are rational, they can reject the sacred order of feudal ranks and privileges and build a rational order of market individuals, equal, rational individuals. The idea of a rational universe – scientific knowledge – endorsed the ideas of individualism and justified market institutions.

Individualism is based on the idea that everyone is a rational individual. All individuals live in a rational universe and all have private, rational interests. They are all 'naturally' equal because they are 'naturally' rational, so no class distinctions – no sacred privileges – should create social inequality. The ideas of individualism were intended to undermine the legitimacy of the feudal class structure, a structure of aristocrats and peasants. The idea of rational Nature could be used to replace the Christian idea of God, since the idea of Nature implied equal individuals while the idea of God implied class.

In the name of rational Nature, property must be private and government must be rational. If property is private, individuals are *free* of traditional feudal duties, and everyone, not just aristocrats, has a 'natural' right to own property. If government is rational, all rational individuals must be seen as *equal*. Freedom and equality are the basic commitments of market individualist ideas, the social, legitimating commitments. The market must guarantee freedom and equality, as defined by private property, and freedom and equality must support civility – a decent, just society.

These central issues are explicit in the theory, but they all tend to rest on an implicit assumption, the assumption of an open frontier – endless free land. The original individualists assumed an agrarian market, a market of independent landowners. They assumed, in effect, that everyone could own private land and work that land, a market of owner-workers. This was their vision of civil society, a vision that legitimated the market. Their idea of private property was essentially private farms. They lived in the midst of feudal agriculture and did not envision industry. They simply wanted to end class privilege so all individuals could own private land.

The market they endorsed, however, and the institutions they built, soon led to the rise of industry and a market of owners and workers. Industrial production ended agrarian relations and the open frontier soon vanished. Without endless free land, the original idea that everyone could be an owner could no longer make any sense. The market could no longer be imagined as consisting of *owner-workers*. The industrial market had to be recognized as consisting of *owners and workers*, a new kind of class division, a *market* class division. A few individuals – the owners – could monopolize all the property, and everyone else – the workers – would have to work for those owners, just to stay alive. This was not the market the early individualists sought. Indeed, they feared an industrial market as essentially unjust. The market they created, however, soon became industrial, and a new analysis was needed, an analysis of industrial relations. As the market became industrial in the later nineteenth century, this new analysis was provided by the critical social theorists. The most prominent of these theorists, and still quite influential, were Karl Marx (1818–1883), Max Weber (1864–1920), and Emile Durkheim (1858–1917). These theorists, in general, did not see the industrial market as leading to civil society. Rather, they saw it, from different theoretical perspectives, as leading to class oppression.

The need for an open frontier is always tacit in individualist theory but always clear in the cowboy myth. The images of the myth always distinguish between honest, decent westerners and greedy, selfish easterners. The frontier West is always seen as potentially civil and just, while the urban East is always seen as irredeemably corrupt. The villains in the West want to monopolize all the property, preventing a civil market of equal owner-workers. But these villains, usually from the East, can be defeated in the West by strong, honorable individualists – the cowboy hero – because of the open frontier. The cowboy emerges from the wilderness, so he is closest to Nature, the most free and equal. The myth generally shows what the individualists argue: the market can only be civil on an open frontier. It also shows what the social theorists argue: an urban, industrial market will tend to be oppressive because of class monopolies.

The myth also makes explicit other social issues that the theory always hides. The myth, for example, but not the theory, always celebrates violence as a necessity of individual freedom. It also celebrates, as the theory only assumes, social inequality for women and non-whites. The theory never addresses environmental concerns, but it assumes constant market expansion. The myth, however, makes it clear that the market can only be civil if the wilderness is endless, which means an infinite environment. In all these ways the myth exposes assumptions that the theory obscures, assumptions about violence, sex, race, and the environment. As the myth reflects the theory, it also reveals some hidden aspects of the theory, and these hidden aspects suggest that market individualism was never exactly what it seemed either in theory or in practice.

The myth of the frontier

The image of the frontier hero took shape in America late in the eighteenth century through the popular stories of Daniel Boone. In the early nineteenth century, the idea of the frontier hero became even more popular through the Leatherstocking stories of James Fenimore Cooper (*The Last of the Mohicans, The Pathfinder, The Deerslayer*). As America developed the East, the myth of the frontier moved West, and when it reached the open prairies it became the myth of the Wild West. The first western heroes were mountain men or scouts, and the cowboy appeared in the late 1880s in popular dime novels. He soon became the definitive hero, the symbolic frontier individualist. He is still that hero today, long after the open frontier has vanished from America society. He still rides from the western wilderness to create a civil society, and he still portrays the individualist promise, the promise of freedom and equality.

America had an eastern frontier for over two hundred years but a western frontier for only four decades. Yet the Western defined the frontier hero and the cultural imagery of individualism. So the West offered something the East did not for a market myth of origin. The cowboy in the West could ride through mountains and deserts, while the scout in the East could only walk through forests. The western cowboy could carry a sixgun, making violence more abrupt, while the eastern scout only had a rifle, a rifle that had to be reloaded, through the barrel, after each shot. A greater possibility of violence may be more entertaining, and violence may also seem more symbolic of market competition. Maybe the deserts and prairies of the West could seem more endless than the forests of the East, more open to freedom and opportunity. And maybe the image of free western land – formalized in the Homestead Act of 1862 – made the West seem more symbolic. In any case, the West took over the frontier myth, defining the frontier imagery, and the cowboy became the mythical hero, the hero of individualism.

The mythical cowboy is not always a working cowboy in the sense of herding cattle. Often he is a gunfighter, sometimes a gambler, and he may be a rancher, sheriff, or scout, even an outlaw. The 'cowboy' of the myth is defined by his strength, honor, and independence, his wilderness identity, not by his job. He has no privileged lineage, no aristocratic status. He emerges from the wilderness a free and equal individual. He is the cultural version of the theoretical individualist, and the culture calls him a cowboy hero whether he herds cattle or not.

In 1890, the US Census Bureau declared the western frontier officially closed. Around the same time the image of the cowboy emerged in

American culture as the dominant frontier hero. The basic period of western settlement was 1860 to 1890, and most Westerns are set in this period, the time of the mythical Wild West. Westerns primarily appealed to people in the urban East, where factories and cities had long replaced any sense of a wild frontier. The cowboy became more popular as America became industrial. America was built on individualism, the promise of freedom and equality, but individualism assumed an open frontier. The cowboy, then, in his cultural myth, remembered the original frontier vision of individualism as America in fact became industrial.

All the stories of the cowboy – all the popular Westerns – tell the mythical story or variations on that story. In this standard, definitive story, a new frontier community is threatened by greedy villains, and a stranger rides from the wilderness to help the decent citizens. He is detached from social order, 'naturally' free and equal, and he has the skills of the wilderness, especially the skill of violence. He is not initially interested in the problems of the citizens, and they initially distrust him, even fear him. He finally decides to get involved, usually because he falls in love. Only he has the strength to defeat the villains, and generally he must fight alone since the citizens are weak and fearful. After he wins he is loved and admired, and his dominant authority is accepted. He always, however, surrenders that authority by riding away into the sunset or marrying and settling down, taking off his guns. He only fights reluctantly to save the good community, and he only seeks civil equality, never social control.

This is the standard Wild West story, and many variations have been told (Wright, 1975). Each variation maintains the individualist imagery while changing some of the social relations. Indians, when they appear, are sometimes seen as vicious and brutal and sometimes as noble and innocent. The citizens are often seen as honest and decent but sometimes as petty and corrupt. The hero typically fights to build a social order where freedom and equality are possible. But sometimes he fights to escape social order because of its oppressive controls. Usually the hero fights alone, but sometimes he fights with other individualists, other cowboy heroes. Each variation makes a different cultural point about the ideas of individualism. But all the variations always remember that the cowboy needs a frontier. The frontier defines the cowboy, and the cowboy defines individualism. The frontier enables freedom and equality, the basis for civil society, but the frontier is gone in the urban East and no hope for civility remains.

Throughout the twentieth century the myth of the Wild West permeated market culture in novels, films, television, songs, and advertising. The cowboy has been a potent symbol of individualist values, and Henry Kissinger, for example, used this symbol in 1972 to explain his diplomatic achievements as Secretary of State. He was asked in an interview if he had any theories:

Yes, but I won't tell you what they are. Because they don't coincide with the common theory ... My theory is quite different ... Well, why not? I'll tell you.

What do I care, after all? The main point stems from the fact that I've always acted alone. Americans admire that enormously. Americans admire the cowboy leading the caravan alone astride his horse, the cowboy entering a village or a city alone on his horse ... He acts, that's all: aiming at the right spot at the right time. A Wild West tale, if you like ... This romantic, surprising character suits me, because being alone has always been part of my style, of my technique if you prefer ... Independence too. Yes, that's very important to me and in me. And, finally, conviction. I am always convinced of the necessity of whatever I'm doing. (Fallaci, 1972: 21)

Kissinger used cowboy imagery to explain his social actions and shape his view of himself. He relied on the myth to explain the success of his individualist approach. The images of the myth, in his view, explained his success much better than any theory. He saw himself as a true individualist with the cowboy as his model. He wore a suit and tie, not western cowboy clothes. But he saw himself as a cowboy, and his diplomatic strategies followed this image. Many years later, in 1997, Secretary of State Madeleine Albright wore a cowboy hat on a diplomatic trip to Europe. President Clinton also once gave cowboy hats as gifts to all world leaders at a global economic summit. He argued for more free trade at that summit, greater market individualism, and the cowboy hats, as the leaders understood, were symbolic of that argument. As Kissinger makes clear, the cowboy myth is a model for social action. Individuals see themselves as shooting straight, acting alone, and riding tall in the saddle. The cowboy portrays the market ideal, the ideal of independence, and he shapes our social relations as he wanders the Wild West.

The popular cowboy

From dime novels to dude ranches, Americans have been enchanted with the cowboy. Fads come and go, as Elizabeth Larson has written in *Utne Reader*, but 'all things cowboy and cowgirl seem to get more popular with every passing decade' (1993: 27). Novels first carried the cowboy myth, and hundreds of millions of Wild West novels have now been sold. Louis L'Amour is the best-selling novelist in American history, with almost 225 million cowboy novels in print worldwide in 1993. Movies grew up portraying the cowboy hero, and they have always been the source of his greatest cultural success. According to Edward Buscombe:

Between 1926 and 1967, apart from a brief period in the early 30s, Westerns consistently formed around a quarter of all feature films made in Hollywood. This one genre, with its highly formulaic content and steady market, can be seen as the absolute bedrock of Hollywood, the foundation upon which its glittering palaces were erected. (1988: 35)

Westerns were also pervasive on the radio in the 1940s and 1950s, and then on television in the 1950s and 1960s, with 35 Western shows on television in 1959, eight of them in the ten-most-watched category. In her book on Westerns, *West of Everything*, Jane Tompkins summarizes their impact:

> From roughly 1900 to 1975 a significant portion of the adolescent male population spent every Saturday afternoon at the movies. What they saw there were Westerns ... People from all levels of society read Westerns: presidents, truck drivers, librarians, soldiers, college students, businessmen, homeless people. They are read by women as well as men, rich and poor, young and old. In one way or another Westerns – novels and film – have touched the lives of virtually everyone who has lived during the first three quarters of this century. (1992: 5)

Tompkins's account is impressive but also probably conservative. In a deeper sense the imagery of the Wild West influenced everyone in the twentieth century, despite the relative decline of Western movies and TV shows in the latter part of the century. Leslie Fiedler (1966), for example, has argued that most of the great American novels are really Westerns in disguise, and Robert Ray has similarly argued that 'many of Hollywood's classic genre movies' are essentially 'thinly camouflaged Westerns' (1985: 75, 84). Westerns became less prominent in movies and television beginning in the 1970s, but the image of the cowboy, the model of individualism, still permeates our consciousness.

Most American popular stories, then, are in some sense versions of Westerns, because they are always versions of individualism. George Lucas, for example, has said that *Star Wars* is essentially 'a fast-paced action-adventure film in the tradition of the American Western' (Rogers, 1997: 4D). Also, and perhaps most significantly, the heroes of our modern urban action films – the films of Clint Eastwood, Arnold Schwarzenegger, Bruce Willis, and others – are usually denounced as 'cowboys' by their bureaucratic superiors. These action films have replaced the Western as our most popular genre, and while they are not set in the Wild West, they are still focused on the mythical image of the cowboy as someone who acts independently, defies authorities, and 'shoots from the hip'. In effect, these are our modern versions of the Western, only now they show the 'cowboy' trapped in the urban East, where industry, technology, and bureaucracy have triumphed and frontier freedom is gone.

Not only is the Western, in disguise, still prominent in film and television, the image of the Wild West is still prominent and popular, even increasing in popularity, in other areas of culture – clothes, music, dances, rodeos, festivals, vacations, furniture, magazines, advertising, art. Western clothes, from hats to boots, western jewelry, western furniture, and western decor have lately entered the realm of good taste, even the realm of fashion design. Accordingly many slick cowboy magazines have recently appeared, selling and discussing western style and accoutrements, including western art and western vacations. Western art, both cowboy art and Indian art, has been rapidly growing in appeal and success, selling at record levels, with classic paintings by Charles Russell and Fredric Remington recently bringing millions of dollars.

In less wealthy and rarefied circles, truck drivers have commonly identified themselves with cowboys, since the drivers, like the cowboys, tend to be alone, independent, and moving. Presumably for similar reasons, millions of Americans wear cowboy clothes, visit cowboy bars, and dance to cowboy music. Country-western music is enormously popular, with Garth Brooks about to become the best-selling recording artist in American history, surpassing the Beatles. This music is performed by singers who dress like cowboys as a strategy to increase their appeal, a very successful strategy according to Cecelia Techi. They consciously discarded an earlier, hillbilly image in order 'to move from a hick to a hero in one change of clothing' (1994: 115). Cowboy clothes give country music a mythical individualist power. The cowboy must be solitary and taciturn, a quiet loner, so the music lets him speak while still remaining silent:

> The music becomes the voice of the individualist otherwise consigned to silence … When artists perform in western garb, their stage clothes mean West, and that West, in turn, is an individualist, self-reliant America speaking its heart and soul. The cowboy suit becomes a license to sing about – in effect, to talk about – anything under the sun. (Techi, 1994: 129, 130)

The image of the Wild West is also popular in rodeos, where prize money is in the millions, champions become superstars, and television coverage is national. Rodeos celebrate the working cowboy, and they are increasingly popular overseas, specifically as a reflection of the wild American West. Brazil, for example, has become quite enthusiastic about American rodeos, according to a *Chicago Tribune* report in 1997. Despite it own tradition of 'Brazilian cowpunchers … the rodeo that is capturing the imagination of Brazilians has a distinctly US flavor' (Astor, 1997: 3C). Dude ranches in the West have also been thriving lately, with many people seeking a cowboy, frontier experience. And advertising, of course, has increasingly relied on Wild West imagery to sell many kinds of products, most obviously the cigarettes smoked by the Marlboro Man. This was one of the most successful and longest running advertising campaigns in history. A rugged cowboy smoked a cigarette while riding through the West, and Marlboro became the world's best-selling cigarette, the first cigarette to be named to the Marketing Hall of Fame. This advertising campaign was studied by Richard Kluger, who describes the Marlboro Man as 'a throwback hero, strong, stoic, self-reliant, free (though not without responsibilities), potent – the kind of man women are drawn to … And he was classless … though his white hat, confident gait, and effortless handling of his mount tagged him as a leader' (1996: 295).

In all these ways and many others, the imagery of the Wild West has maintained and even increased its cultural prominence in America, even with fewer Western films. This imagery has also been enormously successful in other countries, especially over the last few decades. Western films have been popular in Europe, Africa, Asia, and South America. Many Western films, in fact, have been made in foreign countries, most famously in Italy but also in Spain, Germany, Mexico, Japan, and India. In Germany, Karl May wrote Westerns in the nineteenth century but never visited America. He became the most popular novelist in German history, the favorite novelist, for example, of Einstein and Hitler. In Mexico, Marcial Lafuente Estefanía is probably the most popular novelist in Mexican history. He has written over 2200 Westerns and all are set on the American, not the Mexican, frontier. A country television network, Country Music Television, has gone on the air in Europe and Asia, is moving into Latin America, and is reaching nearly 90 per cent of the world's television audience. There are cowboy festivals in Japan and Germany as well as in other parts of the world. Each summer throughout Germany, cowboy melodramas are performed in mock Wild West villages, where, according to the *Los Angeles Times*, 'Germans are crazy about cowboys and Indians, possibly more so than Americans' (Petty, 1996: 1A).

Wild West images are routinely used to discuss politics and business by journalists, executives, and government officials (like Henry Kissinger). These images are used in America and also internationally. In India, for example, in 1996, Tarun Das, Director General of the Confederation of Indian Industry, criticized multinational corporations for taking a 'cowboy approach' to partnerships with Indian companies (Karp, 1996: 78). Also in 1996, a headline in the *New York Times* business section read, 'Cowboy in the Black Forest: Daimler Chief's Tough Style Isn't Business as Usual for Europe'. The article made the point that the new chief executive was defiant of industrial custom in Germany ('Cowboy in the ...', 1996: 1C). A *Wall Street Journal* headline in 1995 said, 'US Brings to Bosnia Tactics that Tamed Wild West,' and the article included these comments: 'The US Army is coming to the Balkans big, slow, and uncompromising – like John Wayne or Errol Flynn in an old Western movie ... The American message ... is that a new, tougher sheriff has come to town' ('US Brings ..., 1995: 7).

Such cowboy references can be multiplied endlessly, from newspapers, magazines, interviews, memos, books on business. The cowboy myth offers a metaphorical shorthand for thinking about our society. It permeates politics and commerce, news and entertainment, work and pleasure. It is a myth of social origin that reflects our social theories, our legitimating market ideas.

The theoretical cowboy

Many efforts have been made over the years to explain the continued popularity of the cowboy. Most interpret his myth in terms of specifically American history and culture – the frontier experience, the idea of manifest destiny, the American issue of race, the American issue of masculinity. In general, these are interesting and revealing efforts. From the perspective of this book, however, they are too specifically American and not sufficiently theoretical. The cowboy is a uniquely American character, but he represents the ideas of America, the American civil vision, not the specific history of America. He represents individualist values, and those values were first put into practice, and most completely put into practice, in American market institutions. America was the first market nation, and the cowboy is an American character who symbolizes market individualism, not simply American individualism.

The myth illuminates abstract theoretical concepts through dramatic concrete images. The abstract individuals of the theory become specific characters in the myth, characters that are male or female, black or white, young or old, strong or afraid, confident or confused, honest or dishonest. The myth makes the theory engaging and entertaining, so theoretical ideas become fun to understand. The myth gives the theory life by putting abstract concepts in an immediate, emotional context. It tells us how to think about the market and act as individualists in a practical, relevant way.

As a result, these mythical stories may be our most important and effective source of social understanding. We certainly need the abstract theories for constructing and maintaining market institutions. We also need the critical theories for correcting and improving those institutions. But the mythical images of popular culture complement and complete the theories, and like Henry Kissinger we probably use them more than the theories to conduct and make sense of our lives. The cowboy interprets individualist values for daily social life, often telling us more about those values than we really want to know, so the cowboy will be used in this book to explore individualist theory, the theory embodied in the image of the Wild West.

Outline and terminology

The first part of the book (Chapters 1, 2, 3) focuses on the rise of market individualism in the seventeenth and eighteenth centuries, and its portrayal in the myth of the West. Chapter 1 addresses the issues of social contract theory, particularly the theory of John Locke, the theory that defined individualism. Chapter 2 explores in more depth the basic assumptions of individualism, and how those assumptions are reproduced in the cowboy myth. Chapter 3 is concerned with the market analysis of Adam Smith – the idea of the *invisible hand* and its implications for market government. In the second part of the book (Chapters 4, 5, 6), the three social critics of the market are discussed, the central social theorists of the nineteenth century – Karl Marx, Max Weber, Emile Durkheim. These social theorists analyze the new industrial market, not the earlier agrarian market assumed by the individualists. The third part of the book (Chapters 7, 8, 9) explores three important issues of market individualism; issues that are always clear in the myth but always tacit in the theory. These are the issues of women and sex (Chapter 7), Indians and race (Chapter 8), and wilderness and the environment (Chapter 9). The Conclusion summarizes the social importance of the myth of the Wild West as our central cultural reference for understanding the market.

Some terminological conventions will be used to clarify some of the issues. The idea of rational Nature (capital N) will be distinguished from the ordinary experience of physical nature (small n). All societies experience natural processes (nature) in the ordinary, everyday sense – rivers, trees, seasons, lightning. Each society, however, interprets and explains these natural processes differently, according to specific cultural concepts. The idea of rational Nature is the scientific version – the scientific interpretation – of the common human experience of nature. This scientific idea of Nature arose in the seventeenth century and became the basis for market individualism.

In another convention, the term 'natural' will be put in quotation marks whenever it is used to describe *social* qualities. In this way such ideas as 'natural' social qualities – rights, individuals, freedom – will be distinguished from natural physical phenomena – rain, crops, winter. The idea of 'natural' freedom, for example, asserts that individualist freedom is legitimated by rational Nature. All individualist ideas were derived from the idea of Nature, just as all feudal ideas were derived from the idea of God. Individualist theorists claimed their social assertions were 'natural' in exactly the same sense that feudal priests claimed their social assertions were sacred. Both the individualists and the priests appealed to the truths of the universe to validate a particular social order. The individualists simply saw those truths as rational while the priests saw them as divine. For the individualists Nature endorses social relations, the relations of the market, and this social use of the adjective 'natural' will be distinguished by quotation marks.

In the discussion of individualist ideas, the terms 'rational society,' 'individualist society,' and 'market society' will be used interchangeably. All these terms will indicate the idea of a social order based on rational, autonomous individuals. The term 'civil society' will also be used but with an added normative judgment. The idea of civil society will suggest that market society will also be a *good* society, a society of freedom and equality, justice and decency. In a civil society social order emerges from rational individuals pursuing their self-interests, not from sacred truths imposed from above, that is, from the gods, tradition, or government. The idea of civil society is the legitimating individualist promise. It asserts the need for market relations, and it also *justifies* those relations in the name of freedom and equality.

Finally, the idea of agrarian society, a society based on agriculture, will be contrasted with the idea of industrial society, a society based on industry. All of modern society will be characterized as industrial, despite the arguments of some recent theorists that society is now post-industrial. The important distinction to be used in this book is between agrarian and industrial society, so modern society will be seen as industrial: a society based on science and technology.

Using this terminology we will explore individualist theory and the critical reaction to that theory as reflected in a popular myth. The idea of Nature justified the theory, since market relations could be seen as 'natural'. Social relations could now be rational, as opposed to sacred and traditional, and rational relations, according to the theory, would lead to a good society, a civil society of rational individuals. The idea of a civil market, however, emerged under conditions of agrarian production, and the issue for the critical social theorists was whether it could ever make sense under conditions of industrial production.

Certain popular films of the Twentieth Century will be suggested in the analysis that illustrate aspects of the argument. The date of each film will be given when first mentioned and again in the film index.

Part 1

INDIVIDUALISM

Preface

The market idea

Many familiar images are included in the cowboy myth: the lone stranger (cowboy, gunfighter, gambler); the frontier community (farmers, ranchers, miners, wagon train); the untamed wilderness (mountains, deserts, prairies); wilderness dangers (Indians, rivers, storms, thirst); the greedy villains (bankers, land speculators, railroads, large ranchers, claim jumpers, hired gunfighters); attractive women (schoolteachers, daughters, entertainers, prostitutes); tenuous law (no law enforcers, weak law enforcers, corrupt law enforcers); incipient violence (guns everywhere, fights and brawls commonplace); decent westerners (strong, knowledgeable, fair); urban easterners (weak, arrogant, corrupt). These images are generally combined into a standard cowboy story, where the hero saves the good community from villainous violence and cruelty. The cowboy emerges from the wilderness with a special skill at violence. The citizens are honest and decent but they are also weak and afraid. They want to build a society of equals, a civil society, and in the frontier West everyone can claim and own land. But the citizens are always threatened by the villains, and they always initially suspect and fear the detached cowboy hero.

The villains are selfish and greedy and they try to monopolize all the property. They want to achieve dominant privilege – to 'own all the land in the valley' – and they are willing to lie and kill to do it. Usually, they are associated with the East – bankers, developers, railroad executives, large ranchers – and they only own property to maximize their wealth, not to build a good society. Honest, decent westerners are generally contrasted with corrupt, deceitful easterners. Indians are sometimes also a threat, but the primary danger to the good citizens comes from villains in the society, not from Indians in the wilderness. The cowboy finally fights the villains, saving the community and winning respect, even the love of a woman. But he never uses his victory to take social control. He always rides away or settles down, either returning to the wilderness or becoming a civil equal.

This standard cowboy story is a cultural drama of individualism. The cowboy symbolizes individualist ideas as does the rugged scenery of the American West. All the images of the West – cowboy hats, horses, buffalo, red rock canyons – carry the cultural message of freedom, equality, private property, civility: the promise of individualism. The cultural story reflects a theoretical story, a story of rational individuals building a civil market. This theoretical story was originally told by the early individualist theorists: Thomas Hobbes and John Locke in the seventeenth century and Adam Smith and Thomas Jefferson, among others, in the eighteenth century.

There were two basic parts to this original individualist story, a political part and an economic part. The political part was told in the seventeenth century, first by Thomas Hobbes and later, most influentially, by John Locke. The economic part was told in the eighteenth century, most famously by Adam Smith. The political part was the idea of the *social contract*. This idea established the basic individualist assumptions about rational individuals, and it also established the requirements for a rational government. The economic part was the idea of a self-regulating market, the idea of laissez-faire. This idea suggested how social order would arise from a market in private property, a market with limited government. These two parts of the individualist story, the political and the economic, established the general theory of market society, a theory of freedom and equality. Civil society would emerge from rational individuals pursuing their private interests through market order and competition. All individuals would have an equal opportunity to own private property, and all individuals would be free to maximize that property.

Private property was the central individualist issue, the pivot of market society. The idea of private property contradicted the feudal class structure. The feudal idea of property was basically land, and land was an issue of class privilege. In general, land could only be inherited, not bought or sold, and the aristocratic right to land involved sacred class duties as well as privileges. Aristocrats benefited most from the traditional class order, but that order also protected peasants to some degree. Peasants had traditional duties to the lords – the duty to work the land – but they also had some limited traditional rights to the land under the lord's control. The feudal idea of property supported the class structure, and the idea of private property undermined that class structure. If property is private, it no longer supports traditional relations – sacred duties. Private property implied individual equality and the removal of all traditional constraints on land and production.

In seventeenth-century Europe, and particularly in England, a rising class of merchants struggled against aristocratic privilege. Trade was increasing and merchants were achieving wealth and influence. Aristocrats, however, still had dominant power because the social order was still feudal. The increasing wealth of the merchants was threatened by aristocratic control, so the merchants supported the idea of private property and the rejection of feudal tradition. In particular, they supported the individualist theorists who argued for private property in the name of rational Nature. The merchants wanted to maximize their property through rational production and trade, so they needed a market in private property, not the feudal structure of class.

In the middle of the seventeenth century Thomas Hobbes published an influential version of social contract theory, *Leviathan*. Later, in 1690, John Locke published an even more influential version of that theory, the *Second Treatise of Civil Government*. Locke's version then became the primary basis for building market institutions. Locke agreed with Hobbes on most aspects of the theory, but he disagreed significantly on its implications for government. Hobbes used social contract theory to justify a strong, absolute government, a government beyond the control of the citizens. Locke, however, used social contract theory to justify a weak, representative government, a government controlled by the citizens. Locke's version was far more compatible with the individualist idea of freedom and so it was far more appealing. Locke's vision, then, became the basis for shaping market ideas and institutions, particularly as they developed in America.

Locke told a theoretical story, the story of the social contract, and this story influenced the American and French revolutions and shaped market institutions. Social contract theory was primarily concerned with government – a rational government for market relations. Government, according to Locke, should always remain limited and passive, controlled by and responsive to rational citizens. This political argument, however, did not include an economic analysis of the market, a discussion, that is, of how the market would work. If market relations were to replace feudal relations so rational government could replace aristocratic government, what would this really mean at the level of production? Locke's political ideas needed economic support, and Adam Smith supplied that support in 1776 with his book on the market, *The Wealth of Nations*. He analyzed the market laws of supply and demand, and this analysis made him world famous. A market in private property, he argued, will regulate itself with no need for government controls. If rational individuals are free to pursue their private interests through supply and demand, a decent civil society will result. This economic argument supported Locke's politics and completed the individualist conception. Together Locke's politics and Smith's economics defined the individualist vision, the vision of a civil market.

1

THE SOCIAL CONTRACT

Thomas Hobbes lived from 1588 to 1679, and John Locke lived from 1632 to 1704. Both were English and lived primarily in England, but both also left England and lived in exile for certain periods of time fearing the possible repercussions of their political ideas and associations. According to Ramon Lemos, Hobbes was 'the first postrenaissance philosopher to present an original and comprehensive system of political philosophy' (1978: 3). This was a theory of the social contract, a theory of rational individuals creating a rational government, a government not based on class.

Hobbes's social contract theory became very important, but its importance was soon eclipsed by the later social contract theory of John Locke. Locke's version of the theory was influenced by Hobbes but was different in crucial ways, and Locke's version was much more amenable to the Europe of his time. As a result, in the words of Peter Laslett, he helped 'to change the philosophical and political assumptions of humanity' (1960: 16). As John Dunn has observed, Locke's career 'ended in an extraordinary eminence'.

> It left him in his own lifetime as one of the luminaries of the European intellectual scene and, after his death, as the symbolic forerunner and philosophical foundation of the Enlightenment and of what has become fashionable to call the Age of the Democratic Revolution. (1969, 11)

Locke built on Hobbes to create a political vision, a vision of individualist government. And both Hobbes and Locke assumed in their theories an image of wilderness America; a place of 'natural' individuals (Indians) and thus of new beginnings. Hobbes began and Locke defined the basic individualist conception, and this conception always included the idea of a wilderness frontier.

Agrarian civil society

The basic individualist idea was that rational individuals would compete for private property in a context of equal laws. A limited, democratic government would enforce those laws and protect private contracts, the basis for market exchange. Government would otherwise remain minimal and passive, with no dominant power to enforce sacred rules, tradition, or morality. Social order would be based on market relations, and this would be a civil, not a sacred, social order. No sacred tradition or morality would be necessary because the market laws of supply and demand would create a good society, a society of freedom and equality. This was the vision of the early individualists, a vision from within European feudal agriculture in the seventeenth and eighteenth centuries. Essentially this was a vision of letting everyone own land and work that land, a vision of owner-workers, independent agrarians. Neither Locke nor Smith foresaw the rise of industry, although their individualist ideas soon led to the rise of industry. They thought market relations would lead to a good society, a civil society, but only if all individuals could own and work their own private property, their own land.

In the later eighteenth century, Smith began to see a rising group of 'merchants and manufacturers', in his words, as opposed to independent farmers. This would mean a structural division between owners and workers, and this, Smith thought, would undermine any possibility of a civil, just market. He assumed, that is, along with Locke and Jefferson, that the market could only be civil in a context of agrarian owner-workers. He also assumed, as Jefferson clearly states, that all individuals can only be agrarian owner-workers as long as there is free wilderness land. In 1787, Jefferson wrote in a letter to James Madison:

> I think our governments will remain virtuous for many centuries; as long as they are chiefly agricultural; and this will be as long as there shall be vacant lands in America. When they get piled up upon one another in large cities, as in Europe, they will become corrupt as in Europe. (1903: 392)

Jefferson lived from 1743 to 1826. He saw the early beginnings of industry, and he thought an urban structure of owners and workers could not be compatible with civility. This perspective was also shared by other founding Americans, including Benjamin Franklin, Thomas Paine, and George Washington. Civil society, in their view, required agrarian owner-workers, and this required endless free land. As a consequence, many proposals were made in early America to restrict the amount of land an individual could own so all individuals would always have a chance to own and work land.

This was the original individualist idea of equal opportunity – the equal opportunity to become an owner of property, specifically land. If everyone can be an owner of property, then everyone will be equal. Everyone can be an owner-worker, and no one will have to be only a worker. In this book I will call this *real equal opportunity*, the original idea of equal opportunity. This idea of equal opportunity requires endless free land, an open frontier. In our modern industrial society there is no longer an equal opportunity for all individuals to claim and own real property, such as land. Today we tend to understand equal opportunity as the equal opportunity to get a job, that is, to become a worker. This is a necessary industrial adjustment of the legitimating market idea of equal opportunity, but it is not the idea of the early individualists. For them, market relations could only be civil and just in a context of real equal opportunity, a context of endless free land.

In a context of real equal opportunity, such as an agrarian frontier, everyone can be an owner-worker, which means everyone can be *structurally equal*. In an urban, industrial context owners and workers are structurally unequal. Workers must work for owners – sell their labor – in order to live, so owners have far more structural power than workers, who are structurally dependent. Owners can make money from their property (land, factories, patents, minerals, etc.), while workers can only make money from their labor. Further, the labor of the workers helps make the owners richer, while the workers generally have little chance to get rich. In an industrial city a class of owners can essentially monopolize all the productive property, all the factories, machines, railroads, etc. Everyone, then, who is not an owner must be a worker. Industry creates *class monopolies* and thus a structural inequality between owners and workers. The frontier, however, prevents class monopolies. If free wilderness land is available to everyone, no class monopolies of property can exist. No matter how rich some people get, all other people always have a chance to claim and own productive property (land). This is why Jefferson saw free western land as necessary for civil society, and why the cowboy myth sees the western frontier as the basis for justice and decency.

The early individualists argued for *legal equality*, where everyone has an equal legal right to own private property – equal legal opportunity. They argued for this equality to end the legal class inequality of feudal society, where aristocrats had exclusive legal rights to own land. But the early individualists also assumed that the legal equality of private property would also imply structural equality, a context of agrarian owner-workers. That is, they also assumed endless free land where no class monopolies could exist. They thought legal equality with private property (equal opportunity) would create civil society because all individuals could become structurally equal. Their market institutions, however, including legal equality, soon led to urban industry and structural inequality – owners and workers. In our modern industrial market, then, we have legal equality with structural inequality, and this contradicts the original individualist vision. The implicit image of an endless agrarian frontier – real equal opportunity – was essentially an individualist fantasy, a civil market hope. This theoretical fantasy, however, justified individualist ideas and market relations. It also generated a legitimating individualist myth, a myth of market origin, the myth of the Wild West.

The individualists did not argue for *economic equality* – equal individual wealth – as Karl Marx would, for example, in the nineteenth century. Some could be richer than others, in their view, because some would be better, or luckier, at market competition. They did think, however, that everyone should have an equal opportunity to claim and own productive property, such as land. They worried about class monopolies and structural inequality, issues of feudalism and the cities. The legitimating individualist vision, then, the vision of civil society, was always a frontier fantasy, and this vision created urban industry. This is what the cowboy myth portrays through its imagery of the West and the East. The frontier West can be civil and just if greedy, corrupt villains, usually from the East, can be defeated. The West offers real equal opportunity while the urban East does not. This implicit frontier fantasy is clear in the myth, and market culture in general, particularly American culture, has generally romanticized agrarian life. Small family farms and rural communities are typically seen as more humane and fulfilling than industrial cities and corporate factories. This romantic, pastoral image is inherent in individualism, as Jefferson remarks and the cowboy remembers.

Heroes

Individualism is essentially the assertion that all individuals are 'naturally' equal. If all individuals are 'naturally' rational, in a rational universe, then they are also 'naturally' equal. They are 'naturally' equal, that is, in the sense that no 'natural' reasons exist – no reasons derived from Nature – to justify traditional class privilege. All rational individuals should have equal opportunity – legal equality. They should not have economic equality (equal wealth), because some will compete better than others in the market. But they should all have equal opportunity – no class privilege. For the individualists, the reference to Nature replaces the reference to God as the basis for social order. And the reference to Nature implies that all individuals are 'naturally' equal.

If Nature replaces God and the market replaces feudalism, then a new kind of individualist hero must replace the traditional aristocratic hero. The individualist hero – the frontier scout, the cowboy – always defends equality, while the traditional hero – Achilles, Arthur, Lancelot, Robin Hood – always fights for privilege. The cowboy hero emerges from the wilderness as a 'natural' individual. He has no social lineage or rank, usually not even a family. He has a lowly or illegal job, or he may be unemployed. He is still, however, a social hero, the equal of anyone and superior to many. The traditional hero must have a family: he cannot be a hero without the proper lineage. He fights to save the social order just like the cowboy, but he also fights for fame and glory and he is proud of his class privilege. The cowboy does not fight for fame and glory and he only fights reluctantly. He never expects or accepts social superiority and dominant authority, but the traditional hero must be superior and dominant in order to be a hero.

The knight is the hero of feudal institutions and the cowboy is the hero of market institutions. But the cowboy is a hero on an agrarian frontier where everyone can claim free land. The cowboy is the hero of civil society, but civil society, according to the theory and the myth, requires structural equality – an open frontier. So what happens when the frontier is gone and market institutions become industrial? What happens when the cowboy, as the individualist hero, has to live in the city amid structural inequality? In mythical terms this is the urban East, a place of greed and corruption, a place of class monopolies.

In classic cowboy imagery, classic Western films, the cowboy must purge greedy villains from decent agrarian (or mining) communities – *Dodge City* (1939), *Tall in the Saddle* (1944), *San Antonio* (1945), *Man Without a Star* (1955), *The Far Country* (1955), *Blood on the Moon* (1948), *War of the Wildcats* (1943), *The Violent Men* (1955), *The Sheepman* (1958), *The Outlaw Josey Wales* (1976), *Joe Kidd* (1972). The villains are typically identified with the East. They are from the East, they wear eastern clothes and they have eastern, as opposed to agrarian values: that is, they seek to monopolize all the property and create structural inequality. In other popular Westerns, the frontier is closing and the cowboy hero can no longer fight to save a civil society. In these films the hero can only try to remain free by seeking remaining frontiers, and he must fight to escape western towns that are now greedy, petty, and corrupt, just like the urban East – *The Magnificent Seven* (1960), *Lonely Are the Brave* (1962), *Butch Cassidy and the Sundance Kid* (1969), *The Wild Bunch* (1969), *Dances With Wolves* (1990), *The Professionals* (1966), *Unforgiven* (1992).

When the frontier is completely gone, the individualist hero must live in the industrial city amid inequality, bureaucracy, and corruption. But the individualist hero is a cowboy who fights for freedom and equality, and he needs an open frontier. The films that tell this story, the story of the industrial 'cowboy', are our modern urban action films, the films of Clint Eastwood, Charles Bronson, Sylvester Stallone, Arnold Schwarzenegger, Bruce Willis, and other stars – *Death Wish* (1974) and it's sequels, *Die Hard* (1988) and it's sequels, *First Blood* (1982) and it's sequels, *Dirty Harry* (1971) and it's sequels, *The Eiger Sanction* (1975), *Armageddon* (1998), *The Terminator* (1984) and it's sequel, *Eraser* (1996), *Clear and Present Danger* (1994). Over the last few decades these action films have essentially replaced Westerns as our most popular cultural entertainment, our mythical version of individualism. In these films the hero still fights for freedom and equality, justice and decency, but he can only hope to survive pervasive corruption, he cannot hope to build a good community.

These are films of urban paranoia where no one can be trusted and betrayal is everywhere. The hero must exist in a bureaucratic structure – the police, the government, a newspaper – where all his bureaucratic superiors are incompetent or corrupt. He must defy those superiors to defeat the villains, and he is commonly denounced and condemned as a 'cowboy' – not a team player – by outraged bureaucrats. When the cowboy lives on the western frontier, he is filled with individualist honor. He does not draw first, shoot in the back, kill the unarmed, or harm women. The 'cowboy' in the city, however, must abandon all honor to win and survive. He must shoot in the back, kill unarmed men, even kill women. Honor only makes sense, these films tell us, when civility is possible, and civility requires an open frontier. The industrial 'cowboy' hero is desperate to be free, desperate to the point of massive, excessive violence. Sometimes he finally tries to return to the wilderness, or at least to the rural West, as the original source of individualist freedom – *First Blood*, *Blade Runner* (1982), *L.A. Confidential* (1997).

When the frontier is gone the cowboy myth becomes the urban action myth. In this version individualist freedom, the freedom of the open frontier, is no longer compatible with market relations. The market cannot be civil, according to the myth and the early individualists, in an urban context of class monopolies and structural inequality. The frontier cowboy hero must become the industrial 'cowboy' hero. The frontier hero can combine honor and violence, freedom and civility, but the industrial hero can only combine violence and freedom in a context of absolute corruption. This industrial version of the cowboy myth reflects the original individualist assumption of a civil *agrarian* market, a market of structural equals. But the market the individualists created in turn created industry and the structural inequality of the cities. This industrial market was analyzed by the social theorists – Marx, Weber, Durkheim – who generally saw it as oppressive and degrading, just as the individualists feared. The cowboy myth portrays both these visions, the agrarian frontier and the industrial city, and it shows how the cowboy hero, the true individualist, must respond to each as he fights for freedom and equality.

A theoretical story

The basic individualist conception derives from social contract theory. And this theory, though stated abstractly, was always essentially a story, a story that became a myth. According to this story, individuals originally lived in a completely 'natural' condition with no government or laws – the *State of Nature*. In the State of Nature, individuals were perfectly 'natural' and free. They were free, that is, of all artificial social roles and duties, the roles and duties of class, religion, tradition. These 'natural' individuals only had 'natural' characteristics, characteristics given to them by Nature, and these 'natural' characteristics, then, had to be the basis for creating a rational government.

This idea of 'natural' characteristics was the crucial individualist vision. People were to be understood in terms of their similar 'natural' qualities, not in terms of their traditional class differences, and a rational social order would then be created based on these 'natural' qualities. The idea of the State of Nature was essentially an idea of seeing people in terms of Nature rather than God. According to the feudal version of God, there are fundamental sacred differences between people, specifically between families, and this justifies class structure. According to social contract theory, however, no class differences exist in the State of Nature, so no class structure can be legitimate in a rational society.

The central individualist issue, then, is what these 'natural' qualities are. The idea of the State of Nature – 'natural' individuals – rejects the traditional social order, so what kind of rational social order should now be established? This rational social order must be based on these 'natural' individual qualities, so what are the basic characteristics of all individuals in the original State of Nature? According to social contract theory, individuals in the State of Nature are *rational, autonomous,* and *self-interested.* They are rational in the sense that they can understand their own world and control their own destiny. They do not need the obedience and submission of faith. They are autonomous in the sense that they have no 'natural' social duties. They are 'naturally' free as rational individuals to do whatever they want, with no sacred, traditional obligations. They are self-interested in the sense that what they 'naturally' want is to maximize their wealth, that is, their private property. Individuals in the State of Nature, according to social contract theory, are perfectly independent and detached, perfectly autonomous, and they rationally seek to maximize their property any way they can. This is the defining individualist vision, the vision of the State of Nature, and all social efforts to build market institutions will be based on this 'natural' vision.

In particular, the idea of the State of Nature defines the central individualist values of freedom and equality, the values that legitimate individualism. The value of equality is derived from the assumption of rationality. If all individuals are 'naturally' rational, they are also 'naturally' equal, since no 'natural' differences of class and rank exist. All rational individuals, therefore, should have legal equality – the equal opportunity to claim and own property. The value of freedom is derived from the assumption of autonomy. If all individuals are 'naturally' autonomous, then they are 'naturally' free to do whatever they want, with no concern for class, tradition, or even for family. In particular, they are 'naturally' free to maximize their property any way they can, using their rationality and their equal opportunity. Further, if all individuals are 'naturally' self-interested, then they all have a 'natural' right to own private property. The idea of private property follows from the assumption of self-interest, and the idea of private property defines individualist freedom and equality. 'Natural' individual equality means an equal opportunity to own private property with no concern for class privilege. 'Natural' individual freedom means the complete individual freedom to maximize private property with no concern for traditional constraints.

Rationality, autonomy, and self-interest are the basic assumptions of individualism, the qualities of individuals in the State of Nature. From these assumptions Hobbes and Locke told the social contract story, a story of rational individuals choosing to leave the State of Nature to form a rational government. According to this story, individuals are perfectly free and equal in the State of Nature as they compete for private property. But this means they are also free to lie, cheat, steal, and kill. They are essentially too free in the State of Nature, so their property is always in danger and their lives are always at risk.

Because they are 'naturally' rational, they all agree to leave the State of Nature and enter a social contract. Through this social contract, they agree to accept a rational government, a government to enforce rational laws. The point of this government is to enable rational competition for private property, a rational market order. Thus, the rational laws must guarantee legal equality and private property, giving everyone equal opportunity. More generally, government must be strong enough to enforce rational contracts, mutual agreements between rational individuals. Individuals must still be free to compete, but now they must compete in a rational market. They must make rational agreements for production and trade, and then they must fulfill those agreements even if they change their mind. Government, that is, must prevent lying and cheating, coercion and violence, so that all individual competition takes place through market relations.

According to this story, a government can only be legitimate for rational individuals if it assures an equal market opportunity to own and accumulate private property. Hobbes and Locke agreed on the social contract story up to this point. They disagreed, however, on how much power this government must have to protect a rational market. Hobbes thought that rational, autonomous individuals could only be constrained and controlled by a strong, dominant government, a government with absolute power. Locke, however, thought that rational, autonomous individuals would only agree to accept a government (the social contract) with limited, minimal power, a government controlled by its citizens. Locke supported the idea of laissez-faire (let it work), the idea that the market would regulate itself with no need for active government control. The market would 'naturally' generate a prosperous civil society based strictly on individual self-interest and rational competition. As a result, government could always stay limited, simply enforcing rational contracts and assuring legal equality. This idea of limited government was far more appealing to early individualists than Hobbes's idea of absolute government, so Locke's version of the social contract, together with laissez-faire, became the basis for market institutions, particularly in America.

In either version of the theory, rational individuals surrender some of their 'natural' freedoms when they accept a rational government, the freedoms, for example, to lie, cheat, steal, and kill. In Hobbes's version, they must simply trust government to protect their other freedoms, the freedoms of private property, since they also surrender any ability to control or influence government. In Locke's version, however, they accept the need for government but they also distrust the government, so they always retain some power over it. Government must be controlled by its citizens, a representative government. From Locke's perspective, government can easily begin to take too much power and restrict too much freedom. Government will tend to become corrupt and serve special interests, the interests of a privileged class. Rational individuals, then, must always retain some power over government for the sake of freedom and equality. Government must always maintain a delicate political balance, a balance between too much power and not enough power. Without enough power, government cannot end the dangerous State of Nature and assure a rational market. With too much power, however, government will undermine a rational market by serving a privileged class.

Through this delicate balance, government must maintain maximum *market freedom*. This is the freedom of rational individuals to maximize their property in a rational market context. Market freedom is compatible with market society, but complete 'natural' freedom is not. Government must restrict the 'natural' freedoms that threaten market relations, the dangerous, disruptive freedoms of the State of Nature. But it must also let individuals remain as free as possible – market freedom – to maximize their property within a social order.

This issue of freedom, then, is the central problem for market government in Locke's social contract theory. Government must restrict just the right amount of individual freedom, not too much and not too little. Rational individuals form a government, according to the theory, to serve their rational interests. Their property and their lives will be more secure in a rational market order. But they must also always be wary of government and fear its potential power. Government can easily become arrogant and corrupt and threaten market freedom. So government must always be responsive to its citizens, a representative government, and those citizens, according to Locke, should overthrow the government if it becomes oppressive. Rational individuals always have the right to reject and fight their own government, since they created government to serve their interests and protect their freedom. Locke made this argument while Hobbes would not, and Jefferson in America agreed with Locke as he helped create American government. This was the ultimate endorsement of the individualist conception. Rational individuals have the 'natural' right to defy the government and disrupt social order simply to protect their 'natural' freedom.

This social contract story created the individualist vision and justified market government. It is a mythical, theoretical story about a dim, distant past, an imagined individualist story. But it still serves to justify our modern market government through the idea of implied consent. According to this idea, all individuals are equally rational, so they all would choose the same form of government, the government of the social contract. Modern individuals did not leave the State of Nature and enter a social contract. The government created by that contract, however, is exactly the government modern individuals would choose. The original individuals gave explicit consent and later individuals give implied consent. Rational individuals created market government as the best way to serve their rational interests, and since we are all rational, we are still bound, implicitly, by the original social contract.

Social contract theory tells a story, a theoretical story of social origin. It is a story about rational individuals leaving the State of Nature, and the cowboy myth simply retells that story for popular, cultural understanding. In effect, social contract theory is a theoretical myth, a 'metahistory', a 'myth of human origins', according to historian Carl Pletsch. Locke recognized 'the need for a modern myth to organize thinking about modern relationships, whether political, economic, or social'. He was quite 'successful in supplanting the biblical story [and] establishing [the social contract] as the dominant social and political myth of the succeeding centuries' (Pletsch, 1990: 133, 135).

While European nations were still immersed in tradition and class, America was created on individualist ideas and market institutions. As a result America developed the definitive market myth, the cultural myth of individualism. This was the myth of the wild frontier, a myth of 'natural' individuals emerging from the wilderness as the original State of Nature. This myth followed the social contract story as told by Hobbes and Locke, and Hobbes and Locke had told that story with America as the image of the State of Nature. Hobbes wrote in 1651 that the condition of 'the savage people in many places of America' represented the State of Nature (1958: 108). And Locke wrote in 1690 'in the beginning all the World was America' (1966: 319).

In effect, the image of wilderness America helped to create and legitimate individualist ideas. America embodied the State of Nature and the bounty of rational Nature. It was dangerous, promising, pure, renewing, and opportunistic. Individuals could return to Nature in wilderness America, leaving class and tradition behind, and then they could emerge with freedom and equality to build a civil society. America was an endless frontier where everyone could own and work land, and this was the image of social contract theory, the image of civil society. The frontier was the boundary between market freedom and 'natural' freedom, between social order and the State of Nature. Social contract theory implied an open frontier, and America offered a real frontier, a frontier on endless wilderness. America was always implicit in the social contract story, and America told that story in its institutions and its culture, a story of market individualism.

Morality

One of the central early appeals of market individualism was the idea of eliminating moral constraints, the traditional moral constraints that characterized feudal Europe. Morality had long been associated with religion and class, the morality of feudal order. Sacred moral rules had been used for centuries to endorse the arrogance of the aristocracy and the subservience of the peasants. The aristocrats, of course, were happy with this sacred morality, but the peasants were not and neither were the merchants. The merchants in particular wanted more control over their property and their wealth, and this would mean less power for the aristocrats, less moral commitment to class. The sacred feudal morality supported the feudal idea of property – aristocratic power and control. The merchants wanted private property, property divorced from feudal morality, so they supported the individualists and the idea of market society.

Christianity supported feudal morality, and the individualists did not want to challenge Christianity. So individualism did not assert an alternative morality, it simply asserted no need for morality. This was the idea of laissez-faire, the idea of a self-regulating market. According to individualist assumptions, 'naturally' rational individuals are also 'naturally' autonomous, and they 'naturally' pursue their private self-interests. They will therefore 'naturally' compete to maximize their property. They need a minimal government to prevent cheating and coercion. Otherwise, they will 'naturally' create a decent civil society with no need for sacred moral rules. From the perspective of laissez-faire, a good society only needs rational individuals pursuing their private interests. It does not need a strong government to enforce moral rules. Moral rules tend to support one group or class over another, as in feudal Christianity, so they tend to be incompatible with individualist equality. The market will work just fine by itself, based strictly on rationality and equality, and any commitment to moral rules would tend to corrupt the market, not maintain it.

This individualist perspective on the market follows very closely, in early modern Europe, the new scientific perspective on the universe, the idea of rational Nature. The Christians had argued for a thousand years that God maintained a mysterious universal order, an order beyond human understanding, and He also maintained the feudal social order, requiring moral rules and judging human actions. The scientists, then, began to argue that the universe is simply a rational machine, working strictly by itself and available to human understanding. They did not reject the Christian God but rather simply sidestepped him. God could still remain in the background as the Creator of the universe, but He was no longer active in the universe and humans could easily ignore Him. The early individualists, then, used this same image to justify laissez-faire. The market would work by itself, just like a rational machine, creating a good society. Both the universe and social order could now be seen as rational, and neither would involve sacred moral rules.

This rejection of morality, however, presented a serious problem. Morality, it was generally thought, was what kept people from lying and cheating, from abusing and killing each other. From this perspective, morality would be necessary for a good society, and any society without morality could only be mean and violent. Individualists wanted to argue that public morality would not be necessary for a good society – only rational self-interests would be necessary. Individuals should only be privately selfish and greedy; they would not need to act morally.

The serious individualist problem, then, was how to expect private, greedy selfishness to turn into social decency. For laissez-faire to work, perfectly selfish individuals should 'naturally' generate through market competition a just, civil society. This was an appealing individualist image: individuals should only think about themselves and everything would work out fine. It was not completely convincing, however, because it seemed more likely that completely selfish individuals would create a society that was cruel, vicious, and oppressive. This was the individualist problem of morality, and it became known in early modern Europe as the problem of egoism versus altruism. The market would be based on egoism – complete private self-interest. But a good society would require altruism – mutual sharing, caring, respect. Somehow, civil altruism had to be seen as 'naturally' emerging from market egoism, and this meant that selfish market individuals would also have to act morally, altruistically. No society could be decent without a sense of trust, and trust would require shared social commitments. Some sense of morality, then, would have to infuse the market, but it could not come from sacred moral rules; that is, it could not come from religion.

For Hobbes this individualist problem of morality implied the need for absolute government. If individuals can be perfectly selfish and greedy in market competition, only a strong, dominant government can maintain social order. Government must have more power than any individual or any group of individuals; that is, it cannot be controlled by the people. Hobbes was willing to abandon morality altogether, unlike Locke or Smith. In this sense he fully embraced the implications of individualism. But his only solution, then, to the problem of morality – the problem of a good society – was to create an absolute government and hope it would not become corrupt.

When Locke faced the same moral problem, he solved it quite differently. Essentially he assumed that rational individuals are also innately moral, innately kind, decent, honest. Because of this innate morality – a 'natural' morality – the market would 'naturally' be civil and government could always remain limited. Individuals would always be honest and trustworthy even in market competition, even in pursuit of private self-interest. In this way Locke solved the problem of morality simply by a moral assumption. No sacred moral rules, and thus no dominant, moralistic government (aristocrats), would be necessary for a decent social order. Government could always remain passive, simply enforcing rational contracts, because rational, self-interested individuals would always constrain their selfishness through 'natural', innate altruism, creating a good society.

This was an appealing solution and Locke became quite famous. But it was also finally unconvincing because it contradicted individualism. From the individualist perspective, individuals are 'naturally' rational, autonomous, and self-interested. They are not 'naturally' moral. Indeed, the basic point of individualism was to envision a good society that did not depend on morality. If individuals are assumed to be moral, then they are not autonomous and self-interested. If individuals are inherently moral, then private property is not strictly private; that is, the owners of property always have moral obligations to others. Locke did not solve the moral problem but rather just assumed it away. His basic moral assumption made his theory very appealing as a political individualist vision, but it also guaranteed the quick return of the individualist moral problem, the problem of egoism and altruism.

This problem remained for nearly a century after Locke until Smith finally solved it, or at least he appeared to solve it. Hobbes and Locke had analyzed the political issues of government for rational individuals, but they had not analyzed the economic issues of the market. Before the work of Adam Smith, the idea of laissez-faire was essentially an individualist hope that the market would be self-regulating so government could be limited. Smith provided the necessary economic analysis, an analysis of supply and demand. He showed in great detail how market competition between selfish individuals would 'naturally' lead to a civil society, with no need for government control. Smith even argued for less government than Locke, and his economic analysis of market relations solved the problem of morality. He showed indeed that laissez-faire would work, that private, selfish egoism would 'naturally' generate public, civil altruism.

At least this is what he *seemed* to show and how he was generally interpreted. He became world famous for proving the individualist vision, that the market could be just and civil based strictly on selfish greed. In fact, however, this was not what he argued. Rather, like Locke, he assumed innate morality. Innately moral individuals would temper pure self-interest, and the market would be civil. We will look more carefully at Smith's market analysis in Chapter 3, but he could only solve the market problem of morality by assuming it did not exist, just as Locke had done. Locke assumed that all individuals belonged to a 'community of nature', and Smith assumed innate 'moral sentiments', a shared 'sociability'. Both could support the idea of laissez-faire only because they assumed individuals were not perfectly selfish, although Smith was interpreted quite differently.

The market problem of morality, then, was not truly solved. Hobbes faced it directly and recommended absolute government. Locke and Smith refused to face it and recommended limited government. Locke and Smith became the basis for market institutions, but they assumed an innate morality that made no sense within those institutions. If rational individuals are autonomous and self-interested, why would they be moral? But if they are not moral, the market cannot be civil according to Locke and Smith. The early individualists, including Thomas Jefferson, generally assumed that rational individuals would also be honest and honorable. Only this assumption could make the market vision work, as Adam B. Seligman points out:

> The workings of a free-market … are not sufficient preconditions for the existence of civil society … civil society rests first of all on the idea of the autonomous individual and the terms of association, trust, and mutuality between these individuals … (… the classical idea of citizenship …) … civil society calls for the generalization and the universalization of trust. (1992: 178–179)

Locke and Smith, it seems, could not fully face the implications of individualism, the idea of pure self-interest. From one special perspective, however, their assumption of innate morality can be seen as compatible with individualism. This is the perspective of an *agrarian market* on an endless, open frontier, a frontier of free land. This is the market both Locke and Smith assumed and that Jefferson clearly wanted. On an agrarian frontier, all individuals can always be owner-workers, working the land they own. As a result, they can always be structurally equal. Some individuals may become richer than others, but no class structure can arise, no class monopolies of property. As a result, no individual or group of individuals will be able to achieve structural dominance, the dominance of owners over workers.

Owners are not very likely to be honest and honorable with workers, moral and altruistic, because owners make profit from the exploitation of workers. This is why the moral assumption of Locke and Smith cannot make sense in an industrial market. If a rational owner can make more money by exploiting and oppressing a worker, and that owner will not be punished because of structural privilege, then no innate morality is likely to prevent that owner from making more money.

If everyone can be structurally equal, however, as on an open frontier, then individuals will tend to be honest and honorable, and trust will be easy to achieve. This is not because of innate individual morality. Rather, it is because everyone will have a rational, private interest in acting with honesty and honor. If no individual or group of individuals can achieve structural privilege, then a context of trust and respect is generally best for maximizing rational self-interests. In such a market context, agreements are most reliable, investments are most secure, and business plans are encouraged. In a context of structural equality, it makes the most rational sense for all individuals to compete with a shared morality. Anyone who lies and cheats for immediate market profit will tend to be exposed and punished and lose market access. In a context of structural inequality, however, it often makes most rational sense for an individual to lie and cheat, particularly an owner. Owners will not tend to be punished for deceiving and abusing workers, so there is far less rational incentive for a shared, civil morality.

From this perspective the moral assumption of Locke and Smith was really an agrarian assumption, an assumption about endless free land, as Jefferson understood. On an open frontier in a context of owner-workers, mutual trust and honor make rational market sense, and this is what the cowboy myth always portrays. On the mythical frontier the villains try to achieve monopolies of property – 'own all the land in the valley' – and the good, decent citizens act with honesty and trust – 'a man's word is his bond'. The villains represent the eastern market, a market with no frontier, and the western market can only remain just and civil as long as the frontier lasts. In this sense, then, the only solution to the problem of morality is an open, agrarian frontier. This was Jefferson's point as he helped construct America on the ideas of Locke and Smith. The market could be civil based on independent agrarians, and America was an image of endless free land.

The ideas of market individualism derive from the social contract theory of John Locke and the market theory of Adam Smith. Both these theories rest on basic individualist assumptions, assumptions that are most clearly articulated in Locke's social contract theory. These are assumptions about 'natural' individual qualities, the qualities of the original State of Nature according to Locke and Hobbes. These assumptions shaped all individualist ideas and market institutions. They were intended to replace traditional morality although they were also laced with morality. They were not always clear and they were often contradictory, but they led to the rise of our modern society – to all our modern wealth as well as our modern dilemmas.

Illustrative films

Some Westerns and action films are listed in the chapter. Other typical Westerns to view would be *The Westerner* (1940), *Shane* (1953), *Silverado* (1985), *Pale Rider* (1985). In *The Westerner* and *Shane* (and *The Violent Men*), the villains are essentially still in the State of Nature, unwilling to submit to law. They are early, rugged westerners who resist the civilizing newcomers. In *Silverado* and *Pale Rider* (and also *Tall in the Saddle, War of the Wildcats, Dallas, Man Without a Star, The Far Country*), the villains are more identified with the corrupt, greedy East. *Pale Rider* is more or less a remake of *Shane*, and in *Shane* the villain is an early rancher who denies the rights of the homesteaders. In the later version, however – *Pale Rider* – the villain owns a mining company and is identified with the East. Part of the imagery of his villainy in this film is the use of industrial mining technology. In *Shane* the hero is clearly identified with the wilderness, typically filmed against the mountain glory of the Grand Tetons. But the villainous gunfighter, though not from the East, is never seen in a wilderness setting. He is only filmed against the backdrop of a building or in the saloon. All these films show the morality of small agrarians (or miners) and the threat from greedy monopolists.

2

'NATURAL' INDIVIDUALS

Assumptions

The basic assumptions of individualism – the qualities of the State of Nature – are rationality, autonomy, and self-interest. These assumptions were intended, by the early individualists, as a rejection of feudal class structure, particularly the privilege of the aristocrats. In place of this structure, these assumptions asserted 'natural' individual equality (rationality), 'natural' individual freedom (autonomy), and a 'natural' right to private property (self-interest). These assumptions can never be consistent with a need for social morality, including innate morality. If individuals are 'naturally' selfish, they cannot also be 'naturally' kind and caring. The point of these assumptions, however, was to create a good society, a decent, civil society. This civil society must generate trust and honor, but these moral qualities must somehow arise from 'naturally' selfish individuals, not from a sacred morality. The assumptions of individualism undermined the feudal morality of class, but they also had to generate a just, civil society, a moral society that did not depend on morality. This was always the central individualist problem, the problem of generating public altruism from private, selfish egoism.

According to Locke, one central requirement for a just, civil society was a limited, minimal government, a representative government. As the new American nation began to be developed from Locke's ideas, his idea of representative government gradually became an American idea of democratic government. The difference, essentially, was that Locke thought only some individuals should be allowed to vote, only landowners, and the early Americans generally agreed. Soon, however, America began to accept the idea of democracy, an idea rejected by Locke, and all individuals were eventually given the vote, that is, all white male citizens.

It should be remembered, of course, that for all their concern with equality, the early individualists – Hobbes, Locke, Smith, Jefferson, and others – only meant white male equality, not equality for women and non-whites. These individualists wanted to end the class inequality of feudalism through the idea of private property. They were not concerned with other forms of racial or sexual inequality. When they assumed all individuals are rational, they only meant that all white males are rational, so all white males should be able to own property. The abstract concepts of social contract theory, concepts like 'rational individuals', always tend to hide this white male bias. But when American institutions were built on the theory, this bias was made obvious, and it has also been made obvious in the dramatic cultural images of the frontier myth.

According to the idea of implied consent, all rational individuals have implicitly agreed to accept a rational government, a limited government that only maintains market order. Government, in turn, has agreed to protect private property and to maintain as much freedom and equality as is compatible with a rational, competitive market. This all sounds good in theory, and it sounded particularly good to the early individualists in a context of aristocratic government. It becomes quite complicated in practice, however, as we have found in our modern market. A constant and difficult problem it creates is how much freedom should government restrict to maintain market order? This is not just a problem of freedom versus order, the State of Nature versus civility. It also tends to be a problem of freedom versus equality, because the two basic values of the individualist market often come into conflict.

According to social contract theory, a legitimate rational government should maintain maximum market freedom (the freedom to accumulate private property) as well as equal opportunity (the legal equality to own private property). How much market freedom, however, is compatible with equal opportunity? When does the great market wealth of some individuals begin to restrict the equal opportunity of other individuals? To what degree should the government act to protect equal opportunity by restricting market freedom? These are difficult theoretical problems, and they become difficult political problems. They were difficult in the debates over the American Constitution, and they are still difficult today.

In most market nations, opposing political parties have been organized more or less around this issue. One party, generally the conservatives, supports market freedom over equal opportunity, and another, generally the liberals, supports equal opportunity over market freedom. In America this is the difference between Republicans and Democrats, where Republicans tend to want individuals to have more market freedom to maximize their wealth. So they generally support fewer taxes, less welfare, and less government regulation, and they are willing to accept greater economic inequality. Democrats, in contrast, tend to want individuals to have more equality, so they support more taxes, more welfare, and more government regulation, including unions, health care, and affirmative action.

Freedom and equality are appealing goals, but they are difficult to achieve and are not always clear. In the individualist conception they are defined in terms of private property, so a legitimate market government must always protect private property and then try to reconcile freedom and equality. Some people, however, will always think that government has taken too much power and restricted too much freedom. So a final difficult problem arises: when does government become illegitimate, that is, too arbitrary and oppressive, too dominant and biased? When do individuals have a legitimate right to resist and defy their government, even to the point of violent revolution?

All these problems arise from the assumptions of individualism – rationality, autonomy, self-interest. These assumptions defined the values of freedom and equality, and they created modern market society. Their meanings are not always clear, however, and they are not always compatible. We will look at these assumptions more carefully to see their social implications, and we will also look at their mythical, cowboy imagery to see what the theory has hidden and what the culture reveals.

Theoretical rationality

All of individualism rests on the assumption of rationality. It follows from the idea of rational Nature, so individualism is essentially an aspect of science. Hobbes thought he was developing the social implications of Galileo's physics, and Locke and Smith, as well as most individualists, thought they were developing the social implications of Newton's physics. If Nature is rational, then individuals are 'naturally' rational. But if individuals are 'naturally' rational, then they are all 'naturally' equal, and the feudal class structure cannot be legitimate. The early individualists understood that all individuals are not truly equal, not in the sense that they are all equally smart, strong, tall, lucky, rich. All they meant, and all they thought Nature implied, was that no traditional class distinctions creating unequal opportunity can possibly be legitimate. All individuals, they argued, are more 'naturally' equal than they are socially unequal. The only legitimate society, then, is one that gives all individuals an equal chance to succeed, and then their relative success will depend upon their individual merit, that is, upon their effort, intelligence, skill, luck, personality.

The underlying idea was that all individuals (all white males) should be able to own property. Property meant land to the early individualists, so all individuals should be able to own land. Further, they should all be able to own land as private property, with no traditional duties or privileges. In feudal society, aristocrats controlled all the land, but they did not 'own' the land, not in our modern sense of private property. They could not buy or sell the land, and they could only use it in traditional ways, that is, for feudal agriculture. The peasants lived on and farmed the land. They supported the wealth and privilege of the lords, but the peasants had a traditional feudal right to live on and off the land. The lords had sacred, traditional duties to the peasants, essentially providing protection and security. The lords needed the peasants and the peasants needed the lords, and the sacred traditions of feudalism maintained this class arrangement.

The idea of private property undermined this class structure and asserted individual equality. If property is private, everyone can own and work land with no sacred duties. Land can be used simply for private interests – to maximize private wealth – and no class or Church or God will care. For the early individualists, private property meant legal equality and thus equal opportunity. Everyone would have an equal chance to compete in the market. Some would get richer than others, but wealth would be based on individual merit, not on birth and lineage.

The original idea of equal opportunity meant real equal opportunity, the opportunity to claim and own real property (land). The original idea of civil society was a society of equal landowners, independent agrarians. In our modern industrial society we mean something else by equal opportunity – the equal opportunity to get a job. We no longer expect that all individuals will have an equal opportunity to claim and own productive property, particularly land. The original idea of equal opportunity assumed an endless frontier of free wilderness land. According to social contract theory, individuals in the State of Nature (America – the untamed wilderness) had an equal opportunity to claim and own land, and those individuals – equal landowners – then left the State of Nature to form a social contract. This was the original civil vision, and Locke took it quite seriously, as did Jefferson and the early Americans.

Locke recommended that only landowners should vote, and early America only gave landowners the vote. Locke's argument was that only freeholders (free owners of land) would be rational enough to vote. If non-owners (workers) could vote, they would not vote wisely. They would be too ignorant, dependent, easily manipulated, and civil society would fail. Today this sounds arrogant and elitist, and America, of course, slowly and reluctantly gave workers the vote. Locke assumed, however, that everyone could claim free land, and early Americans shared this assumption. From this perspective, anyone who was not a landowner was clearly lazy, ignorant, and dependent, and would therefore be a threat to civil society. In America, according to John C. Miller, Jefferson worried about 'the mobbish workingmen of the cities'. Jefferson often disagreed with the Federalists, who essentially defined the Constitution, but the 'Federalists began to fear the proletariat of the cities no less than did Jefferson' (1960: 120). Jefferson thought, along with many others, that civility depended on independent agrarians, and he and others supported political efforts to limit the size of individual landholdings (agrarian laws) so there would always be enough free land.

The problem, of course, was that the new individualist market quickly undermined agrarian relations and ended the open frontier. Private property means no traditional constraints, and without traditional constraints individuals become inventive and innovative in order to maximize their wealth. The idea of rational Nature encouraged scientific knowledge and thus new technology, and new productive technology led to the rise of industry and the decline of agriculture. The idea of a civil market assumed agrarian relations, but the productive activity of the market destroyed agrarian relations. The early individualists feared industrial cities because of their structural inequality, but the market created industrial cities and all their problems for civility. We now only think of the market in terms of industrial cities, but the cowboy myth always reminds us that the original idea of civility required an agrarian frontier.

Cowboy rationality

The mythical cowboy emerges from the wilderness to save the threatened community. The wilderness is the theoretical State of Nature, the source of 'natural' rationality, 'natural' equality. The wilderness is dangerous and untamed, and the cowboy has special wilderness skills, special wilderness knowledge. He is or has been a scout or a guide. He has lived with or fought against the Indians. He knows the language, the customs, even the leaders of the Indians. Indians are identified in the cowboy myth with the wilderness State of Nature, so the cowboy's connection with the Indians certifies his wilderness identity. He also knows how to survive in the wilderness, how to find food and water, how to cross rivers, how to stop stampedes, how to break wild horses. He has a special skill at violence, and this is also a wilderness skill. Violence is necessary in the dangerous wilderness where law and government are absent.

In all these ways the cowboy is a 'natural' individual, with no rank or family or lineage. He is alone, detached, a stranger, and he has no important position, if he even has a job. He sees himself as an equal, however, and treats all others as equals. He may have a reputation – as a gunfighter, for example – that makes him special and feared, but his reputation is based on individual merit, not on inherited privilege. He may also respect certain individuals more than others, but only on the basis of merit. He fights for individual equality regardless of importance or wealth, and his commitment to equality derives from the wilderness as the source of 'natural' equality.

His wilderness identity also represents rationality. He is a 'natural' individual who can know and tame the wilderness. He can survive in the wilderness, fight Indians, find trails, break horses, herd cattle, use violence, and build society. If the wilderness represents Nature, the cowboy represents the rational individual who can understand and manipulate Nature – the scientist, the engineer, the entrepreneur. The cowboy knows the truths of the wilderness as the scientist knows the truths of Nature.

The cowboy's mastery of the wilderness symbolizes the mastery of Nature, and that is the point of rational Nature, the point of individualism.

The cowboy fights for individual equality, but he is clearly superior to other individuals – stronger, tougher, smarter, a savior, a hero. His superiority is based on merit, and through it he wins social success – respect, authority, land, even a woman's love. The cowboy, then, represents a 'natural' social hierarchy within 'natural' equality, a hierarchy of market winners and losers. He fights not only for equal opportunity but also for superior individual success based on that opportunity. Jefferson envisioned a 'natural' aristocracy arising in market society, an aristocracy of ability, not of lineage.

The cowboy is just such a 'natural aristocrat', as Owen Wister describes his cowboy hero in his 1903 novel, *The Virginian*. This novel became quite famous, and it essentially defined and made respectable the basic elements of the emerging cowboy myth. Its hero, the Virginian, is never called by name, suggesting the unimportance of family and lineage. He is a lowly, working westerner, but he is clearly superior, as Wister notes, to all the snobbish, arrogant easterners. The beautiful eastern schoolmarm initially sees him as a social inferior. Finally, however, she accepts his 'natural' authority, his 'natural' superiority, and this means she also accepts western individual equality, the equality of equal opportunity. This novel, by the way, is where the hero tells the villain, after an insulting epithet, 'When you call me that, smile', a phrase that became famous for reflecting individualist equality. A man can only be insulted and belittled by his friends.

In an important sense, the idea of an aristocracy, even a 'natural' aristocracy, contradicts the idea of individual equality. Jefferson and Wister, of course, assume a context of legal equality. Some individuals can be more successful – the 'natural' aristocrats – but they cannot have legal (class) privilege. Even in this context, however, the idea of a 'natural' aristocrat seems to imply special political authority and power. If some people are 'natural' aristocrats, they should probably be social leaders and have dominant power. This contradicts, however, the market commitment to equality and democracy. The idea of a 'natural' aristocrat can only mean superior market success; it cannot mean superior political privilege and control.

The cowboy always makes this clear by never seeking dominant control. He always rides away or settles down after the community has been saved, surrendering his social authority. He is clearly a 'natural' aristocrat with superior strength and honor. He is always granted respect and authority from the decent citizens, but he always rides away or settles down, relinquishing dominant control. He only seeks social equality, not privileged power. He is a reluctant and retiring social hero, unlike the traditional hero who always fights for class privilege and often becomes a king. The cowboy only fights for market equality, not for privileged power. He can only be a 'natural' aristocrat if he surrenders social control.

Often, indeed, he must fight a villain who previously 'cleaned up the town'. But this previous hero then became a villain by keeping his dominant control and staying to oppress the citizens.

When the cowboy emerges from the wilderness – the State of Nature – the young, fledgling community is also still in the State of Nature. The citizens are trying to leave the wilderness and build a rational society, but the villains rely on strength and violence because no government exists. The cowboy hero must defeat the villains and end the State of Nature, enabling a civil society. This means, in effect, that he becomes the necessary government, imposing a rational order for market competition. After that order is established, the cowboy must leave or settle down, because government must be limited and passive. After the State of Nature a market of equal individuals will regulate itself. Government (the cowboy hero) does not need to maintain that market, only to protect it occasionally.

The villains who threaten civil society want to own all the land, the water, the gold, the right-of-way. They want to monopolize all the property, preventing all others from becoming owner-workers. The individualist cowboy, however, can still defeat these monopolizing villains because of the open frontier. On the western frontier, according to the myth, any effort to monopolize property defines an individual as a villain. In the East, however, where the frontier is gone, monopolies of property are inevitable and no civil society is possible. The frontier enables a civil market including a passive government. Government can only stay weak and minimal if everyone is a structural equal and acts with honesty and trust. On the frontier the cowboy can defeat the villains (defeat monopolies) and then relinquish power (passive government). Laissez-faire is possible (market self-regulation) when everyone is an owner-worker and honesty is rational self-interest.

In the urban, industrial East, however – a context of owners and workers – honesty and trust are not always rational. As a result, government must generally exercise more power, become more active, in order to support equal opportunity and minimize class arrogance. In the industrial city, that is, the cowboy cannot protect freedom and equality by simply riding away. Government must become a dominant presence if the market is to work at all, much less remain civil. This is why Locke and Smith assumed a frontier and Jefferson worried about its end. They wanted equal opportunity – real equal opportunity – and they also wanted limited government, which means maximum market freedom – the freedom to maximize wealth. In a context of owners and workers, however – class monopolies – the freedom of some individuals undermines the equal opportunity of others. Government must be used to protect equality or a new class system will emerge. Only on the frontier is freedom compatible with equality. The cowboy must fight for both if the market is to be civil, and neither freedom nor equality, in the original individualist sense, is compatible with urban industry.

Theoretical autonomy

According to social contract theory, individuals are 'naturally' autonomous. They are autonomous in the sense that they have no necessary duties, no sacred, traditional duties. They are born 'naturally' free, free of all moral rules and social responsibilities. The assumption of autonomy is the assumption of individual freedom, the freedom to pursue private interests. More exactly, the assumption of autonomy means the freedom to pursue private property. Only if property is private can individuals truly be free. If property is private, its owners are free of all social obligations. They can use their property any way they wish, strictly for private interests. If property is not private, individuals are always bound by social obligations, obligations imposed by the property. Property in feudal society imposed social obligations, the obligations of class structure, so the idea of 'natural' autonomy was asserted to end this idea of property.

The assumption of autonomy follows from rational Nature, that is, from scientific knowledge. In the sacred, Christian universe, God watched and controlled everything, and God had moral rules. Morality was built into everything, the entire universe, and so all aspects of the universe – all natural events (rain, seasons, crops, etc.) – imposed moral constraints on all individuals. The idea of rational Nature, then, eliminated morality from the universe. The universe was only a rational machine, so individuals could now be seen as 'naturally' autonomous. They were free of any sacred morality, and they could use their rationality however they wished. They could use their rationality to maximize their wealth, and they could build a rational society to maximize their freedom to maximize their wealth.

According to Locke's theory, private property exists in the State of Nature as a 'natural' individual right. Government does not exist, so no social obligations exist. Private property, then, is the 'natural' way individuals would use property (land) prior to any government. Individuals are rational and autonomous in the State of Nature and they compete for private property. This competition, however, has no rational limits, no legal or moral constraints. Thus, this 'natural' competition is often violent and vicious, a state of constant warfare. Individuals in the State of Nature are perfectly free, so they are free to lie, cheat, steal, and kill. No individual is safe and no property is ever secure. For Locke, the State of Nature is not always a 'State of War', but it tends to become this way, dominated by 'violence and injury'. This is 'one great *reason of Men's putting themselves into Society*, and quitting the State of Nature' (1966: 299–300, italics in original). In the State of Nature, the individual right to property is 'constantly exposed to the Invasion of others', and life 'is full of fears and continual dangers' (1966: 368). Hobbes also saw the State of Nature this way. It is a 'condition ... called war, and such a war as is of everyman against

everyman ... the life of man is solitary, poor, nasty, brutish, and short'
(1958: 106–107).

Government, then, is necessary for rational individuals. They willingly
(rationally) surrender some of their freedom in order to achieve security.
Government must have enough power to end the State of Nature. That is,
it must have enough power to dominate all individuals so no individuals
will be tempted to lie, cheat, steal, etc. But government with this much
power also becomes a potential threat to freedom. Government may
begin to abuse its power and serve special interests, class interests. So
government must always be limited. It must end 'natural' freedom and
enable market freedom, but it must enable as much market freedom as
possible, as much, that is, as is compatible with rational market equality.
Government must maintain this delicate balance between too much
power and not enough power, so it must be closely watched and controlled to prevent potential abuse.

Locke's concern with limited government translated in America into
democratic controls as well as structural controls. The democratic controls
put in the Constitution included regular elections, free speech, a free
press, trial by jury. The structural controls included internal checks and
balances among separate branches (legislative, executive, judicial), independent state governments, and a Bill of Rights. Jefferson insisted on a
Bill of Rights to prevent government abuse, and he also argued, following
Locke, that rebellion and revolution might sometimes be necessary to
fight government corruption. Individuals always have a right to resist
their government in defense of their 'natural' right to freedom, even to
resist violently.

The idea of democracy is a commitment to constant criticism.
According to the theory, rational individuals create their government to
serve their rational interests, so they always have a right to criticize that
government in terms of their rational interests. This is what it means to
have free speech, a free press, and trial by a jury of peers. Social contract
theory, in effect, makes criticism of government a 'natural' individual
right. And criticism, of course, is built into the market. Rational individuals who want to compete must be critical of what their competitors are
doing and try to do it better. Rational criticism is built into science, since
any given theory of Nature can always be improved and corrected, and
criticism can lead to new ideas, new technology, innovation. Criticism and
innovation are inherent in individualism. More specifically, they are
inherent in individual autonomy, in the individualist idea of freedom.
When individuals are free from all sacred tradition, they are free to criticize others, including the government, to challenge accepted wisdom, and
to explore new ideas, new frontiers.

Criticism, however, can often lead to resistance and defiance and even
to violence. Both Locke and Jefferson endorsed the possible necessity of
violence against corrupt government. Government must always maintain
a delicate balance between chaos (too little law) and oppression (corrupt

law), and this delicate balance, indeed, may never satisfy everyone. Criticism is a necessity of democracy – that's what elections are about – and sometimes criticism must 'take to the streets' and defy the law outside the political process. In some cases in American history this defiance of the law is later seen as noble and just because the law was biased and corrupt. Both Susan B. Anthony and Martin Luther King, Jr, for example, went to jail for breaking the law. But their defiance of the law led to changes in the law, changes that gave more freedom and equality to women and non-whites.

Anthony and King used non-violent resistance, but the student activists of the 1960s often used violence to protest the Vietnam War. Many of these students went to jail, but now they are generally seen as having supported American ideals while resisting an unjust war. In another example, however, the bombers of the Federal Building in Oklahoma City in 1995, where 164 died, also claimed to be fighting for freedom by resisting oppressive laws. Unlike Anthony and King, though, and unlike the student protesters, these bombers have not been vindicated by history and are not likely to be. Their criticism of government fell on the wrong side of the delicate government balance, while these other government critics – breakers of the law – are seen as defenders of freedom.

In their own time, Anthony, King, and the student protesters were often condemned by government officials as threats to the nation, to its ideals of freedom and justice, just as the Oklahoma City bombers have been condemned. Anthony, King, and the protesters, however, but not the bombers, were later vindicated and even celebrated in the name of these same ideals, the ideals of individual defiance, the ideals Locke and Jefferson supported. The idea of legitimate resistance, then, even violent resistance, is always confused and uncertain, and the 'proper' use of government power can never truly be clear. Any individual, that is, may decide in any specific case that resistance and violence are justified regardless of the opinions of others because freedom is at stake, as history will later show. This idea is built into social contract theory, the legitimating theory of modern market society and specifically of America. It should not be surprising, then, that many market societies have problems with violence, and America is known for its violence.

Social contract theory essentially states that violence is inherent in freedom. It is a necessary condition for freedom. Violence is endemic in the State of Nature where individuals are most 'naturally' free, perfectly free. Individuals then surrender some of their freedom in order to escape the violence, but they always retain the right to be violent because violence is required for freedom. Violence may be necessary against oppressive government, so violence will probably increase in market society as government becomes more dominant. As the market becomes industrial and divided between owners and workers, government must become more dominant, and this may imply, according to the theory, that violence is likely to increase.

When Locke and Jefferson endorsed the possible need for periodic revolutions, they did not anticipate industry. They only thought that a market government of equal, independent agrarians (owner-workers) might tend to become corrupt. Jefferson clearly thought that an urban, industrial market could never be civil, so violence could only defend civility on an endless agrarian frontier. The frontier would enable structural equality and thus a civil society, so violence would only be necessary at the beginning, to end the State of Nature, and occasionally under government to end excessive control.

This is the implicit agrarian image of social contract theory. Violence will always be potentially ready to protect individual freedom, but in a context of structural equality (an open frontier) it will not usually be necessary. On an open frontier laissez-faire will work – the market will regulate itself amid individual honesty and trust. Government can thus stay limited and passive, and freedom will only require potential violence, perhaps sporadic violence, not constant, defiant violence. The cowboy myth, of course, makes this implicit theoretical image an explicit cultural image, an image of the civil frontier. This is the image Jefferson used when he worried about urban corruption, and this is the image the cowboy portrays when he must use violence to fight monopolies of property.

Cowboy autonomy

American popular culture tends to focus on heroes who defy established authority. They defy established laws and rules – government, corporations, bureaucracy – to defend individual freedom. The cowboy is the individualist hero, the symbol of market freedom, and he often has to break the law to maintain a decent society, a society of freedom and equality. The cowboy must use violence to end the State of Nature (violent, vicious villains) or remove corrupt officials (the sheriff, the judge, the mayor). His violence, however, is always tempered by honor. The violence enables a decent market society, and honor must be part of any such society, honor in the sense of honesty, courtesy, morality. The cowboy must fight for freedom but he must also fight with honor. He must combine violence with honor to build a good society, and this is always possible on the open frontier where all individuals can work their own land.

When the 'cowboy' moves to the city, however, in the urban action film, he must become more violent and far less concerned with honor. On the open frontier the citizens can be civil, but in the industrial city virtually no one can be trusted. The individualist hero is denounced as a 'cowboy' because he breaks laws and rules. He lives in a context of owners and workers and there is no western frontier, no real equalizing opportunity. Honor can no longer create civility but rather will only get him killed.

Freedom is constantly threatened and violence is always necessary, so the 'cowboy' can never take off his guns.

The cowboy is the symbol of individual autonomy, the 'natural' autonomy of the original State of Nature. He emerges from the wilderness with no social connections – alone, independent, self-reliant. He is a rational equal of everyone, and he is free to pursue his own interests and shape his own destiny. He represents individualist freedom in its pure, 'natural' form. He has wilderness knowledge and skills – he knows the Indians, he knows the trails – and part of his wilderness identity is his special mastery of violence. Violence is necessary in the wilderness State of Nature, an inherent aspect of freedom, and it is also necessary to end the State of Nature and build a civil society. Violence is only implicit in social contract theory, but the myth makes it explicit, celebrating violence to celebrate freedom. The myth reveals what the theory hides. Individualist freedom depends on violence because individualist freedom derives from the wilderness. As Robert Warshow remarks in his classic essay, 'The Westerner', the Western maintains a 'hold on our imagination … because it offers a serious orientation to the problem of violence such as can be found almost nowhere else in our culture' (1962: 151).

The cowboy's connection with the wilderness makes him stronger than the decent citizens. Only he has the necessary strength, the necessary violence, to save the threatened community and build a civil society. The citizens want to leave the State of Nature and form a social contract, but they have become too far removed from Nature, that is, from the wilderness. Their participation in society has made them weak, while the cowboy emerging from the wilderness still remains strong. As the myth portrays the theory, civil society needs the decency of the citizens, but it also needs the strength and violence of the wilderness. Social order must never take away too much 'natural' freedom, and this is what the cowboy represents as a lonesome wilderness stranger.

The villains are also strong and especially good at violence. They are part of the State of Nature, the part that prefers full 'natural' freedom over rational market freedom. In the imagery of the myth, however, the cowboy hero is far more connected with the wilderness than the villains. The central villain is usually from the East, although he hires western thugs, and when the villains are not from the East, they only know about money and property, not about Indians and trails. The cowboy is the true individualist emerging from the State of Nature, the enabler of civil society. What he brings from Nature (the wilderness) is exactly what society needs. Part of what he brings is wilderness strength and violence, but the villains are also strong and violent though not identified with the wilderness. What the wilderness gives the cowboy, then, as the true, enabling individualist, is strength tempered by morality, a wilderness sense of honor.

The cowboy is a man of honor, perhaps his definitive trait. His commitment to individualist freedom is always constrained by honor, and this makes civil society possible. The villains have no honor, so their 'natural' freedom is destructive. The citizens are moral and decent but they are also weak and afraid, and honor requires confidence and strength, even a need for violence. The cowboy, then, is uniquely a man of honor, and he is also uniquely identified with the wilderness. The wilderness is not only his source of 'natural' freedom, it is also his source of 'natural' honor, an honor that tempers his freedom. In effect, the myth reproduces Locke's assumption, an assumption of innate morality, an assumption also made by Smith and Jefferson. The 'natural' (wilderness) individual has 'natural' (wilderness) honor.

The wilderness is the State of Nature, a place of violence and war. But it is also a place of 'natural' truths, a place of reason and hope. It provides 'natural' freedom and equality, but these can generate a civil society, and civility requires a shared morality, that is, a sense of honor. The wilderness, then, is something to escape but not something to abandon entirely. It provides the freedom and equality, the violence and honor, necessary for a good society. So it must always be close at hand, just across the endless frontier. It is not a place for social life, but it is a place for social renewal, a place that confirms the individualist vision.

This image of the wilderness was imposed on America as individualist ideas arose. America was the State of Nature, a place of 'natural' freedom. Individuals could pursue their rational destiny and build a new society, a society based on Nature. According to Yehoshua Arieli:

> In the eighteenth century, America becomes for Europe as well as for its own inhabitants the stage for the realization of mankind's hopes. 'Nature,' the magic masterwork of the Enlightenment, iridescent with the complex meanings which the revolutionary hopes for the transformation of society instilled, reigned in the New World ... The vast empty spaces, unobstructed by the past, invited man to live freely ... Here the eternal beneficence of nature could be observed and reason became the guide of action. Unhampered by the accumulation of customs, prejudices, and the follies of ages, men could work out their own salvation by their own powers. (1964: 43–45)

The vast eastern forests were originally this realm of Nature, but later, and mythically, the West symbolized the wilderness. The West had scenic grandeur beyond imagination – soaring mountains, rugged canyons, brutal deserts, endless prairies. This scenic grandeur was soon interpreted as validating individualism. Nature had offered a bountiful gift together with spectacular beauty to enable a civil society. The beauty of the West offered social renewal free of eastern corruption. In Europe and the East, the West was first seen in nineteenth-century landscape paintings, the paintings of Bodmer, Bierstadt, Moran, and others. These paintings established the West as part of the individualist vision, as a land of rational destiny.

Moran's paintings in particular convinced members of Congress to establish Yellowstone as the first national park in 1872. Other national parks soon followed – Glacier, Yosemite, Grand Canyon, and others, mostly in the West – and all were established as wilderness monuments to certify individual freedom and validate American society. National forests were also established, and according to Congressman Ralph Regula, 'Average working men and women consider the national forests the last bastion of personal freedom, where they can practice self-reliance' (Miniclier, 1998: 1B).

This image of wilderness freedom, the freedom of the Wild West, soon transcended America as the cowboy began to be an international star. In America and around the world images of the American West, and particularly of the red rock canyons, have become identified with freedom. Pictures of these canyons are repeatedly and successfully used in advertising campaigns to sell different products – cars, cigarettes, cell phones, software, investment advice, politicians – and the point of these ads is always to associate these products and people with a vision of individual freedom.

The wilderness defines the endless frontier, and the frontier depends on the wilderness. The frontier can enable civility based on free wilderness land. Violence can be constrained by honor, and freedom is compatible with order, the order of laissez-faire. Most importantly, freedom is compatible with equality. With endless free land, the (market) freedom of some to get as rich as possible will never undermine the (real) equal opportunity of others to claim and own productive property. All aspects of the individualist vision can work on the open frontier, with wilderness renewal always close at hand. Violence will still be occasionally necessary, since government is always a risk. But the market should usually be civil and free without the need for violence.

When the frontier is gone, however, class monopolies can arise and market freedom begins to undermine equal opportunity. Government must restrict more freedom to protect equality, but as government takes more power, individuals feel more threatened and violence seems more necessary. From the original individualist perspective, the market cannot be civil in a context of class monopolies since government cannot remain passive. This was Jefferson's point about free western land, and it is also the point of the corrupt East in the cowboy myth and in the violent urban action film.

Theoretical self-interest

The assumption of 'natural' self-interest completes the individualist conception. It adds the necessary motivation for free and equal individuals. What are these individuals free and equal *to do*? What do they seek in the original State of Nature, prior to any social involvement? The traditional assumption was that individuals want to go to heaven, so they are motivated to act morally. But if individuals are rational and autonomous, what is their motivation, their 'natural' motivation?

The assumption of self-interest says their motivations are strictly private and selfish, strictly egoistic. They are motivated by no social, altruistic concerns, not, that is, by love, friendship, compassion, generosity. More exactly, 'natural' self-interest means, for the early individualists, the desire to maximize private property. Individuals 'naturally' want to accumulate as much property as they can and to use that property any way they wish. They want this property because it will help them survive, and they are only concerned with their own survival, not with the survival of others. This idea of self-interest means, for example, that winning the love of another is not in your 'natural' self-interest. We tend to think of falling in love as compatible with our own self-interest, but this is not what the individualists mean. When you fall in love, it generally means sharing your private property, and this means it is not in your 'natural' self-interest.

The individualist ideas of rationality and autonomy – freedom and equality – were rejections of feudal traditions and institutions, specifically the class structure. But what kind of new institutions, new 'natural' institutions, did these new ideas suggest? What kind of social institutions – government, property, production, law – could be seen as appropriate for rational, autonomous individuals? The assumption of self-interest provided the answer. These new social institutions would have to guarantee and protect private property for all individuals. If individuals are 'naturally' self-interested, then institutions can only be legitimate ('natural') if they support private property. Private property is a 'natural' individual right, a right in the State of Nature, but it is always at risk in the dangerous State of Nature. Individuals form a government to make their property secure, but government can only be legitimate if individuals are free to maximize that property through rational competition.

The idea of private property was the fundamental threat to feudal institutions, the fundamental social change. Freedom and equality were appealing ideas, but they only became disruptive ideas – the basis for a new social order – when they were defined in terms of private property. Private property meant the complete destruction of all feudal traditions, all sacred moral rules, the rules of class privilege. For the early individualists, and throughout feudal society, property was always understood as land, and feudal land always involved traditional rights and duties. Individuals did not 'own' the land in the sense of private property – it could not be bought and sold. Rather, the land (the feudal manor) bestowed traditional rights and duties upon individuals in accordance with class position. According to Richard Lachmann, 'Land was not the property of persons or institutions. Rather, land was held in manors, while persons and institutions derived land rights from their positions, as landlords or tenants, on the manor' (1987: 42).

Land was therefore the basis of all feudal wealth and power. When the individualists endorsed private property, they simply wanted land to be available to everyone with no traditional constraints. For them, removing traditional constraints meant removing class structure, class limitations and privileges. It did not mean for them, in the seventeenth and eighteenth centuries, what it soon came to mean in the nineteenth century – encouraging innovation and new technology, encouraging industrial production. Primarily, the individualists wanted to end the aristocratic control of land, but they still saw land as the basis of social relations, of social wealth and power. Private property, however, meant that land could be bought and sold with no concern for tradition, and this meant, in turn, that money, not land, became the basis for wealth and power. If land could be bought and sold, then it was no longer valuable for bestowing traditional rights, but only for how much money it was worth. As money replaced land and tradition collapsed, new ideas were encouraged for making more money, and industry began to arise.

The idea of private property, then, has been crucial for modern society. In particular, Locke's argument for private property has defined our market institutions, and specifically our market government. Locke saw private property as a 'natural' individual right, a right existing in the State of Nature prior to the social contract. But if government does not exist, how does an individual establish a right to property? Locke's answer to this has shaped much of our modern market. His answer is that an individual can establish a right to property – unowned, available property – simply by adding labor to that property, that is, by working the property.

> Whatever he then removes out of the State that Nature hath provided, and left in it, he hath mixed his *Labor* with ... and thereby makes it his *Property* ... His *labor* hath taken it out of the hands of Nature, where it was common and belong'd equally to all her Children, and *hath* thereby *appropriated* it to himself. (1966: 306–307)

Locke is assuming that property is land. Thus individuals, in his view, can claim and own available land (free land, land in the State of Nature) simply by working that land and making it productive.

This is an image of an open frontier, a frontier on an empty wilderness of free available land, the original State of Nature. All individuals would have an equal opportunity to claim and work the land, becoming owner-workers. Individuals would have a 'natural' right to claim private property, and government would be created to protect that property and keep competition rational. Locke saw America as this empty available wilderness, and Jefferson and other American founders built American institutions on this image of Locke. Locke envisioned and Jefferson hoped for the equality of endless free land. According to A. Whitney Griswold, 'Jefferson from the outset directed his thoughts to small frontier farmers ... Agriculture, to him, was not primarily a source of wealth but of human virtues and traits most congenial to popular self-government' (1948: 30). Other early Americans shared Jefferson's hope, including Benjamin Franklin, George Washington, and Thomas Paine. Jefferson even joined with other Americans in support of agrarian laws – legal limits on how much land an individual could own – as a way to preserve available free land.

This image of working free land and owning that land became the American promise. American institutions were built on this promise and it attracted many Europeans. This promise was legally formalized in 1862 when the Homestead Act was passed. Title to a parcel of free western land was offered to anyone who worked that land, and this offer continued until the frontier closed. According to many historians, this Act generated far more speculation and corruption than real equal opportunity. But what it offered in practice was never as important as what it offered in theory – a vision of freedom and equality on a wilderness frontier, the American civil promise.

Locke's idea of 'natural' private property helped legitimate the market. But Locke had to add another argument to justify this idea. He had to show somehow why adding labor to unowned property creates a right to that property. He had to make this convincing to make his theory work, so he asserted another idea that became crucial to the market, the idea that *labor is property*. If labor is seen as property – a 'natural' form of private property – then all individuals already own some private property, their labor. Locke argued that all individuals own their labor as property in the original State of Nature: 'Though the Earth, and all inferior creatures be Common to all Men, yet every Man has a *Property* in his own *Person* ... The *Labor* of his body, and the *Work* of his Hands, we may say, are properly his' (1966: 305–306). In the State of Nature the earth and the animals are 'Common to all Men', yet all individuals already – 'naturally' – own their own labor as a form of private property.

This idea that labor is property justifies, for Locke, his idea of working and claiming available land, wilderness land. Private property 'naturally' exists – an individual's labor – so when that labor is added to real property (land), it gives that individual a 'natural' right to own that real property, that free land. Locke asserted that labor is property to justify equal opportunity, the real equal opportunity to claim and own land. Everyone owns labor, so everyone has a 'natural' right to claim and own real property, to become an owner-worker. If free land is endless (the assumption of an open frontier), then independent agrarians will make the market civil and only landowners should vote.

Locke saw labor as property so that people could claim unowned land as a 'natural' individual right. He did not intend this idea to mean that workers in fact are owners because they own their labor. Locke thought people who only owned their labor (the workers) were clearly lazy and ignorant and would threaten civil society. They should not be allowed to vote, and early Americans generally agreed, only giving freeholders the vote. But Locke justified the market and Jefferson built that market, and that market soon generated industry and closed the agrarian frontier. In the new industrial market, class monopolies were inevitable and real equal opportunity was lost. Many individuals, indeed most individuals, could only become workers, but according to Locke's theory they should not be equal participants, they should not be able to vote. They were not really property owners according to Locke's vision, but that vision assumed they could claim unowned property. Now they could only sell their labor.

Essentially, a new class structure emerged, a structure of owners and workers. This was not what the individualists wanted, but their market ideas created it. The market, however, was a rejection of class and it depended on equal opportunity – the real opportunity for everyone to be an owner. Thus either the market had failed – it could not be civil, as Jefferson feared – or a new legitimating version of equal opportunity had to be achieved, a version for industrial relations. Individuals could no longer be structurally equal – the original individualist vision. But individualism was based on legal equality, which meant no legal class privilege. Legal equality, for the early individualists, meant legal equal opportunity, and the assumption of an open frontier, then, meant *real* equal opportunity, a structure of owner-workers.

For the market to be legitimate after the frontier closed, legal equality had to be maintained as a minimum form of equal opportunity. If only a few individuals could own real property, those individuals could not have special legal privileges and special political power. But Locke had argued that they should, because only property owners (landowners) should vote. From this perspective the new class of workers could never have legal equality – equal political access. The market, it seemed, would have to settle for legal equality and structural inequality because of industrial production. But this would mean workers should have the vote. Locke had argued that only property owners should vote – real property owners, owners of productive property – but he also provided an argument to justify the vote for workers.

If labor is seen as property, then all individuals own some property, and everyone should have the vote. This idea of property essentially justified legal equality in a context of owners and workers. Locke did not intend this use of his argument, but the idea that labor is property was used in the nineteenth century to give American workers the vote. The market idea of equality depended on everyone owning property, and Locke, Smith, and Jefferson all assumed that everyone could own real property – land on an open frontier. When the market became industrial, either the market could no longer be seen as equal, because of class divisions, or everyone would have to be seen as owning property, even the new class of workers. The idea that labor is property solved this problem. It essentially justified market equality by guaranteeing equal access to the market. If all individuals owned some property, even if only their labor, then all individuals had something to sell in the market and thus had equal opportunity. The idea that labor is property created the necessary minimal version of equal market opportunity, the version the market needed to still seem legitimate in a context of owners and workers.

If everyone has something to sell because labor is property, then everyone has a chance to compete in the market. In a context of class monopolies, workers only have a chance to sell their labor, not to claim and own real property. In the new industrial market, then, the legitimating idea of equal opportunity had to become the equal opportunity to get a job, not to claim free land. This idea of equal opportunity could be used, and has been used, to justify our modern market, a market of owners and workers. But this was not the original market vision, a vision of owner-workers. Indeed, Locke implied, and Smith and Jefferson stated, that an urban, industrial market would destroy that original vision, a vision of civil society. Locke gave an argument – labor is property – that supported legal equality (everyone owns property) in a context of structural inequality (owners and workers). But Locke and the individualists only thought the market could be civil with legal *and* structural equality.

In the nineteenth century Karl Marx attacked market theory for its idea that labor is property. When workers sell their labor, he argued, they essentially sell themselves. The idea that labor is property, in his view, turned workers into slaves (wage slaves). Marx understood, as Locke and Jefferson did not, that the market would be industrial. It would generate class monopolies and a structure of owners and workers. He called this market *capitalism* and he saw it as deeply oppressive. Marx essentially analyzed, along with Weber and Durkheim, the market that Jefferson feared, a market of cities and factories and great class differences. Marx attacked the industrial market with great insight and effect, as we will see in Chapter 4. It should be noted, however, that his attack focused exactly on Locke's legitimating idea that labor can be seen as property.

Jefferson assumed, following Locke, an *agrarian* version of the idea that labor is property, where labor can be used to claim free land. This version supports a commitment to structural equality, a society of independent agrarians. But Marx attacked an *industrial* version of the idea that labor is property, where labor is the only property most people will ever have, and workers can only sell their labor. The idea that labor is property justified the individualist vision, a vision of 'natural' property rights and equal owners of land. But it also came to justify, as industry arose, a market of owners and workers, the equal opportunity to get a job. This was a central idea for building a market society, but as the market changed from farming to factories – as the frontier was lost – the idea that labor is property changed the market idea of equality.

For the early individualists the assumption of self-interest was an assumption of equal access to private property, equal access to land. The idea of the State of Nature was an idea of endless free land, and this was the basis for the vision of civil society. Everyone could claim free land because everyone owned their labor as property and everyone could work unowned land. This was the vision of individualism, a vision of freedom and equality, and this was portrayed in the frontier myth, the market myth of origin. The myth understood the need for a wilderness because the wilderness meant structural equality. The West could be free *and* equal, and the market could be civil. But the East could only be corrupt. In the West, self-interest would encourage trust and honesty because no class dominance would be possible. The cowboy is 'naturally' self-interested, just as he is rational and autonomous. But he is also 'naturally' honorable because he always has a chance to work and claim free land.

Cowboy self-interest

The decent citizens in the cowboy myth generally work their own land, as farmers, ranchers, miners, homesteaders. They seek to accumulate private property but only through honest competition, where 'a man's word is his bond'. They are 'naturally' self-interested but they are also 'naturally' moral, just as Locke and Smith assume. They do not own their property (their land) just to maximize their wealth. Rather, they want to participate in a civil society, a free and equal society with churches and schools. They help each other build homes and barns, and they work together in crises such as fires, floods, and illness. They compete in a context of morality because they are structural equals, and they can all be structural equals because of the open frontier, where no class monopolies are possible. They all pursue their rational self-interests as private market individuals, but honesty and trust serve rational self-interests in a context of structural equality. The market can be civil on an open frontier because laissez-faire will work and government can always be passive.

The villains are villainous in the cowboy myth because they seek to monopolize property – 'all the land in the valley'. They want to be the only owners, forcing everyone else to be workers. They use force and violence, deceit and corruption, as ways to achieve monopolies, so the myth clearly associates monopolies of property with a lack of civil morality. Monopolies of property mean owners and workers, and owners have little rational interest in treating workers as equals, that is, with honesty and respect. When everyone is an owner-worker, everyone has a rational interest – the interest of maximum profit – in treating all others as equals. Trade will work better for a longer period of time if everyone always remains honest. Owners, however, always have a chance to maximize their profits by oppressing and exploiting workers. This is what Locke and Smith assume, what Jefferson worries about, and what the cowboy myth portrays. Trust is only possible and the market can only be civil if everyone is a structural equal.

Villains are villainous on the open frontier because monopolies are not inevitable. The villains cannot succeed in their efforts to create class because of free wilderness land. The frontier, in effect, defeats all monopolies at least in the vision of the myth. In a context of structural equality, strong, honorable individualists, like the cowboy hero, can defeat the occasional villain, but no dominant control is necessary, no dominant government, because of civil equals.

Individuals are villains in the cowboy myth, on the agrarian frontier, if they do what urban industry encourages. They are villains, that is, because they seek to be owners and live off the work of others. The myth only sees owners as decent if they also work their own property and help everyone else become an owner/worker. In the industrial market, however, owners cannot simply be identified as villains. This market needs owners and workers, and it is always much better to be an owner.

Owners in the industrial market, owners who employ workers, are often called *capitalists*. Capitalists are owners who think of their property as capital, and capital is property (wealth) that is only used for investment. Capitalists, therefore, are people who invest their property – land, factory, stock, company – and live off the profits it makes. Capitalists do not work their property but rather they use it for investment. So profit can only be made from the property if other people work the property. Capitalists, that is, make money from the labor of workers, so capitalists need class monopolies to create a class of workers. These are normal market relations when the market becomes industrial, and these are exactly the market relations the early individualists feared. They wanted a market of owner-workers, not a market of capitalists, so the cowboy myth shows, reflecting the individualists, that capitalists can only be villains.

In the imagery of the myth, the decent citizens – the owner-workers – do not think of their property simply as investment. Rather, they think of it as the basis for civil society. They want to maximize private wealth, but only in a context of public decency, a context of trust and honor, home and family, justice and fairness. If owners can be capitalists and live off the labor of workers, then the hope for civil society will be lost, according to the myth. This is what happens in the urban East, the East Jefferson feared because the frontier is gone.

Following this original individualist imagery, the myth not only denigrates capitalists, it also tends to denigrate workers. Workers in the myth are also usually villains but only as hired hands. They generally work for the villainous owners and oppress the decent citizens. On the open frontier where everyone can own property, workers must be lazy, ignorant, and dependent. They are always a danger to civil society unless they try to become an owner, that is, to start a ranch. The cowboy hero is usually just a worker, if he is even employed, but he always rides away or he plans to start a ranch 'down at the bend of the river'. Sometimes another worker – a young cowhand – will also talk about finding some land and starting a ranch or farm. He is then seen as honest and civil, and he will usually be killed by the villains. He makes the mythical point, however, along with the cowboy hero, that civil society depends on owner-workers. In the imagery of the myth, both owners who are only capitalists and workers who cannot be owners are generally seen simply as villainous threats to honest, decent citizens.

Sometimes, but not very often, a large, dominant rancher is also a decent citizen, not a selfish villain. This image has appeared in popular films – *Chisum* (1970), *McClintok* (1963), *Saddle the Wind* (1958) – and also in popular television shows – *Bonanza* (1959–73), *The Big Valley* (1965–69), *The Virginian* (1962–71). These large, decent ranchers, however, can still be seen as owner-workers – they ride the range, work the roundups, mend the fences, and fight their own fights. They do not own their land as capital but rather as civil participants. They encourage their cowhands to claim their own land, not to simply remain workers. They also encourage and help new settlers, unlike the villainous ranchers. These decent ranchers make the mythical point that great market success, great wealth, is not the source of villainy. Wealthy owners can also be decent if they do not seek monopolies and if the frontier remains open. Only when the frontier is closed do wealthy owners become capitalists and threats to civil society.

The civil need for an open frontier was always implicit in individualism, as Jefferson made clear in his letter to Madison. The idea of private property assumed free wilderness land, as did the ideas of laissez-faire, democracy, and innate morality. America provided an open frontier and its wilderness could easily seem endless, so this frontier assumption could simply be taken for granted until the frontier began to close. The closing of the frontier, however, could threaten market civility. Fredrick Jackson Turner made this point in 1893 in his famous 'frontier thesis'. The frontier officially closed in 1890, according to the US Census, and Turner then wrote a historical essay that soon became seminal: 'The Significance of the Frontier in American History'. He argued that American democracy and equality had always depended on free western land. Without an open frontier America would succumb to bitter class conflicts, and freedom and civility would be lost:

> Whenever social conditions tended to crystallize in the East, whenever capital tended to press upon labor or political restraints to impede freedom, there was this gate of escape to the free conditions of the frontier. These free lands promoted individualism, economic equality, freedom to rise, democracy ... American democracy is fundamentally the outcome of the experience of the American people in dealing with the West ... the West gave, not only to the American, but to the unhappy and oppressed of all lands, a vision of hope. (1949: 28, 33)

Jefferson hoped for an endless frontier at the end of the eighteenth century, and Turner announced that the frontier was history at the end of the nineteenth century. Jefferson saw an endless frontier as the only hope for civility, and Turner saw the end of the frontier as also the end of civility. They both had the same social vision, the vision of market individualism, but Jefferson and the early individualists saw that vision as a promising future and Turner saw it as the past.

Turner turned the individualist vision into a historical perspective. His frontier thesis shaped the direction of American history for much of the twentieth century. From this perspective, the history of the frontier West was seen as a history of equal opportunity, the equal opportunity of the original vision, the opportunity to claim free land. In the later twentieth century, however, Turner's view of the West was severely and effectively challenged by many western historians – Patricia Limerick, Richard White, William Cronon, Richard Drinnon, and others. In their view, the frontier West was more a place of conquest and greed than a place of freedom and equality. It was most clearly characterized by blatant sexism, brutal racism, corrupt speculation, and cynical greed. From this perspective, Turner did bad history, and he influenced much more bad history. He distorted frontier history to serve the legitimating myth. In effect, he simply repeated the legitimating myth and asserted it as history.

According to this critique, the western frontier primarily provided opportunity for rich white males, not for all individuals. Turner's frontier vision was never very good history, but it was always very good theory, the legitimating theory of market individualism, the legitimating theory of America. His frontier thesis, then, became influential because it supported the American ideal, the ideal of civil society. If American institutions were to make any sense, they had to be based on equal opportunity, and the frontier had always provided the idea of equal opportunity. As the market became industrial during the nineteenth century, many theoretical efforts had to be made to keep the market legitimate. It was only originally legitimate, as Jefferson pointed out, for a context of independent agrarians, but it had to somehow become legitimate, if at all possible, for a context of owners and workers.

In the midst of this theoretical effort, Turner simply announced, asserting theory as history, that the market had truly been legitimate (civil) as long as the frontier was open, but it could not remain legitimate after the frontier closed. He clearly articulated what many people feared, that industrial America would be oppressive and corrupt, not free and equal. His argument opposed the contemporary efforts to legitimate the industrial market. It also, however, reasserted the legitimacy of original market institutions, institutions on an open frontier. In this sense, his frontier thesis was always a legitimating argument, not a historical argument. The image of the frontier had always validated freedom and equality even if the reality of the frontier did not. The end of the frontier, then, ended that validating image, and that image had been crucial to America. Turner became influential by capturing that historical moment. He disguised a theoretical necessity as historical interpretation, and America needed its legitimating theory more than it needed accurate history.

Turner's idea and influence show that the frontier never really closed in American theory or institutions, nor in American culture. The image of a frontier is inherent in market theory, an image of equal opportunity, so some implicit frontier permeates all market issues – private property, limited government, democracy, freedom and equality. Turner was right to think that the western frontier legitimated the American market, even if that frontier never worked as he thought. The frontier provided the *image*, at least, of real equal opportunity, a place where everyone could claim free land and become an owner-worker. When workers in the urban East, or in traditional Europe, could find no chance to improve their lives, they could always imagine going West and claiming frontier land. This frontier hope could keep the market stable even if the frontier reality was dismal. But once the frontier was gone all this hope would be gone, and this is what Turner feared. This is also what Jefferson feared, and what the cowboy myth condemns, particularly in the urban action film. This is the image of the urban East, a place of corruption and oppression, a place of class monopolies.

The image of an open frontier pervades the individualist assumption of 'natural' self-interest. Individuals 'naturally' want to maximize private property, and all individuals can own private property if they are willing to work free land. In much the same way, the image of a frontier pervades the assumptions of rationality and autonomy. Rational individuals are all 'naturally' equal, and they can only be equal if they all own private property. Autonomous individuals are all 'naturally' free, and they can only be free if they can maximize private property, without destroying equality. These three assumptions define the individualist conception, the conception presented in social contract theory, and all these assumptions are threatened, and civil society is doubtful, when the open frontier is lost.

Locke's social contract theory argued for limited government. Government would be necessary to end the State of Nature. But freedom and equality would only be compatible, and the market would only be civil, if government could remain passive. This argument for government implicitly assumed an open, endless frontier, a frontier of equal opportunity. But it also assumed laissez-faire – market self-regulation – so government could always remain limited. The idea of laissez-faire was necessary for freedom and equality, including democratic government, but Locke did not show how laissez-faire could work, not in economic detail. Laissez-faire meant, in essence, that public altruism would emerge from private egoism. It meant, that is, that strictly private selfishness and greed would create a good society. Locke essentially finessed this issue by assuming innate morality. But the idea of innate morality contradicted individualism, and egoism leading to altruism was very difficult to believe. The issue of laissez-faire – of egoism and altruism – continued to haunt individualism until Adam Smith analyzed the market in 1776. Self-regulation, he argued, would follow from supply and demand. Egoism would become altruism simply through rational self-interests, and this market vision completed the individualist conception and influenced the American Constitution.

Illustrative films

The hero in *Shane* emerges from the wilderness of the Tetons wearing buckskins, and he rides back into that wilderness after saving the community. *Shane* is a classic illustration of most of the themes of the cowboy myth. Perhaps the greatest visual entrance of a hero from the wilderness is when John Wayne is first seen against the backdrop of Monument Valley in *Stagecoach* (1939). Heroes with special knowledge of the wilderness, knowledge that saves threatened lives, are seen in *Northwest Mounted Police* (1940), *Unconquered* (1947 – sort of an eastern western), *Smoke Signal* (1955), *Winchester 73* (1950), *The Last Wagon* (1956), *Arrowhead* (1953), *Duel at Diablo* (1966), *The Last of the Mohicans* (1992) – another eastern western, *The Indian Fighter* (1955), *The Scalphunters* (1968), *Shalako* (1968).

Shalako and Vera Cruz (1954) are two good examples of European class arrogance confronting western individual equality. The western commitment to equality defeats wealthy eastern arrogance in *War of the Wildcats* (also titled *In Old Oklahoma*), *Dallas, Man Without a Star, The Tall Men* (1955), *Pale Rider, The Professionals, Joe Kidd*. Images of monopolizing villains appear in *War of the Wildcats, Blood on the Moon, Dallas, Shane, The Violent Men, Silverado, The Sheepman, The Far Country, Pale Rider, Joe Kidd*. In *The Outlaw Josey Wales*, the hero essentially organizes his own agrarian frontier community, a community of outcasts and misfits who all become equal.

In *Shane, Man Without a Star, Shalako, Pale Rider*, the hero rides away back into the wilderness. In *Stagecoach, The Westerner, Angel and the Badman* (1947), *Blood on the Moon, War of the Wildcats, Tall Man Riding* (1955), *Yellow Sky* (1948), *The Violent Men, The Sheepman, The Last Wagon, Silverado, The Outlaw Josey Wales*, he settles down to start a family. In *Silverado, Rio Lobo* (1977), *Rough Night in Jericho* (1967) the villain is a gunfighter who previously cleaned up the town and stayed to abuse his power.

All these films, and all Westerns generally, show the hero's special skill at violence, and the social necessity of violence to achieve civil society and maintain individual freedom. When the frontier begins to close, freedom and civility begin to be lost, so the heroes must ride away seeking a new place for freedom – *High Noon* (1952), *Man Without a Star, Lonely Are the Brave, The Professionals* – or they must fight a hopeless battle trying to maintain their freedom – *The Magnificent Seven, Butch Cassidy and the Sundance Kid, The Wild Bunch*.

3

THE *INVISIBLE HAND*

If John Locke helped establish the Enlightenment, Adam Smith was one of its most important thinkers. He was born in Scotland in 1723 and he lived most of his life there, dying in 1790. He taught at Glasgow University and first became well known when he published the *Theory of Moral Sentiments* in 1759. He knew and interacted with many Enlightenment figures, including James Watt, the inventor of the steam engine, Benjamin Franklin, and probably Thomas Jefferson. His later book, the *Wealth of Nations* brought him great fame during his lifetime, and it is still influential today. Its original and full title was *An Inquiry into the Nature and Causes of the Wealth of Nations*, and it was published in 1776. This book captured and completed many of the ideas of the Enlightenment, as did the creation of America. As George Soule has remarked:

> That this classic of economic liberalism happened to appear in 1776, the year of the American Declaration of Independence, is not mere historical coincidence. Similar forces led to both famous documents. (1952: 40)

For Edmund Burke, a contemporary of Smith's, the *Wealth of Nations* was 'probably the most important book that has ever been published'. This book solved the individualist problem of market order, the problem of egoism and altruism, or at least it seemed to solve this problem for the Europe of Smith's time, as well as for early America.

Egoism and altruism

Smith's solution to the individualist problem was the idea of supply and demand. He showed in great economic detail how the market would generally regulate itself to maintain a good society in a context of private property. If rational, autonomous individuals pursue their private self-interests and government only acts to enforce rational contracts, not to enforce morality, a prosperous civil society will result. Smith changed the individualist discussion from politics to economics. Both Hobbes and Locke had understood individualism as essentially an issue of government. If government could be based on rational individuals, as opposed to sacred morality, then a decent civil society could emerge. In the midst of seventeenth-century feudalism, aristocratic government could be seen as the primary class problem, the source of arbitrary power.

The idea of rational government, however, raised the problem of selfishness and morality, the problem of egoism and altruism. If no dominant government could enforce moral rules, how could a society of selfish individuals possibly be pleasant and just? Hobbes faced this problem directly, unlike Locke, and recommended an absolute government, an absolute *rational* government. This government would not enforce moral rules, but it would have such absolute power to enforce rational contracts – power not subject to the people – that no one would ever lie or cheat. Hobbes essentially wanted to replace a sacred absolute government with a rational absolute government, and this was never very appealing from the perspective of individualism.

Locke solved the individualist problem by recommending limited government and assuming innate morality. The idea of limited government appealed to early individualists, but the idea of innate morality in 'naturally' selfish individuals could never seem quite convincing. Government could only be limited if the market would regulate itself – laissez-faire – but how could a civil market arise from 'natural' selfishness? The idea of innate morality could seem to solve this problem, but it only raised another problem within individualist assumptions. Locke's idea of limited government was the solution the individualists sought, but they needed a better argument to envision a civil market.

Adam Smith provided that argument by shifting the focus from politics to economics, the economic relations of supply and demand. Supply and demand, he argued, would 'naturally' turn egoism into altruism, private, selfish greed into public, civil decency. He accepted Locke's individualist assumptions and he agreed with Locke that government should be limited. Indeed, it should be even more limited, according to Smith, than Locke had recommended. He showed how the market would work when rational individuals use their private property to compete for private profit through rational market relations. Government should let the market be free, as free as possible in a context of rational order. In such a free market, strictly selfish individuals will 'naturally' generate a decent, just society, and the individualist problem is solved.

This is the argument Smith seemed to make, the argument he was interpreted as making, but it was not exactly the argument he actually made. The argument he seemed to make made him world famous because it solved the problem of civility, the problem of egoism and altruism, with no need for an additional moral assumption. All of individualism could now make sense, according to this interpretation of Smith, because of the civil logic of market supply and demand.

Smith, however, actually made a different argument, and he made a moral assumption, an assumption similar to Locke's. The market laws of supply and demand, he argued, would only turn honest, honorable egoism into civil altruism. The market would only be self-regulating – laissez-faire would only work – if private, rational self-interests are constrained by innate morality. A market of perfectly selfish individuals, according to Smith, would only generate social disorder and collapse, not a civil society. Smith could assume innate morality because he also assumed, just like Locke, independent agrarians and endless free land. In both Locke and Smith the moral assumption was really an agrarian assumption, and the coming dominance of industry was not foreseen. Smith could only solve the individualist problem by making a moral assumption, the assumption of an open frontier. But his economic analysis allowed him to be interpreted as solving it more completely, with egoism truly becoming altruism. This *interpretation* was what the market really needed, a vision of perfect selfishness becoming civil decency. This interpretation of Smith became even more important as the market became industrial and private moral constraints became even less convincing. So this interpretation of supply and demand is still used today and still makes Smith famous in our modern market society.

Supply and demand

Government should enable the market, Smith argued, by protecting private property and enforcing rational contracts. Otherwise, it should leave the market alone, letting it work by supply and demand. In this market context, each individual will always try to supply what other individuals demand. If individuals are rational and self-interested, they will always try to make and sell what people want to buy. This is the best way to maximize property, and it makes the market self-regulating. No class tradition or sacred morality will be necessary to constrain individuals. All individuals will pursue their rational interests by making and selling what others want to buy. If government keeps the market honest and equal but does not interfere, the logic of supply and demand will shape productive activities toward a civil society.

In this market context all individuals will try to make money, and they will all use their reason to decide what to do. They will not, that is, be told what to do by tradition, religion, or government. They will all to some degree analyze the market to decide their best options in accordance with their talents. They will make various rational calculations, like what others need or want, what would be the cost of production, and how much profit could be made. If individuals are rational, they will not choose to make and supply what no one wants to buy.

Because of this market logic, according to Smith, a division of labor will arise. People will specialize in different things – extraction, manufacturing, marketing, sales – in order to maximize their profits. Individuals will invent new things and try new strategies as a way to minimize competition. As more people specialize in a division of labor, market trade will increase. People will no longer make or grow everything they need, as they did on feudal farms. Instead, individuals will tend to make one thing very well – buggies, hats, plows – and then they will trade in the market for the other things they need. This is why money is necessary for the market division of labor and was not very necessary for feudal agriculture. Individuals who specialize must be able to make money so they can then use that money as the basis for necessary trade.

Because of the division of labor – specialization – products will be made in greater volume and with improved efficiency. As a consequence, both costs and prices will go down. More things will be made that people want or need, and they will be made better and cheaper. Constant competition will also encourage producers to make things better and cheaper, so they can have an advantage over their competitors. Competition will tend to bring prices down, and it will also tend to encourage innovation and more efficient production. This is the self-regulating logic of supply and demand. Individuals will know what to do from their rational calculations. They will make needed products and they will constantly make them cheaper and better. Further, individuals will be able to buy what they need at lower prices with higher quality. Market trade will increase, everyone's life will improve, and civil society will result.

Wars will even be less likely because market relations require peace. Feudal estates were generally self-sufficient – no division of labor – and feudal wars were common. But the market division of labor depends on peaceful trade, including trade between nations, so wars between nations are discouraged. In the case of international trade, Smith wanted a more limited government than Locke. Locke thought trade should be free within a nation – no government interference – but that government should protect the national economy from foreign competitors. This made Locke a *mercantilist*. For Smith, however, all trade should be free, even across national borders, and government should always stay out of the market. If government tries to protect a business, that business will become less efficient and the interests of society will suffer. All competition, even foreign competition, keeps producers lean and competitive, while protection creates bias and special interests. Without the logic of supply and demand, the market cannot be civil. Further, if governments try to protect their nations, the likelihood of war will increase, and war is not good for trade or civility.

The issue of government protection is a crucial one for Smith. The market logic of supply and demand will punish certain businesses because they fail to be competitive. It will also reward other businesses that succeed at competition. The market will eliminate waste and inefficiency and generally contribute to civil society if the government leaves it alone. But if government begins to protect certain interests, as it protected the aristocrats under feudalism, privilege, arrogance, and corruption will result. Market competition must always be free, as a basic issue of principle, so government can never be used to protect the interests of powerful, connected individuals. If the market is free, all businesses, no matter how successful, must always stay competitive – efficient – or they may become vulnerable to aggressive competitors. But if government can be used to protect certain businesses for whatever reason – morality, decency, patriotism – then those businesses and those individuals become privileged. If government can control market relations, it will tend to be used to protect wealth and power and a new class structure can emerge.

When government protects special interests, it also prevents innovation. When the market is free it encourages innovation as a way to maximize profits. Rational individuals will try new ideas in order to be more efficient and competitive. But innovation can be disruptive of established, successful businesses, just as automobiles, for example, were disruptive of the railroads and Microsoft was disruptive of IBM. According to Smith, the market support for innovation is one of its social, civil benefits. Individuals innovate for their private self-interests, but better and cheaper products tend to be created, and everyone benefits generally. Disruptive innovation will not be possible, however, if government protects established businesses. In traditional societies, such as feudalism, innovation would threaten the sacred order, including the class structure, so it was generally discouraged. The market encourages innovation, and thus social disruption, as an issue of equal opportunity, but only if government is passive.

Smith analyzed economic relations to make a political argument, an argument for limited government. He wanted to show that the market could be civil without a sacred morality, a morality enforced by government. If rational individuals can be strictly self-interested, with no concern for sacred duties, then market relations will create a good society, a society of freedom, equality, and prosperity. Private, rational interests would 'naturally' converge into public, civil interests, as though arranged by an *invisible hand*. Smith's idea of the invisible hand became very famous and is still in use today. It suggested for him, and still suggests today, a market process that is 'natural' but unexpected, essentially a form of market magic. The market logic of supply and demand will 'naturally' (magically) turn private, selfish action into a decent civil society:

> Every individual [seeks] the most advantageous employment for whatever capital he can muster. It is his own advantage, indeed, and not that of the society which he has in view. But the study of his own advantage naturally, or rather necessarily, leads him to prefer that employment which is most advantageous to the society … he intends only his own gain, and he is in this … led by an invisible hand to promote an end which was no part of his

intention … By pursuing his own interest he frequently promotes that of the society more effectively than when he really intends to promote it. (1977: 398, 400)

Government would have to remain limited, making no moral effort to improve society. Individuals should only think about themselves because, Smith argues, 'I have never known much good done by those who affected to trade for the public good' (1977: 400).

With this idea of the *invisible hand* Smith solved the problem of civil order and completed the individualist conception. He assumed, like Locke and all individualists, that rational individuals only seek to maximize their wealth. They do not, that is, ever seek particular work – artist, teacher, farmer – because it is fun or fulfilling. Smith's market analysis only makes sense if individuals are always ready to leave a specific job in order to make more money. If individuals are willing to accept less money or be unsuccessful because they enjoy their work, the logic of supply and demand fails. Individuals can only be motivated by private profit, not by passion or beauty or even by friends. People will only supply what others demand if they seek to maximize their property, not to achieve joy and happiness.

This is an austere view of human motivation and also of social order. The market can only be civil if people only want money. This was the point of Rousseau and the Romantics in their attack on market relations. The individualist assumption of rational self-interest always implied this austerity, and Smith's idea of the *invisible hand* made it quite explicit. Or at least Smith *seemed* to make it explicit and was interpreted in this way. He could only be seen as solving the problem of civil order if perfect, private egoism could be magically turned into altruism. The market would create civil order, according to this view, if government would let it be free, regardless of the social context. Unlike later free market advocates, however, Smith only saw the *invisible hand* working in a specific context, a context of independent agrarians with morally constrained self-interests.

The agrarian hand

Smith assumed innate moral sentiments as the basis for the *invisible hand*. This moral assumption was not usually remembered as Smith became famous, but he made it clear. Government should not enforce sacred duties, it should leave the market alone. But people have general moral duties, he argued, 'natural' duties, 'the duties of justice, of truth, of chastity, of fidelity … But upon the tolerable observation of these duties depends the very existence of human society, which would crumble into nothing if mankind were not generally impressed with a reverence for these important rules of conduct' (1911: 231–232). Without this innate morality the market can never be civil. The *invisible hand* only turns moral self-interest, not perfect self-interest, into a good society. Because of the *invisible hand* government can be limited and the market can be free. But the *invisible hand* only works if altruism is innate.

All the early individualists made this moral assumption. As Yehoshua Arieli comments, 'The innate sociability and morality of man explained the belief that a political society, based on natural rights and limited in authority, resolved the apparent conflict between individual rights and the needs of society' (1964: 123). Smith's moral assumption, just like Locke's, was based on independent agrarians. In contrast to 'merchants' and 'manufacturers', 'Country gentlemen and farmers are, to their great honour, of all people, the least subject to the wretched spirit of monopoly' (1977: 405–406). According to Overton H. Taylor, Smith shared an 'agrarian bias' with Jefferson and others of his time. He sought, in the words of Taylor, 'unhampered access by all farmers to the world's best and cheapest sources of supply of seeds and plants, fertilizers, farming tools, etc.'. This was his vision of a free market. He wanted 'to foster growth of national wealth … simply by encouraging its farmers to be as productive as possible', with minimal government control (1960: 84–85).

Smith envisioned an agrarian civil society, and he did not anticipate industry. According to Robert Heilbroner:

> He did not see a revolution – the Industrial Revolution. Smith did not see in the ugly factory system … the first appearance of new and disruptively powerful social forces. In a sense his system presupposes that eighteenth-century England will remain unchanged forever. Only in quantity will it grow: more people, more goods, more wealth; its quality will remain unchanged. (1980: 70)

Also, according to Heilbroner, Smith assumed that people would work their own land. He developed his theory, in Heilbroner's terms, on the basis of 'individual owner-managers'. In this society, 'by and large those who saved were the very same people as those who put savings to use' (1980: 261). These 'owner-managers', that is, would work on and profit from their own private property, their own land. Smith argued that capitalist owners make possible the growth and wealth of the market. They not only make profits, they save and reinvest those profits. The owners, therefore, constantly create new productive *value*, new products and wealth. But Smith also assumed that productive value is only created by labor – the labor theory of value. If owners create productive value, but value is only created by labor, then owners must also be workers, that is, they must be owner-workers. As Taylor comments while discussing Smith: 'All the "classical" economists thought of most "capitalists" as active, "enterprising," owner-managers' (1960: 115).

A capitalist, then, for Smith and the early individualists, is not someone who only makes money from money, that is, from investments. A capitalist, rather, is someone who owns property (land), works that property, makes a profit, and reinvests that profit as capital. This was the market vision in the middle of the eighteenth century, a vision of independent agrarians. By the middle of the nineteenth century, industry was beginning to dominate. Capitalists became far less likely to work their own property and far more likely to live off investments, that is, off workers. Industrial owners, unlike farmers, seldom live on and work their own property as part of a community of independent owners. Instead, they begin to think of property strictly as investment where others do all the work. Industrial capitalists generally cease to be independent ownerworkers. Rather, they begin to maximize their profits in a context of owners and workers.

According to Smith's analysis, however, the *invisible hand* will not work in an industrial context. The market can only regulate itself, and create civil society, in a context of owner-workers. In a context of class division between owners and workers, the rational interests of the owning class will always be to oppress and exploit the working class as much as possible. For the *invisible hand* to work, the rational self-interests of all individuals must 'naturally' converge, through supply and demand, into a general public benefit. But this cannot be possible, according to Smith, if one class can benefit from the oppression and exploitation of another. In such a class context, the private interests of the owners will always contradict and diverge from the private interests of the workers.

Put another way, innate moral constraints cannot be assumed in a context of class division. The civil necessities – honesty and honor – will no longer serve rational self-interests if some individuals can use their structural class dominance to profit from the misery of others. The *invisible hand* will only work, according to Smith, in a context of structural equality. It cannot work, therefore, in industry, with its necessary class division. 'Merchants and manufacturers', according to Smith, have a 'wretched spirit of greed and monopoly', not a civil spirit of trust and honor. Smith envisioned a competitive market among structurally equal farmers, where everyone always has real equal opportunity. He envisioned a market, according to Taylor, where 'nothing is monopolized, protected, or privileged, and everything is open to all comers' (1960: 111).

The *invisible hand* can work and government can be limited when property cannot be monopolized by a dominant owning class. In effect, then, Smith assumed an agrarian frontier of endless free land. When 'the wretched spirit of monopoly' dominates the market, the market cannot be civil. 'Merchants and manufacturers' in the cities are most likely to have this 'wretched spirit', but it can also exist in rural agriculture. 'The rent of land … is naturally a monopoly price' (1977: 131), according to Smith. This means, as Elie Halevy points out, that the *invisible hand* only works when empty land is available. The 'wretched spirit of monopoly' can make the market uncivil when a privileged class of owners, like the aristocrats, control all the land. In any context of monopoly, owners are divided from workers and labor is divorced from profit. If labor is divorced from profit, then profit can be made by exploiting labor. The *invisible hand* requires independent agrarians on an endless frontier. As Halevy summarizes Smith's arguments, 'when all of the land becomes occupied ...' and profit can be made off the labor of others, then 'the identity of interests ... is no longer necessary and there may be divergence' (1966: 100).

Smith assumed an agrarian frontier to solve the individualist problem. Individuals will not be honest and honorable when class monopolies exist, so the *invisible hand* and limited government always depend on real equal opportunity. Smith completed the individualist conception and legitimated market society. But the market was quickly becoming industrial and the frontier could not be endless. So Smith's arguments had to be interpreted as applying more generally, to industrial market relations as well as agrarian. The moral assumption had to be ignored, along with its agrarian frontier context. The legitimating idea of equal opportunity had to be reinterpreted. It had to be based on Locke's idea that labor is property, not on the assumption of endless free land. The industrial market could only be legitimate if it offered equal opportunity. But now equal opportunity had to mean the opportunity to sell your labor and get a job, not the opportunity to apply your labor to unowned land.

According to this interpretation, the *invisible hand* should work, government should be limited, and the market should be civil even in a context of owners and workers. The market would be self-regulating without an open frontier, that is, without the structural equality of independent owner-workers. It could still be civil and provide freedom and equality as long as people, at a minimum, could sell their labor and get a job. In the industrial market, however, many people could not get a job, and certainly not a job that offered much opportunity. The new idea of equal opportunity – selling your labor – began to be unconvincing. The market had always assumed an open frontier as the basis for equal opportunity, and without such a frontier it began to lose its legitimacy as well as its stability. The market freedom of the owners created class monopolies and thus deep inequality, and this new context led to many market failures and finally to the Great Depression.

For the market to remain legitimate, government had to become more powerful. Market freedom had to be restricted and equal opportunity had to be protected, even in the minimal sense of opportunity to get a job. Smith's arguments had to be used to defend an industrial market, even though he had assumed an open agrarian frontier. But the point of Smith's arguments, the point of the *invisible hand*, was to keep government limited and let the market be free. In the context of industry, then, government had to become more active so the market could remain legitimate, but the market could only be legitimate if government remained passive.

Smith's analysis of supply and demand supported limited government. But Smith's analysis could only make sense in a context of equal opportunity, and government had to become dominant, under industrial conditions, to support equal opportunity. So the market idea of government became deeply confused, and with it the idea of civility. The industrial market was still a market, but the individualist arguments that justified the market could not easily apply. According to these arguments, the market can only be civil on an equalizing frontier, so the modern industrial market must have a problem with civility. A problem with civility is also a problem with freedom and equality, and this is what the cowboy myth always portrays as a reflection of original individualism.

The mythical hand

The myth reflects the frontier assumption, the assumption of structural equality. The West can be free and equal as a place of owner-workers, while the East must be corrupt and oppressive as a place of owners and workers. Market theory had to be adjusted to legitimate urban industry, but the myth remembers the original theory, the theory of independent agrarians. It remembers this theory at the level of culture, not at the level of concepts, so it shows us a fantasy of freedom and equality, a fantasy that legitimates the market. The historical West seldom fulfilled this fantasy of individualism, a fantasy of opportunity and civility. Rather, development in the West was primarily characterized by corporate greed and cynical exploitation. The market, however, offered a promise to justify its institutions, and the myth of the Wild West still reflects that original promise even when market history and theory cannot.

The decent citizens in the myth are independent agrarians with no 'wretched spirit of monopoly'. The villains have that 'wretched spirit', but they can be defeated on the open frontier. The cowboy must briefly take dominant power to restore a civil society, but then he surrenders that power to maintain that civil society. The *invisible hand* can work on the open frontier with 'country gentlemen and farmers'. This cowboy imagery reflects Locke and Smith as well as Jefferson and Turner. The myth reminds us of the frontier necessity despite modern market revisions. It also shows the implied corruption of urban, industrial society, a society with no frontier. The 'cowboy' in the city must thus become more violent simply to try to be free. No one can be trusted, civility is not possible, and honor will get him killed. The basic moral duties – 'truth, chastity, fidelity' – are no longer observed. 'The very existence of human society' is threatened. It will 'crumble into nothing' when the 'wretched spirit' dominates, and this is what action films show.

The entire individualist conception focuses on the role of government, as does the myth of the frontier. The original vision was that government could remain limited in a context of structural equality. Industrial production, however, necessitated theoretical revisions, and those revisions have tried to suggest that government can remain limited in a context of structural inequality – owners and workers. The idea of the *invisible hand* justifies limited government, but the myth remembers, as the theory does not, that the *invisible hand* requires an open frontier. Industry greatly complicates the market idea of government, and the cowboy myth reminds us that this complication is an issue of the lost frontier.

Government

American institutions, including government, were based on market theory, and market theory (in Locke and Smith) implicitly assumed equal, independent landowners – an open agrarian frontier. According to the theory, democracy would only work, as Jefferson pointed out, in a context of free land. If the *invisible hand* would work – if the market were self-regulating – government could remain limited and not become a threat. But the *invisible hand* could only work in a market of structural equals, a market of owner-workers, and that required an endless frontier.

Democracy was created in America to constrain government power. Other limits on power were also created, including a written constitution, internal checks and balances, and a Bill of Rights. With a written constitution legitimate government authority is clearly stated. Officials cannot assert arbitrary power just because they are officials. Government power has constitutional limits, and only the citizens, through a complex democratic process, can decide to change the constitution. When a government has internal checks and balances, each of the major branches of the government – executive, legislative, judicial – limits the power of the other branches. Executive officials enforce laws but cannot create laws, and legislative officials create laws but cannot enforce them. Judges can decide if the laws created by legislative officials are constitutional and whether executive officials, particularly the police, obey the laws they enforce. But judges can neither create nor enforce laws, so each branch constrains the others.

The Bill of Rights arose from a struggle during the writing of the Constitution, a struggle between the Federalists, the Anti-Federalists, and the Jeffersonians. The Federalists wanted a more powerful federal government than the Anti-Federalists, and the Jeffersonians were somewhere in between. The Federalists essentially won the struggle and designed the Constitution, but Jefferson insisted on adding a Bill of Rights so federal power would always be limited. Federal power was further limited by the authority of state governments. The states retained independent power over internal state matters. This was the issue of 'states rights', and this issue was contentious at the time and remains contentious today.

All these American efforts to limit government power assumed independent agrarians. In early America only landowners – freeholders – were given the democratic vote. Only agrarians, it was assumed, would have the rationality required for civil society. Farming would generate virtues, the moral duties Smith required, while 'merchants and manufacturers' would have the 'wretched spirit'. As America developed and became more urban, the vote was gradually extended to all male citizens, which meant workers were allowed to vote. But this was not the original vision of a civil market society, and the vote was not given to all individuals (all white males) until well into the nineteenth century. In early America, democracy was clearly an issue of independent agrarians, and 'agrarian laws' were often proposed. These were laws to limit the land an individual could own, so all individuals would always be able to claim free land. Monopolies of land would be prevented and real equal opportunity maintained. Jefferson supported such laws to justify limiting the vote. As Chilton Willamson remarks:

> At one point [Jefferson] suggested that a freehold qualification for voting would not be incompatible with the rights of man so long as all men had the opportunity to take up 50 acres of land. An egalitarian land policy would stave off indefinitely the spectre of a Europeanized America. (1960: 128)

In the nineteenth century, of course, and throughout the twentieth century Jefferson's fears were realized. America became less agrarian and more urban. At the end of the nineteenth century, only about 40 per cent of Americans were farmers, and at the end of the twentieth century, only about 2 per cent of Americans were farmers. As industry developed, the legitimating vision of structural equality, the vision of an open frontier could no longer be sustained. The promise of market civility among owner-workers had to become a hope for market civility among owners and workers. But property could all be monopolized, so owners would no longer have a rational incentive to be honest and honorable. Rather, they would now have a rational incentive to exploit and oppress workers for the sake of greater profit.

As America developed, government gradually became more active. It fought the Civil War, which was centered on an issue of equality, and from time to time it broke up industrial monopolies to protect market competition, that is, equal access. After the frontier closed, America fought in World War I, then a speculative boom took place during the 1920s. The boom led companies to overproduce – to make more products than they could sell – and banks to lend more money than they could afford to lose. The market crashed in 1929, the American economy collapsed, and most of the world entered the Great Depression, which lasted through the 1930s. The market had never worked exactly like Smith envisioned, but the Depression made it seem that the market did not work at all.

According to Smith's theory, the market should be self-regulating, and that meant it should 'naturally' recover from recession and depression strictly through supply and demand. In theory, overproduction would lead to layoffs and thus to cheap labor. This would lower the costs of production so owners would reinvest. Workers would be hired, products would be made, and the market would cure itself. But the *invisible hand* did not seem to work and the market did not recover from the Great Depression. Industry had failed, savings were gone, unemployment was staggering, poverty was brutal, and Smith's market theory seemed far less convincing.

During the 1930s President Franklin Roosevelt began to increase the role of government in direct opposition to market theory. He used government to help the poor through welfare and job creation. He supported legalization of unions – the Wagner Act – so workers would have more power to protect their wages and jobs against the interests of the owners. He began to regulate the economy, particularly banking and investment, so speculation would be limited and savings would be safer. He created government insurance on personal savings to restore confidence in banks. To finance all this new government activity, he began to spend more money than government had; that is, he began to borrow against future taxes – deficit spending. According to market theory, however, government should not go into debt, and all these actions to restore the economy contradicted the idea of limited, passive government.

This kind of active government, according to established theory, would undermine individual freedom, and Roosevelt was indeed often attacked as an enemy of freedom. Market theory, however, was clearly not working, and Roosevelt had decided, in general, to sacrifice some market freedom to try to maintain market relations. Smith's idea of self-regulation had been interpreted as applying to industry, and the Depression made it seem that the theory had failed. Many people, therefore, supported Roosevelt's efforts to regulate the market and constrain market freedom. Many other people, in fact, were much more radical in their critique of the market. These people felt that the market should be rejected as oppressive and illegitimate, and that socialism should be embraced as the only hope for equality.

None of the government efforts under Roosevelt managed to end the Depression. They did not stimulate production and lead to market recovery. These efforts probably did, however, hold America together when it could have fallen apart. Government was used to mitigate the inequality of the Depression, and many historians have argued that these government efforts – far beyond the limits of market theory – probably prevented class violence, maybe even revolution. During World War I, Russia had become communist through a violent revolution, and during the Depression communism began to seem attractive to some Americans since the market had clearly failed. The failure of the market had also created a blatant structure of class inequality, a structure of wealthy owners and poor workers, with extensive unemployment. There was growing class anger in America, anger toward owners and capitalism. In this context

Roosevelt used government to constrain the owners and also to help the poor and unemployed. He managed to contain the anger and keep America stable, but only by defying market theory and increasing government power.

Roosevelt changed the market role of government but only through practical, ad hoc efforts. He saw a market crisis and acted to address its problems, undermining market theory in the process, but he did not have an alternative economic theory. His practical efforts, however, were too weak to end the Depression; the economic collapse was too deep. In the context of private property, government could not spend enough money or take enough power to stimulate sufficient investment for market recovery.

The Depression only ended in America when government began to mobilize for World War II. Because of the war, government took control of the American economy. It ended most market competition and most labor disputes. Market theory, in effect, was set aside for the sake of national defense. The legitimating idea of private property – property safe from government interference – became far less important than the effort to win the war. All productive property could be controlled and utilized by government as part of the war effort. Government essentially put everyone to work, and America became enormously productive while completely dominated by government. It also became quite stable and unified, even more equal, since everyone was willing to sacrifice together for the sake of a common cause.

Economically, the war ended the Great Depression, but after the war, government had to retreat from the economy because of market theory. Property again had to be private. The market had to be competitive, businesses had to be able to fail, owners had to maximize profit and lay off workers, and workers had to be organized and angry. The economic problems of the market returned, including unemployment, labor violence, and recurring recessions. An active, controlling government had ended the Depression, but government could only take control in the name of national defense. Otherwise, according to the theory, it should stay out of market relations. The industrial market, it seemed, contrary to market theory, required an active government to maintain stability and prevent collapse. But the only legitimate reason for such an active government, in a market context of private property, seemed to be war.

In fact, America did enter another war, the Korean War, at the beginning of the 1950s, and that war, economically, ended a recession and increased prosperity. Government put more people to work and bought more products than it normally could in peacetime. But after the war the economic problems returned. America then entered another war, the Cold War, in the middle of the 1950s, and it lasted 30 years. From an economic perspective this was a perfect war. Government could spend money, support production, and put people to work for the sake of national security, but few people had to be killed. In theory, the country could be committed to free market principles – minimal government – but in practice the government could be actively involved in the name of national defense. Among other things, the Cold War supported a long period of growth and stability in America.

John Maynard Keynes

From the Depression through the 1950s many politicians used the government, including defense spending, to regulate trade, support greater equality, and maintain market stability. Smith's market theory could not endorse these increasingly necessary efforts, so a new market theory seemed to be required, a theory for urban industry, not frontier agriculture. In fact, a new market theory had been developed by John Maynard Keynes in England during the Depression. Keynes argued that a free industrial market would not be self-regulating. Rather, it would tend toward overproduction and collapse, just as in the Depression. After such a collapse, no *invisible hand* of supply and demand would be able to stimulate recovery. For recovery to take place and the market to be stable, government would have to be active and involved. If government remained limited and passive under industrial conditions, market relations could not be viable, much less civil. In effect, Keynes gave theoretical arguments that supported Roosevelt's ad hoc efforts. In Keynes's view, government had to regulate the industrial market. In particular, government had to use its power to maintain a minimum, legitimating semblance of equal opportunity.

Government should actively support full employment, so everyone would always have the opportunity to get a job. It should use such strategies, according to Keynes, as deficit spending, market regulation, manipulating taxes and interest rates, and even directly creating jobs. Full employment is important because it legitimizes market relations, at least in the minimal sense of equal opportunity. Also, if unemployment is high, people will have less money, fewer products can be bought, overproduction is likely, and a downward spiral can begin. When the economy begins to stagnate and layoffs increase, government should lower taxes and interest rates to encourage investment, production, and jobs. When the economy begins to overheat and inflation and overproduction seem likely, government should raise taxes and interest rates to slow down production and prevent recession. Government should also spend money it does not have – deficit spending – whenever it is necessary to maintain full employment.

Keynes argued that a free industrial market would not maintain equality or stability, and certainly not civility. It would tend toward economic collapse, severe class division, and massive unemployment – not toward equal opportunity. Smith had argued that free market relations would generate stability and civility strictly through supply and demand. But Smith had assumed an agrarian frontier – real equal opportunity – with no class monopolies. Smith could envision the *invisible hand* in a context of structural equality – independent owner-workers. But Keynes had to analyze a market with structural inequality, essentially a market without a frontier. This market, he argued, could not be self-regulating, so government would have to become active to maintain equal opportunity. In effect, government would have to try to replace the legitimating equality of the original endless frontier.

Keynes's theory contradicted market dogma, and it was not immediately accepted. Until the 1960s politicians in America had gradually increased the market role of government, using such strategies as national defense, but without a supporting theory. In the early 1960s, however, President John Kennedy embraced Keynesian theory as the basis for his economic policies. He identified a strategy he called the 'New Frontier', and part of this strategy was to use an active government to maintain stability and employment. Beginning with Kennedy, Keynes became the basic theoretical reference for understanding market relations. Most market nations for the next few decades followed Keynesian policies into a period of growth and prosperity. Toward the end of the 1970s, however, inflation and stagnation began to increase. As a result, Keynesian policies lost some luster, and a conservative reaction began.

Keynes had offered a liberal perspective. He wanted government to support greater equality by restricting market freedom (government regulation). Conservatives, in contrast, would generally prefer Smith to Keynes. They would endorse market freedom over equal opportunity, even if it meant greater inequality. They would want government to stay limited and passive so individuals could have more freedom to maximize their wealth.

In the early 1980s, in response to inflation and stagnation, President Ronald Reagan led a conservative reaction in America against Keynesian policies. Government regulation was reduced, market freedom was enhanced, and the market indeed seemed to work somewhat better in terms of productivity and growth. But inequality increased significantly. Welfare was cut, unions were broken, companies moved overseas, layoffs increased (downsizing) and unemployment rose. Many good jobs were simply eliminated, and many people moved from well-paid jobs with good benefits to low-paid jobs with no benefits, or into unemployment. Greater market freedom under the conservatives encouraged greater inequality. In the middle 1990s a liberal, Bill Clinton, was elected president, and government became somewhat more active in support of greater equality. But Clinton also tried to maintain many conservative commitments to greater market freedom.

In general, Keynesian economic policies became entrenched during the last half of the twentieth century. Those policies sometimes led to inflation and stagnation, and then to conservative governments. But conservatives could not eliminate all government regulations, all Keynesian efforts. Even under conservatives, the industrial market needed some regulation, some deficit spending, some protection for equality. Conservatives could reduce some market controls, some Keynesian policies, but they could not reduce too many, not without risks of class conflict and market collapse. As the market became industrial and the frontier closed, government had to become more active to balance freedom and equality. Liberals and conservatives still disagree over the proper role of government. But conservatives now accept a far more active government than Locke or Smith envisioned. Government is now integral to the market. It can no longer be minimal and passive. When the modern need for government is compared to the original vision, all current disagreements between liberals and conservatives seem relatively minor.

Indeed, government has generally become more active in America than even Keynes recommended. Among other things, it has increased welfare and funded education as efforts to mitigate inequality. In general, it has acted to redistribute wealth through taxes and spending, restricting market freedom to support equal opportunity. In many ways government has acted to maintain equal opportunity, in some minimal sense, after the frontier was gone, that is, after the original frontier, the wilderness frontier, was gone. But the market needs an open frontier as part of its legitimating idea, so America has often found new 'frontiers' to replace the original frontier.

As the western frontier closed, colonial 'frontiers' began to be announced in other, vulnerable nations. New opportunities could still be found in the land of other people, land to be claimed as colonies. Later, many other 'frontiers' were discovered and announced, 'frontiers' of science, medicine, space, information, global business, the internet. Most if not all of these new 'frontiers' have depended on government help. The original frontier meant limited government, but all the subsequent 'frontiers' have involved an active government. Perhaps the most important of these substitute frontiers has been free public education, our central modern version of equal opportunity. After the frontier closed, free public education in America became a government commitment. And this new commitment, requiring an active government, was explicitly defended by its proponents as a replacement for the lost frontier.

The idea of the frontier remains important, in market politics and culture if not in market theory. Kennedy recognized its importance in his vision of a 'New Frontier', and *Star Trek*'s many versions explored 'Space, the final frontier'. The cowboy rides through the Wild West in the market myth of origin, and he reminds us that the individualist promise assumed an open frontier. A frontier is implicit in market institutions because freedom must be compatible with equality. If freedom contradicts equality, as it does with class monopolies, government cannot be limited and the market may not be civil. This is what the cowboy remembers even when market theory does not.

The market led to industrial production and to enormous wealth and prosperity, at least for some. But the market promised freedom and equality, and industry distorts that promise. Can the market only be civil on an agrarian frontier? Does this mean the industrial market can only be oppressive? Is industry only compatible with equality if private property is eliminated, that is, with socialized property? Can industry be sustained without private property? Can the industrial market be civil and balance freedom with equality through appropriate government intervention?

These are the questions asked by the classical social theorists – Marx, Weber, Durkheim. These theorists analyzed an existing industrial market, not an envisioned agrarian market. They generally agreed with basic individualist values – freedom, equality, rationality – but they were far less convinced that a market in private property would support those values. They saw an industrial reality of owners and workers, not an agrarian fantasy of owner-workers. The early individualists lived amid feudalism and were trying to project a market, a market with a civil promise. But the classical social theorists lived amid the market, and what they saw was not a civil promise but rather class inequality, bureaucratic despair, and moral collapse.

Illustrative films

Lack of government is often the problem on the wild frontier, so some government is needed – *The Westerner, Destry Rides Again* (1939), *The Far Country, Dodge City, Dallas, The Tin Star* (1957). Without the villains, however, government can be minimal and the *invisible hand* will work because the decent citizens – independent agrarians – only compete in a context of trust. Some of the best images of a moral frontier community are in *The Westerner, My Darling Clementine* (1946), *Shane, The Far Country, The Outlaw Josey Wales, Destry Rides Again*. Government is often corrupt, however, so the hero must go outside the law, even become an outlaw, to restore civil society – *Ramrod* (1947), *El Paso* (1949), *The Violent Men, Rio Lobo, The Outlaw Josey Wales, The Missouri Breaks* (1976), *The Sons of Katie Elder* (1965), *Silverado, Rough Night in Jericho*. As the frontier closes, government tends to become more dominant and oppressive – *The Professionals, The Wild Bunch, Posse* (1975). After the frontier is gone, in urban industrial society, government is often seen as deeply corrupt and oppressive – *The Marathon Man* (1976), *Three Days of the Condor* (1975), *The Formula* (1980), *Clear and Present Danger, Eraser, Total Recall* (1990), *The X-Files* (1998), *Mercury Rising* (1998), *Enemy of the State* (1998).

Part 2

INDUSTRIAL PROBLEMS

Preface

The social theorists

In the context of feudal society, individualist ideas had been radical and critical, challenging the established institutions – traditional institutions – in the name of rational interests. Individualism was a form of social criticism, the criticism of feudal relations. By the nineteenth century, however, these individualist ideas had created a new set of established institutions, the institutions of market society. In this market context a new version of social criticism arose, the criticism of market relations. The ideas of individualism had led to reason, science, and industry, but this new society was seen by many critics as failing to fulfill the original legitimating vision. It seemed to be, at least to these critics, more about selfishness, greed, and exploitation than about freedom, equality, and civility. This was what Jefferson had feared at the end of the eighteenth century, and before he died in 1826 he became quite disillusioned with the American form of democracy and individualism.

The new industrial world generated social theorists who no longer thought in terms of agriculture. These theorists generally accepted, like the earlier individualists, the basic values of freedom, equality, and rationality, but they were far more critical of market institutions, the institutions of capitalism. They saw those institutions as generally leading to a new class structure of oppression and exploitation. Three of these critical theorists – Karl Marx, Max Weber, and Emile Durkheim – offered analyses of the market and market society that are still important today. Marx wrote in the middle of the nineteenth century and Weber and Durkheim later in that century and into the early twentieth. They brought social perspectives to the analysis of the market, but they generally agreed that it created inequality and division, not equality and civility. They all shared a commitment to reason and science, and they saw their analytic efforts as contributing to science, the science of social relations. They admired the enormous productivity of industry, and they saw market relations as generating science and industry. But industry also meant a new structure of class, a structure of owners and workers, so these social theorists began to analyze exactly what the early individualists had feared.

They all approached the market from a *social* perspective as opposed to an individualist perspective. That is, they saw individuals as inherently social, as inherently involved in social relations, not as inherently autonomous. Social order, they all agreed, cannot be understood strictly in terms of private, rational self-interests of autonomous individuals. No human individuals, from their social perspective, had ever been completely separate and detached, as the individualists had assumed in the idea of the State of Nature. For these social theorists, individuals can only be human and rational as part of a social order, not prior to social order as the individualists had argued. Individuals are born into social order and society makes them human. For these social theorists, then, social order can never be what social contract theory says it is, a rational, self-interested choice of autonomous individuals.

As a result, social order cannot be understood strictly in terms of 'natural' individuals. It cannot be understood simply in terms of the individualist concepts of rationality, autonomy, and self-interest. Rather, it must be understood in terms of social relations and social concepts, concepts like power, class, organization, and morality. Thus, market theory can be criticized for ignoring social relations, and market institutions can be criticized for sacrificing social relations to the pursuit of private self-interests. From their different analytic perspectives, these social theorists generally agree that market institutions encourage social division, not social unity, and some commitment to social unity is required for a good society.

This social critique of market relations began in the eighteenth century as a part of the Romantic reaction to rationality. This Romantic reaction celebrated love, passion, and beauty, not reason, calculation, and self-interest, and it was led by Jean-Jacques Rousseau. Rousseau argued, against Hobbes and Locke and general market enthusiasm, that humans are 'naturally' kind and generous, not 'naturally' selfish and greedy. Like Hobbes and Locke he envisioned an original State of Nature, but in his version of the State of Nature, individuals were pure and innocent, trusting and communal. The development of reason and civilization, then, did not tame an original condition of individualist violence. Rather, it corrupted an original condition of social decency. Rousseau envisioned 'naturally' social individuals – the Noble Savage – living in virtue and harmony, childlike and happy. This original social innocence, for Rousseau, was corrupted by rational self-interest, and this Romantic perspective influenced the later social theorists.

From the social, Romantic perspective, humans originally lived in a 'natural' condition of community, not a 'natural' condition of war. This suggests that a good society needs public trust and unity, not private selfishness and greed. In the eighteenth century, many people in Europe began to think that the market would strip social life of meaning and value. The market would encourage rational, selfish calculations and discourage all higher, nobler concerns – art, love, beauty, passion, emotion. This was the Romantic reaction – the rational market would undermine basic social needs. And this Romantic perspective was later applied by Marx, Weber, and Durkheim to the analysis of the industrial market.

These *social* theorists of the nineteenth century do not assume an original 'natural' condition of social innocence and purity. Rather, they assume an original *traditional* condition of shared social values and strong social unity. They are far less Romantic than Rousseau, however, about this original social condition, because they also see it as closed, restrictive, and resistant to change. They generally contrast traditional society with rational society, and they see traditional society as more concerned with social relations but also as more rigid and inefficient, more resistant to criticism. They see traditional society as anchored in religion and thus in a strong, sacred sense of shared values and social identities.

Religion, however, tends to protect stability and discourage social change. A commitment to reason, in contrast, encourages criticism, change, innovation. It also encourages industrial production. All these theorists are impressed by reason and industry, and they like many things about the market. But they worry about a society committed strictly to private self-interests. The market in their view will tend to encourage selfishness and cynicism, and industrial market production will tend to create a structure of class conflict, not a structure of individual equality. In particular, they worry about the loss of tradition. Tradition always provided many social protections while preventing social change. But the market will undermine traditional protections and encourage social change while also encouraging greed, selfishness, and class division.

For all of these social theorists the primary market problem is the industrial structure of class. Industrial production in a context of private property will inevitably generate class monopolies of property. Each of these theorists, however, approaches the issue of class from a different analytic perspective. Marx focuses on the structure of productive relations and particularly on the industrial class relations of market owners and workers. Weber focuses on the structure of social organization and particularly on the bureaucratic rationality required by industrial production. Durkheim focuses on the structure of social stability and particularly on the failure of stability in a market context of class. All of these theorists admire the market for its commitment to reason and industry, but they all also criticize the market as the source of structural inequality – class division. They all agree with the early individualists on the need for individual equality. Only Weber, however, laments, along with Jefferson and Turner, the end of the open frontier. They all see industry as inevitable, a consequence of market relations, unlike the early individualists. Yet they also see equality as valuable, so they all worry about the emergence of class and whether equality is compatible with industry.

In general, these theorists are quite pessimistic about this new industrial market, the market of laissez-faire. Marx is the most angry and critical of these three theorists. He sees market relations as deeply oppressive because of their structure of class. He is also, however, the most optimistic of the three about the possibility of combining industry with equality. Capitalism, he argues, cannot long survive because the workers will rise up in revolution. Through this revolution a structure of socialized property will be created – communism – and this will lead to a final social utopia: freedom and equality with industrial prosperity.

Weber, however, cannot share this optimism. He agrees with Marx that industrial market relations will generate class division and class oppression. But communism, in his view, cannot be a solution. Bureaucracy is necessary for industrial organization, and bureaucracy, according to Weber, will always create a structure of class control even if property is socialized. Bureaucracy will dehumanize social life regardless of the structure of property, so he can only be pessimistic about the future of industrial society.

Durkheim is pessimistic about a *free* industrial market, that is, about laissez-faire. But he also thinks, unlike Marx or Weber, that market relations can be improved and made civil through appropriate government controls and actions. If the market is left to the *invisible hand*, in accordance with Smith's vision, division, despair, and instability will result from the industrial class structure. But government, in Durkheim's view, can be used to regulate the market and protect a commitment to equality. There are many positive aspects of the market for Durkheim – support for criticism, innovation, individualism. But a free market, he argues, against Adam Smith, will not create civility. The market will create industry, and industry can only be compatible with equality, and thus with civility, if government is used to constrain market selfishness.

All these theorists share a commitment to reason and science, but Marx has a different idea of rationality than Weber and Durkheim. Marx thinks that rational individuals will first develop capitalism (private property) in their progress toward rationality. But then they will reject capitalism and develop communism (socialized property) as the most rational society. Weber and Durkheim, however, think that capitalism (the market) is the most rational form of society. They agree with the individualists that rational individuals have private self-interests and therefore require private property. Only Marx thinks that a truly rational society is incompatible with private property. He thinks that rationality is necessary for industry and that industry is possible under communism, that is, without market relations. Weber and Durkheim agree that rationality generates industry, but they only see rationality, and therefore industry, as compatible with private property, not with socialized property.

All three agree that a good society must be committed to freedom and equality, the basic individualist vision. For Marx, however, freedom and equality are only possible under communism, while for Weber and Durkheim they are only possible in the market. Weber is simply pessimistic because bureaucracy will undermine freedom and equality. Durkheim, like Marx, remains optimistic about freedom and equality. But Durkheim, unlike Marx or Weber, thinks they can be and must be achieved in a market context of industry.

In general, these social theorists agree with early individualists as well as the cowboy myth. They all see the industrial market as threatening to freedom and equality because of class monopolies. The myth and the individualists envision the structural equality of an open agrarian frontier where the *invisible hand* can operate and the market can be civil. But the critical social theorists can only envision industry, so they must explore whether freedom and equality can be made compatible with industry. Marx thinks they can if the market is rejected, and Durkheim thinks they can if the market is corrected. Weber essentially thinks they cannot since industry requires bureaucracy and bureaucracy inhibits freedom and equality. They all tend to share the mythical cowboy image of the corrupt urban East. Marx and Durkheim suggest possibilities for transcending that urban oppression essentially by using government, either through socialized property or through market regulations. Weber, however, generally agrees with the myth, that the market can only live up to its promise on an open agrarian frontier.

The early individualists were optimistic about market society because they assumed real equal opportunity – structural equality. The social theorists are pessimistic about market society because they see monopolies of property – structural inequality. The individualists endorsed market relations in the name of freedom and equality, and the theorists criticize market relations in the name of freedom and equality. The issue that separates these different perspectives is the idea of an open frontier, the idea the cowboy myth portrays. The myth reflects the early individualists through its image of the civil frontier, and it also reflects the social theorists through its image of the urban East. The myth points out that freedom and equality are defined by an open frontier, so it must become problematic, as the social theorists argue, when that frontier is gone.

The myth shows through cultural images what the early individualists promise and what the social theorists condemn. It also shows what the theorists tend to forget, the need for an open frontier. The entire market vision rested on an assumed frontier, and the later social critiques assumed the loss of the frontier, that is, an urban, industrial context. The myth remembers that the underlying legitimating values, the values of freedom and equality, are defined by an open frontier, so it also remembers why the later social theorists are so critical of market industry. Further, the myth remembers that the values of freedom and equality were always only intended to apply to white males. For all their critical concern, the later social theorists, like the early individualists, tend to ignore this issue. These theorists are primarily concerned with the issues of class inequality, not with the issues of sex or race. But the issues of class inequality are crucial for market society, and the cowboy myth also reflects these issues.

4

KARL MARX

The Revolutionary and the Cowboy

Marx was born in Germany in 1818, five years before Jefferson died, and he died in 1883, 19 years after Weber was born and 25 years after Durkheim was born. Marx was the earliest of these critical social theorists and the most horrified by capitalism. He began developing his radical ideas while still a student in Germany, and after his doctorate he could not teach in Germany because of these ideas. He went to Paris for two years where he befriended Friedrich Engels who became his supporter and collaborator. He was expelled from Paris in 1845, from Brussels in 1848, and from Germany in 1849 after being acquitted in a trial for sedition.

He lived the rest of his life in London where he researched and wrote, but did not finish, his major work, *Capital*. He was supported by Engels during these years, and he lived and died in poverty, holding few jobs. Engels was a capitalist with a successful textile business, but he shared Marx's contempt for capitalism and the hope for a communist future. Industrialization was most advanced in the London where Marx lived, so the workers in London were most exposed to the early brutalities of the owners. Marx studied capitalism in theory and practice with insights from his capitalist friend, and he produced a critique of capitalism that shaped the twentieth century and remains influential today. At the time of his death Marx characterized himself as 'the most hated and calumniated man of his time'.

Marx and market class structure

Capitalism for Marx is the market structure of private property and this market structure unleashes the power of industry. Marx was impressed by industrial production, but he also saw private property as generating a new class structure and new class oppression. In this new structure the class that owns all productive property is only concerned with private self-interests, not with traditional obligations. This means that the class of owners – the bourgeoisie – can exploit the class of workers – the proletariat – with no traditional constraints. As a result, Marx argues, a market in private property not only creates industry; it also creates the most oppressive class structure in history.

When property is private, the owners do not have to think of their workers as people, not even as inferior people as the feudal aristocrats thought of the peasants. Owners only think of their workers as labor, and they only buy that labor to maximize their own self-interests. They do not need to protect or care for their workers, as they would with traditional duties, so workers simply become commodities to be bought and sold in the market. When owners do not need their workers, or can pay other workers less, those particular workers – those human beings – have no social protections. They can only hope to sell their labor to someone else. This gives owners, for Marx, unprecedented class power, and they use that power to create unprecedented wealth as well as unprecedented misery.

Not only are workers denied traditional rights and protections, they are also denied direct access to productive property. Under feudalism, peasants were an exploited class, but they lived on the land they worked and they had traditional, if limited, rights to their land. They had their own homes and communities, they made their own clothes, and they grew food for themselves as well as their lords. Peasants, that is, had a traditional right of access to work productive property (land), while workers in the market have no such right of access to work productive property. Workers can only feed, clothe, and shelter themselves if they can get a job, and they have no traditional right to have a job. Workers, therefore, are only able to survive if they can sell their labor to an owner, that is, if their labor serves the interest of an owner. As a result, owners have far more power over workers than aristocrats had over peasants, and the owners can use that power far more oppressively.

Capitalism, for Marx, is even more oppressive to workers than slavery was to slaves. He sees workers as 'wage slaves', commodities to be bought and sold but only for their labor. Slaves were important as *people*, not simply as labor, because they were essentially owned as people and could not be easily replaced. Workers, however, can be simply discarded and forgotten when they get sick or hurt because owners only buy their labor. Slaves were human investments, investments in particular people, so they had to be protected and tended as people as long as they could work. Slaves and peasants were oppressed as people but were also valuable as people. Workers, however, are more oppressed as people because they are only valuable as labor.

Private property makes capitalism uniquely oppressive, but it also makes it uniquely productive. Owners can maximize their wealth with no traditional constraints and no investment in slaves. This means they can take more risks, be more innovative, invent new machines, buy and sell property. The pure self-interest of the owners encourages innovation and industry, and thus great productivity. But this is only possible if workers have no protections and are treated as market commodities.

Marx and the modern market

For Marx capitalism was brutally, excessively oppressive, with owners having unprecedented class power over their workers. But Marx analyzed capitalism in the middle of the nineteenth century, and capitalism generally seems far less brutal today. In the nineteenth century, as the industrial market developed, workers lost the feudal protections of tradition without yet gaining the modern protections of government. The brutal conditions Marx observed, however, led to greater government protections for workers in the twentieth century, making workers far less vulnerable to owners. To do this, however, government had to become more active, in defiance of laissez-faire. In the nineteenth century government was generally more passive, in accordance with market theory, so workers were more exposed and Marx was horrified. Prior to the nineteenth century European peasants were driven off the feudal estates and into the growing cities. Over the last two centuries the owners of the land (the aristocrats) had fenced off their estates (the enclosures) in order to grow livestock and compete in the market. In effect, feudal aristocrats were becoming capitalist owners. The owners of the land began to abandon peasant agriculture and all feudal traditions in order to trade in the market and maximize private profit.

A new class of workers was arising, and they were desperate to get a job. They no longer lived on the land where they could feed and clothe themselves. They needed work to live, but jobs were hard to find, working conditions were terrible, wages were very low, and everyone could easily be replaced. This was the capitalism Marx saw. Owners had enormous power over their workers, and neither government nor tradition offered much help.

Marx analyzed this new class structure and found it to be brutally oppressive. He thought it could not last long and he predicted a workers' revolution. What happened, rather, in the United States, was that government became more active to restrict the power of the owners and provide protection for the workers. As capitalism became industrial, and particularly after the frontier was gone, various laws were passed to protect children, limit working hours, monitor working conditions, assure a minimum wage, provide welfare, legalize unions, support education, and so forth. Because of these government protections capitalism began to seem far less oppressive. Owners today do not have the enormous, arbitrary power they had in early capitalism, the capitalism Marx observed. Marx thought owners would only get richer while workers would only get more miserable, but government acted to redistribute some of the wealth. As a result, we now tend to see capitalism as far more stable and tolerable than Marx did originally.

Government essentially began to restrict some market freedom to protect some equal opportunity, and according to social contract theory, this is what government is created to do. From this perspective government should always remain neutral and maintain market stability by balancing freedom and equality. Marx, however, argued that government under capitalism would not be neutral and independent. It would always serve the class of owners just as feudal government had served the aristocrats. The owners would control all productive wealth and therefore all political power. As a result, government would always support the market freedom of the owners to maximize their wealth. It would not provide protection for the workers.

From our modern market perspective, however, where workers have many protections, this analysis of Marx may seem to be mistaken. Government has, in fact, acted in many ways to protect the workers by restricting some of the market freedoms of the owners. Apparently, then, government has acted much less like a puppet of the owners, and more in support of equality than Marx predicted. Because of many government efforts, particularly support for unions, workers have not become as miserable as Marx predicted and therefore not as concerned with class oppression and not as revolutionary.

Marx, however, would probably disagree, as many modern Marxists have. From his perspective government under capitalism only serves the interests of the owners. Even if government has seemed to help the workers, it has really been helping the owners. The owners are a ruling class, and the interests of this class are to maximize private wealth while preventing social disruption. The owners, therefore, share a class interest in maintaining market stability. They will allow their market government to provide some help for the workers in order to mitigate dangerous inequality.

Government would still be a puppet of the owners, but it would be able to help the workers as long as profits remain high. The owners, as a class, would have an interest in stability, but they would never let their profits decline in order to support stability. This is what it means to be a ruling class: you protect your power and privilege absolutely. If government could protect the workers by reducing the profits of the owners, the owners would not be a ruling class and government would have dominant power. But this is not possible, according to Marx, in a market structure of private property. The owners will have dominant power because they control the wealth, so the government will serve their interests. As a result, government will only help the workers as long as that help does not hurt the owners.

From the perspective of Marx, owners will never sacrifice their profits and wealth to keep their workers happy. Rather, they will protect their profits by oppressing their workers, and they will rely on government force – the police, the army – to control angry workers and maintain social stability. Government under capitalism will never be neutral and fair. It will maintain stability by helping the workers as long as profits remain high. But when profits begin to decline because of that help, government will abandon the workers and help the owners, with the police and the army if necessary. Government will always claim to be perfectly neutral and fair in accordance with the legitimating theory. But this can only be a strategy – an ideological strategy – to seduce and confuse the workers. Government will pretend to help the workers and may in fact really help the workers. But it will only help the workers as long as that also helps the owners. If owners have to maintain profits by making workers miserable – lowering wages, breaking unions, reducing welfare, increasing layoffs – government will always support the owners against the angry workers.

From this perspective, government in the twentieth century was able to help the workers because that also, indirectly, helped the owners and profits were not hurt. Some individual owners may have lost some profits as they lost some market freedom, but owners *as a class* maintained their wealth and power as government helped the workers. Government can only provide protections by taxing people with money and redistributing the wealth. So during the twentieth century, from this Marxist perspective, the profits of the owners, as a class, must have stayed so high that they were willing to sacrifice some wealth, through taxes, for the sake of market stability.

However, another argument made by Marx is that capitalist profits will tend to decline because of market competition. Owners will tend to lower the prices of the products they sell in order to compete successfully, and this will lower their profits. They will then try to lower production costs in order to maintain profits, and in particular they will lower the wages of workers. In addition to lowering wages, owners will also try to maintain profits by replacing workers with machines and this will increase unemployment. Further, the more owners use machines, the more they tend to overproduce. The logic of market competition, then, according to Marx, will tend to make workers poorer, and it will also lead to recession and depression and thus more unemployment. Capitalism will always experience a *declining rate of profit*, and workers will gradually become more oppressed and miserable. Finally, their anger will lead to a class revolution. Capitalism will be overthrown, and private property will be replaced with socialized property, where everyone can truly be equal.

From the perspective of Marx, this analysis leads to an obvious question in terms of the twentieth century. If the owners always have a declining rate of profit and government is only a puppet of the owners, then how could government in the twentieth century provide so much help for workers? If government can only help workers when profits are not threatened, then profits must have remained quite high during much of the twentieth century. But how could profits have remained so high when government was taxing owners to help the workers and capitalism has a declining rate of profit?

In twentieth-century America government did not do much to help the workers until the market failure of the 1930s – the Great Depression. During the Depression, government tried to mitigate inequality and maintain market legitimacy by offering welfare and creating jobs. This was a special, heroic use of government at a time when all market stability was threatened, even the wealth of the owners. The Depression was finally ended by World War II when government put everyone to work. This was another exceptional use of government, and it stabilized market relations. Both the Depression and the war encouraged the use of government, and in the decades after the war government greatly increased welfare for the poor and protections for workers. Because of this active government, the market generally remained stable and legitimate, with remarkably long periods of growth and prosperity. Throughout this period, then, for about half a century, the profits of the owners remained quite high and the workers generally remained content despite the market logic, from the perspective of Marx, of a declining rate of profit. The profits of the owners remained high enough that they could share some wealth with the workers, through welfare and legal protections, in order to assure market stability.

But how could these profits have remained this high? According to Marx's analysis, profits can only remain this high if workers are increasingly oppressed and sinking deeper into poverty. But capitalist owners, particularly in America, generally retained high profits while workers in America during this period generally felt comfortable and secure, with very little sense of class anger. The poor and unemployed during this period were given increased access to welfare, education, and health care, and class conflict remained quite minimal despite the predictions of Marx. This meant that either the analysis of Marx was wrong and capitalism could in fact make everyone richer, owners and workers together, or some other workers somewhere in the world were being brutally oppressed and exploited. Either capitalism was far less brutal than Marx foresaw, or its brutality had been successfully exported overseas so owners in industrial countries, and particularly in America, could retain high profits while workers in industrial countries could be successfully pacified.

For much of the twentieth century, according to modern Marxists, capitalist owners successfully shifted the worst oppression and poverty to the workers and peasants of the less developed countries, that is, of the Third World. According to this argument, these capitalist owners were able to support government protections and pacify industrial workers because they reaped such enormous profits from colonial and imperial controls of

Third World countries. Colonial controls involve military power and imperial controls involve economic power. Through these controls the owners in the First World exploited the land, labor, and resources in the Third World, where workers and peasants had few protections. The resulting profits could offset the declining rate of profit. As a result, owners could share some of their wealth with workers in the First World (industrial workers) for the sake of market stability. According to this analysis, First World workers were saved from brutal exploitation because Third World peasants and workers were so intensely oppressed – dispossessed, starved, enslaved, and killed. During the twentieth century, class conflict was essentially avoided in countries of the First World because the worst aspects of class oppression were shifted to the Third World.

If this analysis is right, the capitalist strategy of shifting exploitation could not be continued indefinitely. It would only characterize a limited period of industrial development. In particular, this capitalist strategy would not be very compatible with today's global economy. When companies can easily move around the planet to maximize their profits, the First World–Third World distinction begins to evaporate. Industrial workers in the First World have enjoyed good jobs – high wages, unions, government protections. But these workers are now beginning to compete for jobs with workers in the Third World, workers with low pay, no unions, and few protections. As companies become globally competitive, Marx's logic of a declining rate of profit will begin to apply. Prices will be forced down and profits will decline, so wages will come down and protections will be removed, even for industrial workers. In recent years, workers in America, for example, have become more threatened. Unions have been weakened and many have been broken. Welfare, health care, and education have been reduced, layoffs have increased, and many companies have moved overseas. A global economy can recreate many of the original conditions of competitive capitalism. These are the conditions of laissez-faire, the conditions Marx analyzed, where government is limited and workers are exposed. As John Lewis Gaddis has written:

> When corporations can base themselves anywhere … governments have little choice but to live with invisible hands. A laissez-faire economic system is emerging at the global level a century after the invention of the welfare state limited laissez-faire economics at the national level. The social and political compromises that saved capitalism through an expansion of state authority early in the twentieth century no longer constrain it. (1999: 67)

In this context, Marx's original analysis may seem more convincing. In a global, competitive economy, profits may be threatened, government may retreat, exploitation may increase, and class anger may intensify. Government has been able to help for a while, but Marx's bitter predictions may have only been delayed.

Labor, alienation, and ideology

Marx's analysis of capitalism focuses on the issue of production. He assumes, like Rousseau, that humans are inherently social, not inherently autonomous. This means, for him, that people can only be fully human when they work together in social groups. Humans are never isolated and detached, never completely self-interested. We are born into social groups, and we depend on social groups to survive. In particular, we are *productive* in social groups – hunting, growing, fishing, building. We can only produce what we need to live and to reproduce successfully though social organization.

Production is a *social* activity for Marx, and it defines our human identity, our human essence. Other animals can only *find* what they need to live. But humans, uniquely, are able to *produce* what they need to live. Humans must organize production, and the way production is organized shapes all social relations. If production is organized equally, so all individuals share equally in productive wealth, then social relations are just – they are not distorted. But if production is organized unequally, as it is in a structure of class, then social relations are distorted. Indeed, the people in the exploited class are separated – alienated – from all their productive efforts and thus from their human essence.

All forms of class structure are unjust for Marx, but the structure of private property is the most oppressive and unjust, the most alienating. Humans are 'naturally', essentially productive according to Marx. Humans produce what they need to live, and individuals can only be fully human when they are not structurally separated from the products they make. Society can only be just and individuals truly fulfilled when they all have a sense of ownership and control over the products they make. Any structure of class control, therefore, distorts this human essence since the privileged class owns and controls what the working class produces. In all class structures before capitalism, however, the lower class lived on the land and thus had some degree of direct control over what they produced. As a result, they could build their own homes, grow their own food, cut wood for heat, and make their own clothes. But private property inevitably creates industry, and in an industrial structure of private property, workers are completely separated, completely *alienated*, from the products they make. Unlike feudal peasants, industrial workers have no traditional rights, no minimal control, over their own products. They are fully alienated from these products; therefore, for Marx, they are also alienated from their labor, from their own human essence, from all other humans, from all social relations. This is the structure of *alienation* for Marx, the structure of capitalist oppression, and it arises from the structure of private property.

Private property is uniquely oppressive because workers are separated from all productive property – the means of production – and owners can only be self-interested, with no traditional, moral constraints. This means workers become commodities to be bought and sold, and this is another way of saying they are alienated. In another version of this same analysis, Marx argues that private property is a form of theft where owners are stealing from the workers. The idea of alienation is Marx's *social* critique of the market, and this idea of theft is his *economic* critique of the market.

His economic critique follows from the *labor theory of value* as stated by Adam Smith. According to this theory, only labor creates productive value, which means only workers create value, not owners. If the value of a product is the price it sells for, then the owners, not the workers, get that money. Owners take a profit from the money they make, a profit from the value produced. But workers produce all the value, so owners are stealing from the workers. Owners create no productive value, but they get rich off that value, while workers who create all that value are generally poor and oppressed. Owners return some of that value to the workers as wages, but the workers deserve all of that value according to the labor theory of value. Profit, therefore, is a form of theft, and when owners reduce wages to increase profits, they are simply maximizing the theft.

This economic version of Marx's argument reveals an interesting issue, an issue about the lost frontier. Marx adopts the labor theory of value from early individualists including Adam Smith. But he uses it to condemn the market while they used it to endorse the market. Both Marx and the individualists value freedom and equality but they have quite different perspectives, and the difference between these perspectives is the issue of industrial production with its structure of owners and workers. Smith assumed the structural equality of independent agrarians on an open frontier. In this context, as in Locke, the labor theory of value applied to owner-workers and supported the idea of private property. If only labor adds value, then aristocrats had no right to the land. The individuals who worked the land had a right to claim and own the land as private property, and thus to sell and profit from the products they made and grew. This theoretical argument legitimated private property, but it assumed an open frontier – no class monopolies, no structure of owners and workers. In the market class context of industry, Marx used exactly this argument to attack private property as a structural form of theft.

Unlike the industrial market theorists, Marx did not reinterpret Smith to justify the industrial market. Rather, he used Smith's original market arguments – arguments that assumed independent agrarians – to condemn that industrial market. Smith had made a similar point about 'merchants and manufacturers' with their 'wretched spirit of monopoly', and Jefferson also feared these merchants and manufacturers. As Smith was reinterpreted for industry, his labor theory of value was discredited, at least from the market perspective. Defenders of the market began to argue that owners do in fact create value by investing money, organizing production, taking risks, etc. They agree that labor adds value but not that *only* labor adds value. If both owners and workers add value, then owners deserve their profit, workers deserve their wages, and the structure of private property is validated. But if *only* labor adds value, then the owners are essentially parasites, sucking wealth from the workers while contributing nothing themselves.

The owners, for Marx, exploit and oppress the workers, but they also depend on the workers because the workers produce all their wealth. The workers greatly outnumber the owners and they tend to become angry, so the owners have to worry about what the workers think and what they understand. If the workers accept that private property is theft, as Marx argues, they are likely to organize as a class and become disruptive, even perhaps revolutionary. The owners must use their enormous class power to maintain class control, and this means, among other things, they must control what the workers think and what they believe. They must put forward an *ideology* that justifies their class position. An ideology is a set of beliefs and values that supports the existing order and serves the existing authorities. Christianity, for example, was part of the ideology of feudalism since it justified aristocratic privilege in the name of God. All religion, for Marx, is an effort at ideology, an effort to assert class privilege as sacred. So if individuals are ever to be free and equal, all religion must be rejected.

Members of the upper class clearly enjoy their own ideology because it validates their social superiority. Primarily, however, ideology serves to confuse and pacify the lower classes. They will accept their misery and remain docile if they are convinced the class structure is just and proper. In an industrial market structure of owners and workers, the idea of equal opportunity, for Marx, is a version of class ideology. If the workers believe in equal opportunity, then they can only blame themselves for their poverty and dependence; they cannot blame the owners. Similarly, according to Marx, other market ideas serve as ideological controls: the idea that government is neutral, that democracy serves the people, that private property means freedom, that owners deserve their profits. The owners use their power to control all sources of ideas – politics, law, media, education, religion, philosophy, and culture (film, television, news, art, music). The market is validated by a vision of civil society, a vision of freedom and equality, and this vision, for Marx, is cynically offered by the owners to pacify the suffering workers.

History and communism

Based on this analysis of capitalism, Marx envisions an inevitable class revolution, a revolution by the workers against the owners. The owners will use their dominant class power, like all ruling classes, to maintain their wealth and privilege. They will use their control of productive property, their control of ideology, and their control of physical force (the law, the police, the prisons, the military). Finally, however, according to Marx, their efforts to maintain power will not succeed. The declining rate of profit, which means lower wages, will finally make workers too poor and miserable. The workers will finally reject capitalist ideology and recognize their class oppression. They will achieve class consciousness and organize against the owners, creating a communist revolution. Capitalism will make them poor and confused, but Marx will help them become conscious, conscious of their class oppression. Marx's social theory will explain the logic of History, the logic of class struggles, and the workers can finally be free by following his ideas.

As workers become more miserable, they will begin to seek the truth, and Marx has discovered the truths they need, the truths of class and History. Marx understands History (with a capital H) as having a purpose and moving toward a goal. He has understood the true laws of History and those laws lead toward a final classless society, a social utopia – communism. The social laws of History, from Marx's perspective, are similar in their rational necessity to the physical laws of Nature. If people follow the laws of History they will move toward a good society – the End of History, communism. People who do not follow these laws – capitalists, workers who oppose communism, people who disagree with Marx – have failed to understand History and must be seen as social threats. History reveals its truths gradually as societies change, so some people, like Marx himself, understand the necessary laws of History sooner than many others. Marx is the first to understand History, so his social theory can lead the workers to a successful communist revolution. After the revolution, industrial production will make everyone prosperous, socialized property will do away with class, and History will come to an End.

History, for Marx, is a succession of class structures and class conflicts. The laws of History are the laws governing class struggles and class revolutions. One kind of class structure works for a while, but it finally becomes unstable due to class conflict. It breaks down, a revolution occurs, and a new kind of class structure emerges, a structure that is more oppressive and more productive. History moves toward greater productivity and greater oppression until the most productive and most oppressive class structure is created – capitalism. Capitalism is the penultimate stage in History. Only after capitalism can a classless society be created. Capitalism generates industry, and industry creates enough wealth for everyone to be equally prosperous. Capitalism will have to be overthrown for its industrial wealth to be shared, but it finally makes communism possible – the end of class structure and thus the End of History.

Marx sees History moving from early tribal societies, hunting and gathering societies, into class-divided agricultural societies. One kind of agricultural class society was slavery and another was feudalism. Feudalism eventually led to capitalism and industry, and capitalism will finally generate, through a revolution, industrial communism. Tribal societies were poor but communal, an early form of communism. All members of the society shared the limited food and resources more or less equally. Agriculture led to a productive surplus – extra food and wealth could be produced and stored. This made class structure possible, where some people, the privileged class, could live well off the work of others. Agriculture was far more productive than hunting and gathering, but it could not be productive enough for everyone to be equal and prosperous. Only with industrial production could a classless, prosperous society be imagined. Capitalism, for Marx, is brutally oppressive, but it is necessary for the generation of industry and thus the possibility of communism. Capitalism (private property) must be overthrown industry retained. Then everyone can live well and freely as equals – communism. History began with poor communal societies, and it goes through various productive stages to reach a rich communal society, the End of History.

Communism, for Marx, can only emerge from fully developed capitalism, that is, from a revolution by *industrial* workers. The various communist countries in the twentieth century, then, including China, Cuba, and the Soviet Union, were never truly communist in Marx's sense. In each of these cases a communist social order emerged from an agricultural society, a society still dominated by feudal relations. In strict Marxist terms, no communist revolution of workers has yet occurred, only revolutions of farmers and peasants. However, these revolutions in agricultural countries – Russia, China, Cuba, etc. – established communist governments, and these communist governments were explicitly based on the communist vision of Marx.

It is always important to remember, in this context, that Marx was primarily a critic of capitalism, not a theorist of communism. He did not make much effort to analyze how communism would work. He vaguely envisioned communism as an industrial utopia of equal individuals, the end of class division. Communism would inevitably replace capitalism because of the laws of history, and communism would not be oppressive. So Marx saw his primary task as analyzing the relations of capitalism, not the relations of communism. His analysis and criticism of capitalism, however, depends on his idea of communism, the idea of socialized property. So Marx's meager vision of communism was always important to his theory, and when communist government began to be established, they rested on this meager vision. For practical communist governments, Marx's brief but enthusiastic comments had to be expanded and institutionalized by subsequent communist leaders such as Lenin, Stalin, and Mao, and through these communist governments Marx's utopian vision influenced much of the twentieth century.

Communism, for Marx, means that all individuals own all productive resources in common. All productive property is socialized, so all property contributes communally to the general social good, not simply to private individual wealth. In a context of socialized property, private individuals (owners) cannot get rich while other individuals (workers) stay poor and do all the work. Everyone will always have a job, everyone will work for similar rewards (pay, benefits, etc.), and the wealth that is produced – the productive value – will benefit everyone equally. People will do different jobs – janitor, manager, engineer, truck driver – but all jobs will be recognized as necessary and important, and everyone will have equal social prestige and equal living conditions.

Everyone, in effect, will be an owner-worker. Everyone will own productive property in common, and everyone will work that property. No one will be able to exploit the labor of others to accumulate private wealth. No one will be alienated because everyone has a claim of ownership in everything that is produced. In Marx's vision, communism eliminates private property and creates an equal society of owner-workers, a society of freedom and justice. He seeks the same kind of structural equality as the early individualists, a structure of owner-workers, but he wants this structure with industrial production, unlike the early individualists. The individualists did not think that structural equality could be compatible with industry, because industry would create class monopolies in a context of private property. They could only envision structural equality on an agrarian frontier, but Marx understood this was fantasy. So he envisioned structural equality together with industry by eliminating private property. Communism, in effect, would guarantee structural equality without an open frontier.

Marx accepted the individualist goals of freedom and equality, at least in general. He agreed that freedom and equality meant no sacred duties and no class privilege. The individualists, however, could only imagine freedom and equality in terms of private property. Freedom, in their view, meant freedom from arbitrary (traditional) social constraints, the freedom to maximize private property. And equality, in their view, meant equal legal access to owning private property – no traditional barriers. They accepted inequality of wealth as long as everyone had equal opportunity. And freedom included the freedom to profit from the work of others. For Marx, these ideas of freedom and equality only meant class oppression. He wanted communism to embody freedom and equality, so he had to define these values in terms of socialized property, not private property.

He defined equality as equal wealth, not as equal opportunity. And he defined freedom as the freedom to live a good life, the freedom to fulfill your human essence. Production, for Marx, defines the human essence, since humans produce the things that keep them alive – food, clothing, shelter. Whatever an individual produces, then – wheat, tables, steel – becomes part of that individual's essence. If individuals do not own what they make – if they are alienated from the products they produce – they are alienated from their own human essence and they cannot be truly free. People can only be truly free, for Marx, when they own what they work to produce, that is, when everyone is an owner-worker.

This is very similar to what the individualists envisioned. They also assumed that a society could only be free and equal, just and decent, if everyone is an owner-worker – structural equality. If everyone is an owner-worker, all individuals work for themselves, so freedom can never mean the freedom of owners to exploit workers who have no chance to be owners. Marx and the individualists agreed on this vision, a vision of freedom and equality, and they also agreed that private property with industrial production would result in class oppression. The individualists defined freedom and equality in terms of private property, so they feared industrial production and assumed an agrarian frontier. Marx embraced industrial production, so he defined freedom and equality in terms of productive activity, not in terms of private property.

Freedom means owning and having pride in what you produce (not working for the private benefit of others), and equality means sharing all productive wealth equally. All individuals must own everything in common – socialized property, communism. Freedom, then, means everything is owned communally. There can be no private ownership because private ownership, with its version of freedom, destroys the possibility of true freedom. Humans are 'naturally' social and productive, so communal ownership allows equal individuals to fulfill their human essence, that is, to be free.

Marx and the individualists agreed that freedom requires a society of owner-workers. They disagreed over what these owner-workers should own – private property or communal property. They agreed that the individualist idea of freedom – private property – would cause many problems in an urban context of industry, problems of class division and exploitation. Marx tried to solve these problems by defining freedom as socialized property so freedom would be compatible with industry. But his idea of freedom also raised problems, problems the individualists tried to solve by asserting private property. The individualists feared industry because of their idea of freedom, but they also feared a dominant government. Marx redefined freedom to solve the problems of industry, but he then recreated the problems of dominant government.

Freedom and government

For the early individualists, freedom meant limited government. A market in private property with equal owner-workers (endless free land) would regulate itself through supply and demand. The *invisible hand* would operate, the market would be civil, government could be passive, and individuals would be free from excessive controls. This idea of freedom – limited government – assumed an agrarian frontier. The individualists vaguely feared but did not fully anticipate the class inequality and failure of freedom arising with urban manufacturing. Marx, however, had to accept an industrial market, exactly what the individualists feared. So he recommended socialized property to achieve industrial equality.

Individuals could be free, in his terms, as communal owner-workers, but they could not be free in terms of limited government, because communism has no *invisible hand*.

If all property is socialized, market relations cannot exist, the relations of supply and demand. Marx wanted to end the market, which he saw as deeply oppressive. But the market, at least in theory, can be self-regulating – laissez-faire. If rational individuals pursue their self-interests in a context of private property, social order will emerge from supply and demand and government can be limited. Under communism, no logic of supply and demand organizes productive relations and thus social life. Communism cannot be self-regulating, not even in theory. Individuals do not pursue private interests, so they do not create social benefits – needed products, improved efficiency, higher quality – based on private calculations. Without a market to organize production, government must control the economy. In effect, government must control all social relations, and this is exactly the opposite of the individualist idea of freedom.

If all property is socialized, people will not decide what to make and how to make it based on their own private interests. People will not invest their money, start businesses, learn skills, improve efficiency, or try new ideas to maximize their private profit. Rather, resources must be developed, factories must be built, trade must be arranged, and people must be given jobs in accordance with a central plan. All productive activity must be planned, and government must create and implement that economic plan. Government must tell farmers what to grow, factories what to make, shippers what to ship, stores what to sell, individuals what to learn, where to work, and when to work. Government must also set prices, wages, and benefits. It must fund all the science, develop all the technology, support all the artists, and control all the media. Everything must be centrally planned and coordinated. The plan enables communal ownership and thus freedom and equality, in Marx's terms. So individuals should be motivated to support and participate in the plan. Government knows how everything should work and thus what is best for everyone. Communal participation – supporting the plan – serves the interests of all individuals. Government must maintain social order from above, with absolute authority, because no market creates social order from below.

In countries that were communist, such as the Soviet Union, government routinely developed five-year or ten-year plans. These plans controlled productive activities, particularly industrial productive activities, in precise and complex detail. All aspects of society depended on the plan, so government had to have enormous power over all social relations. In particular, a communist government could not tolerate criticism or defiance. All parts of the productive plan were interdependent, so if one part did not work properly (say, not enough trucks for delivery of parts), then all other parts of the plan would fail. If any individuals criticized or disrupted the plan, the entire social order could be threatened. So government control and power could not be questioned. Individuals had to live and work where government said they were needed, and they could not criticize government officials.

In a market, if one company does not have enough trucks, another company will supply the trucks in order to make a profit. The market can accommodate failures and adjust to change because it runs on private interests, not on a central plan. In a market society, individuals can be critical and even disruptive in the sense of innovation. This is the point of individualism – individual freedom from centralized control – and it requires limited government. But communism requires a strong government, even an absolute government, and it cannot accept criticism. In particular, it cannot accept much innovation. Any productive innovation, for greater efficiency or improved products, will change some aspect of the central plan and threaten all other production. So innovation must be inhibited for a communist economy to work.

This is another consequence of Marx's idea of freedom. Individualist freedom means freedom from government controls, freedom to criticize, to innovate, to pursue private interests. Communist freedom means freedom from class oppression, freedom to produce as a social equal, to pursue communal interests. The problem with individualist freedom (private property) is that it generates industrial production and creates class division. The problem with communist freedom (socialized property) is that it assumes industrial production and creates government control.

Marx essentially sacrificed individualist freedom to achieve industrial equality. Individualist freedom, he understood, would lead to class monopolies, so he endorsed socialized property to end class monopolies. Like the individualists, he thought a good society, a free and equal society, required structural equality. But unlike the individualists, he wanted structural equality together with industrial production. He understood that a strong, unquestioned government would be necessary to organize communist production after the communist revolution. This would be the government of the Communist Party, and the Party would understand the truths of History. The Party would control the government and the economy. In effect, it would control all the people in the name of justice and decency, freedom and equality.

Marx also seemed to understand, however, just like the individualists, that a strong, unquestioned government could be a serious problem, even under communism. In his discussion of communist utopia, he vaguely suggested that the need for communist government would eventually 'wither away'. Centralized government control, he thought, would no longer be necessary after a few generations of communism. All corrupting vestiges of the market would be gone, all private attitudes, and everyone would have learned to think and act communally. He never explained how this would work, that is, how industrial order could be maintained with neither a market nor a plan. He seemed to hope, however, that communism would eventually be self-regulating and communist freedom would eventually mean freedom from government control.

Marx wanted freedom, equality, and industry, and equality was his central concern. He recommended social institutions for equality – socialized property, absolute government – and he only hoped for freedom from government control. His arguments legitimated communist governments through much of the twentieth century, and these communist governments did not 'wither away'. In general, they maintained absolute control, inhibited innovation, and punished all defiance and criticism. They had to organize productive activities, so they had to protect the central plan. Officials in these governments belonged to the Communist Party, and members of the Party had enormous social power. There were no alternative political parties and no democratic elections. The Party controlled the government and the government controlled the society, and Party members, then, as a consequence, tended to enjoy special privileges; that is, they become corrupt.

Party members generally used their power to serve Party interests, the interests of power and privilege. They enjoyed more wealth, luxury, and freedom than non-Party members, and non-Party members – most of the citizens of communism – did virtually all the productive work. Party members were the officials, the bureaucrats – the people who organized production and collected all productive wealth. The non-Party members were the workers, the people who produced the wealth and depended on the government (the Party) for communal distribution and fairness. Non-Party members, then, tended to live far less pleasant lives, with far more fear and constraint, than members of the Party. Under communism, of course, no private individuals, not even members of the Party, could 'own' productive property, not in the sense that capitalists in the market could own productive property. But the Party controlled all the productive property and its members, therefore, benefited from that control very much like capitalist owners. Party members, that is, could enjoy the wealth produced from the labor of non-Party members, while those non-Party members, very much like market workers, enjoyed much less of that wealth. Communism, in effect, created a special, privileged group – the Party – and this privileged group was quite similar to, under a new definition of property, a dominant, privileged class. Communism may have ended class structure in the sense of private ownership, but it recreated class structure in the sense of government control. This communist version of class undermined both freedom and equality, even in Marx's sense, and it also turned out to be incompatible with industrial production.

In the Soviet Union communism succeeded somewhat in creating industrial production from conditions of feudal agriculture. Enormous brutality and death, however, were involved in this creation of industry, and communist industrial production never worked very well. In general, communist countries became quite unequal and communist governments quite corrupt. Most communist governments collapsed in the late twentieth century, and formerly communist countries have turned to the market and endorsed private property. These communist governments, however, did not collapse because they were corrupt. Rather, they generally collapsed for economic reasons: they failed at industrial production. Marx envisioned communism as a way to combine equality with industry. But communism generated a form of class inequality – Party privileges – and it could not sustain industry.

Industry depends on science and technology, and science and technology depend on criticism and innovation. The market encouraged industry because the market encouraged new ideas, new strategies, social change for the sake of private profit. Communism discouraged criticism and innovation. Its economy needed to work according to a central plan, so new ideas and social change had to be threatening. Competition did not exist to encourage efficiency, so production was often wasteful and inefficient. In effect, communist industry could not create wealth. That is, products were poorly made, and they often had to be sold for less than they cost to make. Many factories could only be maintained through government subsidies; that is, they could not cover their costs of production through sales of the products they made. As a result, communist industrial production often drained government wealth rather than producing greater wealth. In this sense, communist governments failed at production, and finally they failed as governments.

For this discussion, communism should be distinguished from socialism. As I shall use these terms, communism is a more extreme form of socialism, that is, of socialized property. Communism implies a more complete commitment to socialized property than socialism. A country can be called socialist if private property still exists but government controls a significant portion of social wealth, production, and distribution through high taxation and some government ownership of major industries and utilities. Socialism in this sense is compatible with democratic elections and people can call themselves socialists who are opposed to communism. The idea of communism, on the other hand, implies a one-party government and no private property. Government controls the entire economy and this government is not subject to democratic elections or criticism. A socialist government can be elected, and when it loses an election much of the property it socialized – for example, railroads, airlines, coal mines – may then be privatized by a non-socialist government. But communist governments cannot be voted out of power. The government must run the economy – no private property – and the controlling economic plan cannot be disrupted by an election.

Marx envisioned communism as the ultimate rational society – free, equal, just, industrial, prosperous. This vision required that freedom, equality, and industry all be detached from the idea of private property. Without private property, however, Marx could not make communism rational in the sense of legitimating criticism and innovation, that is, in the sense of limited government. He had to eliminate the individualist versions of reason and freedom – private self-interests – in order to eliminate the market structure of class – class monopolies of private property. He wanted to preserve industry without class monopolies, but industry depended on the individualist versions of reason and freedom, including criticism and innovation.

Marx recognized, two centuries after Locke, that the individualist ideas of reason and freedom would lead to industrial production and thus to class monopolies (no open frontier). He thought, however, that the individualist ideas of reason and freedom were essentially ideological and therefore would not be necessary to sustain industrial production. He thought the individualist idea of freedom – the freedom of private property – was inherently oppressive, and it could easily be abandoned without threatening industry. The individualists, however, thought this idea of freedom was necessary for social decency, and they did not see it, as Marx certainly did, as leading inevitably to industry.

The individualists understood, much better than Marx, that reason and freedom based on private property would support democracy and criticism, that is, limits on government. They worried more about government, and Marx worried more about equality. The individualists assumed an open frontier, so they did not worry about equality. The individualists did not understand that their ideas of reason and freedom – legitimate criticism – would end the open frontier, and Marx did not understand that industrial production depended on legitimate criticism. The individualist idea of private freedom made modern industry possible, but the early individualists only envisioned the structural equality of agrarian owner-workers, the civil frontier of the cowboy myth.

Marx and the cowboy

Marx agrees with the cowboy myth that industrial market conditions – the mythical urban East – will generally be oppressive and corrupt. He seeks a society of owner-workers as the basis for justice and decency, but he has no fantasy of an endless agrarian frontier. On the mythical frontier, individuals own the products they make, so they do not have to sell their labor. In Marx's terms, no one will be alienated because there is no class inequality. Marx, however, knows the market will be industrial and class monopolies will arise. The market will be class divided, not structurally equal, so owners, for Marx, can only be greedy capitalist villains, not decent owner-workers. The myth sees owners from the East as greedy capitalist villains, and Marx generally agrees, only he sees all market society as the corrupt urban East.

There are two types of owners portrayed in the cowboy myth – owners who are also workers and owners who are only capitalists. The former see their property as the basis for community and the latter see their property only as investment. The latter are the villains of the myth, and they are the only kind of market owners that Marx envisions. These owners live off the work of others and they have no commitment to equality or civility, only to maximizing wealth. They seek to monopolize all the land in the valley, all access to the river, all the right-of-way – that is, all the productive property. They seek the structural privilege of monopoly domination, and they cheat and oppress others in order to achieve that privilege. They want to prevent those others, the good citizens, from owning any property, that is, they try to turn them into workers. These capitalist owners in the myth try to achieve a position of class privilege, just as Marx argues, but they cannot achieve that position because of the open frontier. The frontier of free land prevents class monopolies, so capitalist owners will always appear as villains, and they can always be defeated by strong, honest individualists – the cowboy hero.

In the industrial city, however – the urban East – all owners become capitalist owners, and the frontier structure of owner-workers is lost. The original vision of the market – structural equality – no longer makes sense, so capitalist owners and class monopolies must be accepted as normal if the market is to be legitimate. Capitalist owners must be seen, in contrast to the cowboy myth, as necessary and useful, not as corrupt villains. The industrial market depends on owners and workers, so capitalist owners must be seen as decent and civil if the market is to be seen as civil. Also, workers must be seen as having equal opportunity, even if it is only access to jobs (selling their labor), not access to land (becoming an owner-worker). Capitalist owners and a class of workers must become a normal structure, but Marx could only see this structure as oppressive and unjust. As a result, he continued to see capitalist owners as simply greedy villains, just as the cowboy myth does, and he essentially recommended communism to achieve the structural equality of the mythical open frontier.

Marx also agrees with the cowboy myth that villainous capitalist owners will corrupt the law and government. The owners will use their wealth and power to control government officials – the sheriff, the mayor, the judge in the myth. The law will be twisted to serve the interests of the owners, so the decent citizens, like the cowboy hero, must defy the law to achieve a just society. Further, capitalist owners in the myth, just as in Marx, confuse and mislead the decent citizens with oppressive ideology. The citizens want to believe the law is fair and just, and the owners encourage that belief while cynically manipulating the law. The owners mislead the citizens into thinking that government is neutral, and then they use that government to control and oppress the citizens. A social hero, then – the cowboy in the myth – must defy the corrupt government and fight for justice and decency. Marx agrees with the myth that a social hero is necessary, a hero of structural equality, but he sees this hero as leading a revolution and creating socialized property.

Marx and the individualists agree about structural equality and disagree about private property. Their disagreement, however, is really about the open frontier – whether the market will be independent agrarians or industrial owners and workers. They seek the same basic goal, a rational society of owner-workers, and they share the same basic legitimating vision, the vision of a detached hero fighting established corruption and creating a just society. Marx's social theory tells a dramatic story, a story of revolution, and this story is very similar to the individualist story, the story of the social contract. They are both stories of an imagined history, a history that justifies the theory. Marx tells a story about a revolutionary hero who fights market oppression to achieve freedom and equality. Individualists tell a story about an individualist hero who fights 'natural' oppression to achieve freedom and equality. The cowboy myth reflects the individualist story with the cowboy as the individualist hero. But it also, to a degree, reflects Marx's story, and the similarities and differences are revealing.

Both the revolutionary hero and the individualist hero are initially detached from the people they want to help. Each has special knowledge and abilities, and this makes them different, outsiders. The individualist hero knows the truths of Nature (the cowboy emerges from the wilderness), and the revolutionary hero knows the truths of History. The cowboy has special wilderness strength, special 'natural' freedom. He is a stranger and initially resisted and feared by the good citizens. Eventually, however, they accept his truths, respect his abilities, and benefit from his efforts. Similarly, the revolutionary hero has special knowledge of capitalist oppression and class revolution, and he is initially resisted and feared. He understands the logic of History long before the oppressed workers, who are confused by ideology. Eventually, he is also accepted and respected, and the workers benefit from his efforts. Both the revolutionary and the individualist (the cowboy) have to be good at violence, since violence is always necessary to end established oppression. Both are fighting for freedom and equality, in somewhat different versions, and both indeed seek a social context of structural equality.

These heroic similarities show that Marx thinks very much like an individualist. He has the same basic vision – freedom and equality – and he tells a similar story. Both he and the individualists tell a story about a rational individual, an individual who understands oppression better than the oppressed. This rational individual is initially rejected, and he must be violent. Finally, however, he defeats the villain, establishes justice, and receives social admiration. This is essentially an individualist story, a cowboy story, and its use by Marx might help to explain why his vision of communist revolution has often been so appealing. Marx used essentially the same heroic imagery to fight capitalist oppression that the early individualists used to fight feudal oppression. It is the imagery of a rational individual, an individual who knows the rational truths of the universe (Nature, History). This rational individual can resist established rules and oppressive morality. Marx asserted the individualist image of resistance against individualist society, against its class structure, and this made the idea of communism attractive to many people. In particular, it enabled belief in communist heroes, heroes of freedom and equality, heroes like Marx himself as well as Lenin, Stalin, Mao, Castro, Che.

Despite these similarities, however, the differences in these stories are crucial. The differences follow from the different references for rationality, Nature and History. If individuals are rational by Nature, they are all 'naturally' rational and thus equally rational, all the time. From this perspective, all individuals always know their own best interests, simply by definition. But if individuals are rational by History, some are rational much sooner than others. This is what Marx envisions: some individuals – the revolutionary heroes – achieve rationality long before most others. Those others remain confused and misled, so they do not understand their own best interests. The rational individuals, the revolutionary heroes, know what is best for everyone, even when most people do not. The revolutionary heroes know the truths of History, so they must form the Communist Party. The Party, then, must have absolute power over everyone else. Most of the people are not yet rational, so their social understanding, their criticism and judgment, cannot be trusted.

The revolutionary hero is rational by History, so he must achieve and maintain social control. Most people are not yet rational, so the revolutionary hero – the Party – must shape and direct their lives for the sake of freedom and equality. The individualist hero, however – the cowboy – is rational by Nature, so he must establish civil equality and surrender social control. From the perspective of Nature, all individuals are equally rational so no hero or Party should have dominant power. All individuals should be equal – legal equality – and government should be limited. Some individuals may be confused, and resist the hero, because they are weak and afraid. But they do not resist the hero because they are not yet rational. The cowboy hero must defeat the villains, just like the revolutionary hero, but he must ride away or settle down to establish freedom and equality. He fights for laissez-faire, not for centralized power. He must become a social equal, not a privileged authority, because individuals are rationally equal by Nature, not rationally unequal by History.

This is the difference in the legitimating stories that led communism toward government corruption and industrial failure. Marx thought people under capitalism should and would become rational enough to criticize capitalism. He did not, however, seem to think that people under communism would need to criticize communism. Communism, in his view, would guarantee social fulfillment, complete freedom and equality, so no internal criticism would be necessary. Government would always be just, since no class structure would exist, and indeed it would eventually 'wither away'. The individualists, however, thought government could never be trusted, even if everyone was equal, so they wanted it to be small and weak. They saw individuals as rational all the time, rational by Nature, not by History. So all individuals had a 'natural' right to freedom and criticism, a 'natural' right to resist excessive government. Marx only legitimated social criticism against capitalism, but the individualists legitimated constant social criticism. Thus they also legitimated innovation, democracy, industry, and constant suspicion of government. The revolutionary hero can be critical of capitalism but he must demand acceptance and obedience under communism. He becomes the hero of an established order, the hero of the central plan. The cowboy, however, is always a hero of defiance and disruption, a hero of social change, a hero of the market.

Illustrative films

Many Westerns show large, villainous ranchers who only want to drive homesteaders away and claim all the land, that is, prevent equality. These ranchers live on their land but they resist law and order and are essentially still in the State of Nature – *Shane*, *The Violent Men*, *The Westerner*, *Silverado*. Many other Westerns, however, show large ranchers and owners simply as capitalists, seeking only greater wealth with no concern for the land or the community. In *Man Without a Star* an owner from the East buys a ranch in order to exploit and exhaust the land, making as much money as possible, and then return East. In *Joe Kidd* an owner from the East comes West with many gunfighters to kill a local farmer who is organizing other farmers and claiming the land. In *The Sheepman* a villainous owner pretends to be part of the community while secretly claiming all the land to sell to the railroad. In *Jesse James* (1939) the railroad oppresses decent western citizens simply for profit. *Heaven's Gate* (1980) is loosely based on the Johnson County War of 1892 in Wyoming, a war that followed from the arrogance of eastern capital investing in western ranches. A blatant image of oppressive eastern capital versus decent western community is in Sergio Leone's US–Italian tribute to American Westerns, *Once Upon a Time in the West* (1968).

5

MAX WEBER

Bureaucracy and the Cowboy

Weber was born in 1864 and he died in 1920. He became a German professor, but he suffered serious depression and ill-health for many years. He often traveled when he could not work, and he visited America in 1904. He was impressed with its violence and individualism as well as with its emerging class structure. Because of a family inheritance he was able to write extensively despite various bouts of depression. He 'belonged to a generation of universal scholars', according to Gerth and Mills (1958: 23), and he knew a great deal about a great many things – law, economics, history, philosophy, politics, and religion. He was instrumental in bringing sociology to Germany as an academic discipline, and he helped define the sociological approach to the study of industrial relations.

Weber analyzed the market structure of industry just a few years later than Marx. These theorists addressed similar social issues including the issue of capitalist class structure. Unlike Marx, however, Weber saw himself as a detached scientist, not as a social activist. He saw the industrial market as a new structure of social relations, and he tried to identify the central, new characteristics of such social relations. The primary social development, in his view, was the emergence of rationality, and the emergence of rationality implied the emergence of bureaucratic structure as the dominant basis for social organization. Weber greed with Marx's attention to class, but he saw the issue of bureaucracy as even more fundamental to the new industrial society. So he focused his theoretical concerns on the emergence of rationality and on the social impacts of bureaucracy, the organizational structure of rationality.

As we will see, Weber wrote about the American frontier and about the equalizing promise of the idea of available land, an idea soon to be lost. He did not write specifically about the cowboy but he did write about a somewhat cowboy-like figure, the charismatic hero. More generally, Weber lived and wrote in Germany at the same time that the western novels of Karl May, novels about the American frontier, became enormously popular. Germans responded enthusiastically to the image of an open frontier, and Weber was part of that German culture. He understood the relation of that image to the ideal of equality, and he lamented, along with Turner and others, the loss of that frontier.

Bureaucracy

The individualists envisioned a market without industry, and Marx envisioned industry without a market. Both were optimistic about the prospects for a good society, but both were pessimistic about the prospects for an industrial market. Max Weber, writing at the end of the nineteenth century, could not envision a market without industry or industry without a market. He agrees that a good society requires freedom and equality, and he shares Marx's admiration for the productivity of industry. Like Marx, he sees private property as leading to class monopolies and a structure of exploitation. Unlike Marx, however, he sees socialized property as offering no solution, only greater oppression. As a result, he is generally pessimistic about the future of rational society.

Weber agrees with Marx that the emergence of rationality will lead to market relations and thus to industry and class. He also agrees that market class structure will be oppressive. He focuses his attention, however, on the issue of rationality, not on the issue of class. The emergence of rationality will lead to the market and industry and thus to class and bureaucracy. He agrees with Marx that a rational market society will generate class oppression and not be very civil. In his view, however, rationality is the primary problem because rationality will lead to bureaucracy regardless of the structure of property.

Marx thought that rationality would finally lead to communism – the end of class oppression. Weber, however, thinks rationality will inevitably lead to bureaucracy, whether in capitalism or communism, and bureaucracy will always be oppressive. Bureaucracy is necessary for industrial organization, and rationality will lead to industry. Bureaucracy is necessary because it maximizes rational order, that is, rational efficiency. Bureaucracy is a structure of formal rules, and these formal rules create a hierarchy of authority where organizational power comes from the top. In this rational structure the people at the top – the owners or managers – can be most confident that their orders will be carried out, that is, that the workers will act rationally. But this rational structure, for Weber, means that all human emotions and all compassionate values must be excluded from bureaucracy.

Bureaucracy, for Weber, will dehumanize social relations, making them efficient but sterile, and bureaucracy follows from rationality. Rationality will generate the market, the market will generate industry, and industry must be efficient, so it will require bureaucracy. Bureaucracy degrades all social life, and it also, in the market, contributes to class oppression. Bureaucracy is a structure of social control, and it gives the owners, at the top of the hierarchy, enormous and indifferent power over the lives of the workers. Even if communism ends private property, industry would still exist and it would still need to be efficient. From Weber's perspective, then, Marx's idea of a communist utopia can only be a fantasy. Communism would probably be more degrading because government would control all of industry and bureaucracy would be more pervasive.

Bureaucracy is the most rational way to organize social efforts – factories, companies, government. It maximizes rational efficiency, and efficiency is important to rational individuals who want to maximize their interests. Rational individuals (owners) will use a bureaucratic structure when they need to hire workers, organize tasks, plan production, and transmit orders. Bureaucracy is essentially a rational organizational tool, a tool for accomplishing goals – profit, trade, justice, war. Rational individuals will use bureaucracy as the most appropriate tool for rational organizational goals, just as they will use other tools – a hammer, a drill – as most appropriate for other goals. As production becomes industrial, bureaucracy becomes necessary for Weber, because bureaucracy always maximizes industrial production.

Bureaucracy is only concerned with *technical* goals – building a building, collecting taxes, shipping parcels, maximizing profit. It is not concerned with social goals – freedom, equality, a good society, religious values. This is why, according to Weber, it maximizes efficiency and dehumanizes society. Bureaucracy, he says, has a 'purely technical form of superiority over any other form of organization' (1958a: 214). Rational societies are primarily concerned with maximizing productive efficiency. Therefore, they need bureaucracy. Traditional societies, in contrast, are primarily concerned with maintaining traditional values. Therefore, they resist bureaucracy and demand a commitment to religion and honor. Weber compares rational societies with traditional societies. Rational societies are primarily concerned with private interests while traditional societies are primarily concerned with communal values. Rational societies will validate technical goals over social honor, bureaucracy over morality. Traditional societies worry about persons, but bureaucracy, according to Weber, operates 'without regard for persons' (1958a: 215), and so it 'dehumanizes' social life.

Workers in a bureaucracy – bureaucrats – must not base their actions on honor, respect, or moral values. The bureaucracy will work best – be most efficient – when the workers only follow the formal rules and accept the hierarchy. Owners establish bureaucracies to control their workers as much as possible. The workers, in effect, should forget their humanity – their values, their sympathies – and simply obey bureaucratic rules. This makes bureaucracy a rational tool for the owners to apply and utilize however they wish. Orders come down the bureaucratic hierarchy from the owners at the top. All responsibilities at each hierarchical level are clearly defined in formal job descriptions. Records are kept of all activities so everyone is always accountable. All pay, evaluation, and dismissals come from above in the hierarchy, not from below. Bureaucrats at every level should obey orders from above and take responsibility for the levels below.

The industrial market creates a class division, a division between owners and workers, and bureaucracy is the organizational structure that supports that class division. Weber agrees with Marx that the owners will be oppressive. But the primary source of that oppression, in his view, is bureaucracy, not private property. Bureaucracy is necessary for industry, and it creates a structure of social dominance, a structure of class control. The owners or managers at the top dominate and control the workers, the bureaucrats, and would characterize communist government as much as capitalist companies. Owners will use bureaucracy to maximize their profits, and Weber agrees with Marx that they will oppress and exploit the workers. But managers will also use bureaucracy to control their workers, and government managers, according to Weber, including communist managers, can be just as oppressive and exploitative, using bureaucracy, as capitalist owners.

Traditional societies organize social relations primarily through kinship, and rational societies organize social relations primarily through bureaucracy. In a traditional society, survival, identity, and wealth tend to depend on kinship loyalty and trust. Traditional privileges and sacred duties are based on blood and family. Members of a kinship group tend to support one another in work, politics, war. Traditional class structures are based on kinship relations. In a rational society, however, wealth and identity depend on individual achievement, not on family loyalty. An individual's rational interests may require ignoring the family. In particular, rational owners would not want to hire their own family members as workers. Fathers, sisters, and nieces cannot be easily controlled, exploited, or fired in order to maximize profits. Rational owners and managers can control bureaucratized workers much more efficiently than relatives. Kinship organized social life before the rise of the market. But kinship organization served sacred, traditional values, and bureaucratic organization serves private, rational interests.

Relatives operate on loyalty and trust, and bureaucrats operate on formal, rational rules. In a traditional organization – a tribe, a church – authority is established through shared values and beliefs, the values and beliefs that maintain social order. But in a rational organization – a capitalist business – authority is established through shared bureaucratic rules, and these rules are only concerned with achieving a technical goal. This means, for Weber, that bureaucracy will be most rational and efficient when it is most indifferent to all human concerns – all passion, trust, loyalty, friendship. Workers in a bureaucracy must simply follow directions from the top, with no concern for moral values, religious beliefs, or family commitments. Owners and managers must be able to use the bureaucracy for whatever goals arise, strictly as an organizational tool. Bureaucracy, for Weber,

> means a discharge of business according to *calculable rules* and 'without regard for persons.'... Its specific nature, which is welcomed by capitalism, develops the more perfectly the more bureaucracy is 'dehumanized,' the more completely it succeeds in eliminating from official business love, hatred, and all purely personal, irrational, and emotional concerns that escape calculation. (1958a: 214–216, italics in original)

Reason and tradition

Weber distinguishes traditional society from rational society through their different structures of authority. *Traditional authority* derives from traditional values supported by religious beliefs. Traditional leaders have sacred authority based on shared beliefs. In a traditional society tradition always dominates and constrains reason. People can use rationality to try to solve problems but only within the limits of the sacred, traditional beliefs. Reason cannot be used to criticize the tradition, as it can be in a rational society. *Rational authority* derives from rational individual self-interest. Rational leaders must appeal to rational arguments, not to sacred tradition. Religion must be seen as ignorance and superstition, and tradition as blind obedience. All established social relations can be criticized in the name of reason, so reason inevitably destroys tradition. For most of human history traditional authority constrained the use of reason. But reason escaped from tradition in early modern Europe, according to Weber. This was the triumph of rational authority, and the market, industry, and bureaucracy soon followed.

Tradition, for Weber, prevented science and industry but encouraged community and honor. He laments the loss of traditional identities and values but not the loss of traditional rigidity and obedience. He admires rationality for its openness and criticism, its encouragement of individualism. But he thinks that a society based on reason can only be cynical and oppressive, a structure of class dominance supported by bureaucratic indifference. As a result, he analyzes the industrial market with a pervasive sense of despair. Reason has forever destroyed the blindness of tradition but also the humanity of honor. He does not seek a return to religion and faith, but he regrets the loss of communal beliefs where people felt involved and connected.

The emergence of rationality has changed social life in ways that cannot be reversed. Reason creates science and technology and thrives on innovation and change. Humans become more free and equal, more individualistic, but humans also need, for Weber, a sense of social stability and shared values, a sense of identity and belonging. There has always been a historical tension between tradition and reason, a tension between group commitments and rational self-interests, and this tension also characterizes all human actions. Individuals are always torn, for Weber, between their need to belong to a group and their need to maximize their interests. In traditional society individual self-interests must always be dominated by group demand and identity. Rational institutions, however, depend on individual self-interest, so the need for sense of group identity is weakened. From Weber's perspective, the tension between tradition and reason is essentially reproduced in all individuals, particularly in market society, and at the level of individuals it is the tension between *status* and *class*.

Class interests, for Weber, are market self-interests, the desire to maximize income. Status interests, on the other hand, are shared, communal interests based on common membership in a social group. Individuals belong to the same class if they have similar market interests, similar market income and opportunity. They belong to the same status group if they have similar life chances and similar life restrictions, chances and restrictions that differ from those of other status groups. These chances and restrictions are generally based on law and custom, not on market position. Individuals in the same class, for Weber, only share market position and thus economic interests – rational market interests. But individuals in the same status group have similar social values, similar beliefs and commitments, rights and responsibilities. This means that individuals in the same status group – a family, a church, a club – share a sense of status honor.

Honor requires accepting social duties, even sacrificing for those duties, regardless of self-interest. Traditional societies depended on honor, and status groups in rational society also depend on honor:

> *Status groups* are normally communities … In contrast to the purely economically determined 'class situation' we wish to designate as 'status situation' every typical component of the life fate of men that is determined by a … social estimation of *honor* … status honor [requires] a specific *style of life* … from all those who wish to belong to the circle. (Weber, 1958a: 186–187, italics in original)

In market society, however, rational individuals must always try to maximize self-interests – class interests – regardless of status honor. The distinction between class and status, then, is a distinction between self-interest and honor, and honor always restricts rational self-interest.

In feudal society, for example, class interests always depended on status interests. Aristocrats maintained their class wealth and power through a shared status identity, a shared sense of honor. The economic interests of class could not be separated from the traditional values of status, so the feudal structure of class, in Weber's terms, was a structure of status ranks. The emergence of rationality, however, separates class interests from status interests. Market wealth and power is strictly an issue of rational self-interest, not an issue of status honor. Individuals will tend to sacrifice all group identity – community, religion, family – in order to maximize their own private property. As Weber comments: 'the market ... knows nothing of 'honor' ... status honor stands in sharp opposition to the pretensions of sheer property' (1958a: 183, 187). Further, the market generates bureaucracy, and 'a consistent execution of bureaucratic domination means the leveling of status "honor"' (1958a: 215).

This fundamental clash between class and status arises from the emergence of rationality and its dominance over tradition. Weber's entire social analysis focuses on the emergence of reason, and one of his central concerns is how it managed to emerge, how it managed to break free of tradition. Reason escaped from tradition in early modern Europe and this was soon to change all social life. But why did it emerge in early modern Europe, not somewhere else, and how could it emerge at all? In the sixteenth and seventeenth centuries Europe was quite backward and poor compared with many other world civilizations and many earlier civilizations. So why did reason emerge in Europe beginning in the sixteenth century? Weber tried to answer this question in a very famous book, *The Protestant Ethic and the Spirit of Capitalism*, where he investigated the unique qualities of Protestantism. More generally, in a longer set of studies – *Ancient Judaism, The Religion of China, The Religion of India* – he investigated the unique qualities of Christianity in comparison with other great world religions. Christianity, in his view, led to the emergence of Protestantism, and thus to the emergence of capitalism, because of its unique view of God.

Christianity asserted, according to Weber, the idea of a *moral* God. This meant the Christian God could never be strictly a traditional god, a god of traditional order and established authorities (emperors, kings, aristocrats). If God is a moral God, then all the established authorities can still be criticized, at least in theory, in the name of God if they fail to be properly moral. Everyone is subject to the judgments of a moral God, and this means that even the most powerful and privileged may not be the chosen of God. For a thousand years the Catholic Church did its best to minimize this aspect of Christianity. It tried its best, with great success, to identify the feudal aristocracy as indeed the chosen of God. But the underlying idea of a critical God was always inherent in Christianity, contained in the Bible, and this idea finally re-emerged in the sixteenth century in the Protestant Reformation.

At the beginning of that century a Catholic monk, Martin Luther, criticized the Church for not being sufficiently moral. First he tried to reform the Church using the moral authority of the Bible, and then he went outside the Church to create an alternative Christianity – Protestantism. In Catholic Christianity the Church controlled the idea of morality because only the Pope could talk to God and only the priests could know God's rules. In Protestant Christianity, however, all individuals could talk to God so everyone could know, at least in theory, the moral rules of God. All individuals, from the Protestant perspective, could have direct access to the ultimate truths of God, the truths of the universe. This meant, then, that all individuals could criticize the authorities and the established social order in the name of those ultimate truths, the moral rules of God. This Protestant idea, in turn, encouraged the idea of reason and the emergence of rationality. According to the idea of reason, all individuals have direct and critical access to the ultimate truths of the universe, the rational truths of Nature.

Luther, however, only wanted people to be religious, not to be rational. He wanted them to be Christian but Protestant, and this raised the problem of how they would know what it meant to be moral, how they would know how to serve God. They could no longer rely on the sacred knowledge of the Catholic priests, and Luther himself, and the other Protestant ministers, had no privileged access to God. Luther had to show how the faithful would know they were chosen, how they would know they had God's approval, and to do this he asserted the idea of a 'calling'. God had given everyone an individual calling, and this meant a unique talent or ability – a craft, a skill, a task. Those whom God had chosen would show a true commitment to that calling – they would do it well. This meant, in effect, according to Weber, that only success at your calling could demonstrate God's grace in the new Protestant religion. John Calvin was a Protestant minister who followed Martin Luther and led the city of Geneva. He took the idea of calling and interpreted it as an individual's private business, the effort to be a cobbler, a banker, a silversmith. Christian salvation, then, according to Calvin, could only be demonstrated by market success at that business – making a private profit.

Calvin essentially argued, according to Weber, that individuals should only make money for the sake of salvation, not for luxury or privilege. They should try to make a profit but not to enjoy their wealth. They should reinvest their profits in their businesses, turning their wealth into capital. Success at business (making a profit) would indicate success with God (God's grace). Weber called this the Protestant ethic, and it led to the spirit of capitalism. Property should now be seen as private capital, not as class privilege, according to the Protestant God. Through the ideas of Luther and Calvin, the Christian God began to endorse a rational market order, not the traditional order.

This change in religious focus, for Weber, stimulates the rise of reason, the triumph of rational authority. Class begins to be separated from status, and self-interest begins to replace honor. Honor is a crucial issue for Weber, because honor is his version of a moral assumption. Society can only be truly human – not dehumanized – if it retains a commitment to honor, that is, to loyalty, trust, compassion, community. Honor, however, is a traditional quality, a quality of traditional heroes – Achilles, Beowulf, Arthur, Gawain. The market undermines all tradition, so Weber can only lament the loss of honor as he accepts the necessity of reason.

The cowboy, however, is a market hero with a strong sense of honor. Honor, for Weber, arises from traditional values, the values of status over class. And the cowboy, in many ways, is like a traditional hero, as Michael Marsden has observed: 'It is practically a commonplace for people to refer to the Western gunfighter-hero as an American parallel to the medieval Knight' (1974: 94). But the cowboy is not a traditional hero in the most important way: he only fights reluctantly for individual equality, not for fame and glory and aristocratic privilege.

The cowboy, then, represents a Weberian social ideal, an ideal Weber thinks is impossible, which is why he becomes pessimistic. The cowboy is a rational individual in a market context who retains a strong sense of honor, a commitment to civil justice. Weber thinks this cannot be possible because the market will generate industry, class, and bureaucracy. The myth essentially agrees with Weber in its image of urban industry. But it also envisions, like Jefferson and Turner, this rational, Weberian ideal on an endless agrarian frontier.

The cowboy's honor

The cowboy cannot draw first, shoot in the back, betray his word, ignore injustice, or seek to dominate. He must be a man of honor regardless of the danger or sacrifice. In the famous cowboy cliché, 'a man's gotta do what a man's gotta do'. Honor defines the cowboy according to Robert Warshow:

> What he defends, at bottom, is the purity of his own image – in fact his honor. This is what makes him invulnerable … he fights not for advantage and not for the right, but to state what he is, and he must live in a world which permits that statement. The Westerner is the last gentleman, and the movies which over and over again tell his story are probably the last art form in which the concept of honor retains its strength. (1962: 140–141)

The cowboy has the honor of a traditional hero but not the aristocratic values. He is fair, honest, courteous, and just, and he is willing to sacrifice for honor, that is, for social order and decency. His idea of social order, however, does not include class privilege, and he does not fight for fame and glory, the traditional expressions of class privilege. He tries to retain some aspects of traditional honor while rejecting many other aspects. This is what Weber thought could not be possible in a rational market context. Weber understood traditional honor as an issue of status identity, where status is achieved through social exclusion and privilege. Thus, the honor of traditional heroes separated the high-born from the base-born, the proud nobles from the vulgar rabble. It even supported class superiority when aristocrats fought each other. According to Gordon Wood:

> Honor was exclusive, heroic, and elitist, and it presumed ... a hierarchical world in which a few could unabashedly claim a moral superiority over the rest. Even in wartime, gentlemen officers in opposing armies recognized that they often had more in common with one another than they did with the common soldiers in their own armies. (1992: 41)

The cowboy's honor, however, only involves equality. It derives from the rational idea of Nature, not from the sacred idea of God, and so it applies to everyone equally. If honor is an issue of status groups, as Weber argues, then the cowboy's status group is all rational individuals. In the context of market individualism, as the cowboy myth makes clear, the status group of rational individuals does not mean all human beings. Rather, it means, as the theory assumes, only all white males, and it tended to mean, more exactly, only white male owners of land. This implicit assumption of status privilege, however, does not change the underlying issue of honor. A civil market society is *defined* in terms of equality, not in terms of privilege, so all implicit assumptions of privilege, as we have seen, eventually have to be challenged and removed. The cowboy's sense of honor is the individualist idea of morality, the basis for civil society, and this was a morality for equal individuals. Women and non-whites, then, could appeal to this idea of honor, the idea of status equality, for inclusion in legal equality.

The cowboy's honor applies to everyone, so he must surrender dominant power. He has no sacred duty to direct the lives of others, as traditional aristocrats had. The traditional hero could seek fame and glory to validate his sacred authority. The cowboy, however, must ride away or settle down because he has no sacred authority. The cowboy hero has the pride of honor just like the traditional hero. But the traditional hero always has the arrogant pride of class superiority, while the cowboy hero only has the individualist pride of equal self-respect. The cowboy has individualist honor, honor derived from the wilderness, but individualist honor is an odd version of honor, as Weber points out.

If honor validates exclusive status privilege, then duty and sacrifice make sense. An individual's honor protects status identity, and status is important to social life. But if honor does not validate exclusive status privilege, then duty and sacrifice make little sense. Why should an individual sacrifice for honor with no status identity at stake? If individuals are all equal, then they should pursue their private self-interests, not sacrifice for honor. In a context of equality, honor can only mean sacrificing self-interest for no superior position, no status privilege.

The only way individualist honor makes sense is on an open frontier. That is, it only makes sense in a context of structural equality. On an open frontier, property cannot be monopolized and everyone can be an owner-worker. Bureaucracy will not be necessary since no class structure of owners and workers can arise. Bureaucracy is incompatible with honor, according to Weber, but bureaucracy is a tool owners use to utilize and control their workers. In a context of structural equality, a commitment to private self-interest is still compatible with civil trust and honesty, that is, with honor. In this context, honor only constrains private self-interest for the sake of market stability, and market stability is the same as market civility. If everyone is structurally equal, then market stability – a rational, civil context – is always in everyone's rational interest. In Weber's terms, all individuals are in a common status group, and they all achieve status benefits – a civil society – from a shared commitment to morality, exactly as Locke and Smith assumed.

But if some individuals have structural class privilege as owners, then they can maximize their private self-interests without concerns of honor. If workers can be oppressed and exploited because they are structurally unequal, then market stability no longer means market civility, not in the original sense of equal opportunity. In this context owners would not be rational to limit their profits in accordance with a sense of honor. Structural inequality makes self-interest incompatible with honor, but structural equality gives everyone a rational incentive to be honest.

This is Weber's point about bureaucracy and the mythical point about the East. The East is urban and bureaucratic, a place of owners and workers. People have become cynical and indifferent, and the authorities have become corrupt. The cowboy must fight against all eastern influence, all efforts to create monopolies, as the only way to maintain honor. This is Weber's pessimist vision, and this vision is reinforced in the modern urban action film where the 'cowboy' has to live in the city. The open frontier no longer exists, so the 'cowboy' can only fight to survive, not to create civility. If civility is not possible, then honor makes no sense. Deceit is pervasive, no one can be trusted, and violence must be excessive as the only hope for freedom. This urban 'cowboy' will kill unarmed men, shoot in the back, even kill women to escape bureaucratic control. This mythical imagery reflects Weber's despair, where rational market industry 'knows nothing of honor'.

The cowboy is then the 'last gentleman' as Warshow comments and Weber implies. Weber wanted equality with honor, individualism with morality, and this requires structural equality like the cowboy image of endless free land. He recognized the need for an open frontier to maintain a civil society, just as Jefferson did, and he lamented the closing of the American frontier just as Turner did. Weber toured America in 1904 and visited Oklahoma. But he left the same day when he read about a shooting and saw too many people with guns. Later he compared the individualist structure of rural America with the class structure of rural Germany. All the land in Germany, he argued, had been monopolized, and 'monopolies of land always create a political aristocracy' (1958a: 384). But America still had empty free land, and that inhibited a similar class structure. In Germany 'the peasant could not become a rationally producing small agriculturist, as, for instance, is the case with the American farmer' (1958a: 366). But class would also arise in America as frontier equality was lost, and no further hope for honor and freedom would exist:

> The utilization of new farm land will soon have reached an end in America; in Europe it no longer exists … America will also experience this [class] problem in the future, though only after all free land has been exhausted … Yet … it is also the last time, as long as the history of mankind shall last, that such conditions for a free and great development will be given; the areas of free soil are now vanishing everywhere in the world. (1958a: 366, 383, 385)

Weber saw the frontier closing and despaired of any hope for civil market society. He also saw, however, what Locke and Smith, Jefferson and Turner all saw in the image of an open frontier, the image the cowboy myth portrays. He could not envision a social hero because he was too pessimistic, but the cowboy clearly fits his social ideal in the sense of equality with decency, rationality with honor. The cowboy is also a Weberian character in another theoretical sense, at least up to a point. The cowboy always disrupts bureaucratic controls in the name of individual freedom. Indeed, he disrupts all social controls that he finds corrupt and unjust. He is initially outside the established social order, and he leads the oppressed citizens with his 'natural' sense of justice. In this way he is the mythical representation of Weber's most interesting and disruptive character, the *charismatic* hero.

The charismatic cowboy

Weber identifies three types of social authority – traditional, rational, and charismatic. The first two always maintain social stability. Leaders are given legitimate authority (social control) either in the name of tradition – the truths of God – or in the name of reason – the truths of Nature. People in traditional society accept and respect sacred beliefs (traditional roles), and people in rational society accept and respect rational rules (bureaucratic roles). Both tradition and reason, for Weber, establish strong social orders, and both types of authority are quite difficult to disrupt and change. Rational authority in particular always leads to bureaucracy, and bureaucracy he sees as especially difficult to disrupt: 'Once it is fully established, bureaucracy is among those social structures which are the hardest to destroy … A form of power relation is established that is practically unshatterable' (Weber, 1958a: 228).

Charismatic authority, however, always has the ability to disrupt established order, whether that order is traditional or rational. The idea of charisma, for Weber, is basically the idea that no social order is permanent, and a strong social leader – a charismatic leader – can always bring about change. A leader has charisma when people will defy existing social rules to follow that leader. A special relationship is established where people give social authority to the person and vision of the leader. The leader has charismatic authority, and this authority overrides and replaces either traditional or rational authority. In Weber's view, charismatic leaders are not very common, and the source of charisma is not very clear. Charisma depends upon unique personal qualities and special historical circumstances. It can only be recognized after the fact, it cannot be predicted or arranged. Charisma, for Weber, explains social disruptions and social change in terms of personal leadership and devoted followers. Examples of such leaders would include Jesus, Luther, Napoleon, Lenin, Mao.

Weber calls these leaders 'charismatic heroes' (1958a: 247–248). They are '"natural" leaders', with 'specific gifts of the body and spirit' (1958a: 245). They are 'neither officeholders nor incumbents' (1958a: 245), not when they arise. They 'stand outside the ties of this world, outside of routine expectations' (1958a: 248). They know 'only inner determination and inner restraint' (1958a: 246) and they only seek public goals, never strictly private goals. A charismatic leader does not seek wealth and power: '… charisma is never a source of private gain by its holders in the sense of economic exploitation … It is the opposite of all ordered economy' (1958a: 247–248).

All these qualities are also qualities of the cowboy. The cowboy is a hero outside the established order, a 'natural' individual with 'specific gifts of the body and spirit'. He has 'inner determination' (self-confidence, self-reliance) and 'inner-restraint' (honor, morality). He fights for social decency, not for personal gain, he is 'the opposite of all ordered economy', and he leads oppressed people toward his social vision. Weber imagined a charismatic hero as the only way to disrupt bureaucracy, and the cowboy hero is exactly the cultural image of an individualist who disrupts bureaucracy.

Weber asserted the need for an open frontier to support rationality with honor, freedom with equality. So he also asserted the need for a frontier kind of hero – a strong, detached, 'natural' leader – to disrupt social control. The charismatic hero, for Weber, is a self-reliant individualist who brings about change to create a better order. In effect, Weber argues that someone like a 'cowboy' will always tend to emerge to defy modern bureaucracy. As Rosabeth Moss Kanter remarks in a discussion of modern corporations, 'the cowboy personifies a challenge to the very premises on which a large corporation rests' (1989a: 361). In many ways the cowboy is a kind of charismatic hero, but he never builds a social order around his special gifts, his personal authority. He only builds a social order of rational individuals, where everyone has equal power.

This is where the cowboy is different, because the cowboy seeks no authority. The cowboy is a charismatic leader up to the point of victory, but then he surrenders his dominant authority for the sake of market equality. He begins as an outsider with 'natural' gifts and a commitment to justice, and he achieves respect, admiration, and even devotion as he saves the oppressed citizens. But the cowboy is a hero of laissez-faire, not of his own personal truth. He wants to remove all social controls except for limited government. He does not want to establish new social controls based on his special vision. He seeks a society of rational individuals, not of reverent followers, because he is strictly a hero of market individualism, a hero of freedom and equality.

The charismatic hero, according to Weber, must take dominant, personal authority to create the new social order. This new social order rests entirely on the leader, but formal institutions must be established to govern daily life. These formal institutions, however, are subject to the leader, so the leader can ignore their rules or disrupt their functions, as Mao, for example, often did. These new institutions are legitimated by charisma, but charisma only belongs to the leader and cannot be passed on. When the leader dies, the social institutions must begin to legitimate themselves, either through tradition or reason. Weber calls this process 'routinization', and routinized institutions generally remain stable until another charismatic leader comes along.

The charismatic hero, in Weber's terms, can create any kind of social order – religious, fascist, communist, capitalist. The cowboy, then, is a special charismatic case, a hero of market relations. He does not need dominant power because the market will regulate itself. He fights for legal equality, not for obedient followers, and basically he fights for freedom. He will build a civil society if he can, leading the oppressed citizens with his 'natural' strength. But if he cannot, as in the urban East, he will still fight for individual freedom and defy bureaucratic control.

In this sense the cowboy version of charisma is fundamentally an image of individualist disruption, that is, of constant innovation and criticism. Weber envisioned charisma as disruption leading to order, and the cowboy is an image of disruption as a source of order, the market order of laissez-faire. All societies need stability and rules, but the market also needs innovation and criticism. It needs new ideas, new technology, entrepreneurs, even visionaries. People who do these things are always disruptive, but they also keep the market efficient and productive. The cowboy is the opposite of the bureaucrat, and both are necessary in a rational industrial society, as Rosabeth Moss Kanter comments:

> The cowboy breaks rules and gets away with it, but the corporation manager thrives on controls and the uniform application of rules ... The large corporate manager's suspicion of the cowboy, then, is not necessarily a politically motivated bias against mavericks who fight oppressive authority or speak unpleasant truths. It comes from a recognition that the cowboy personifies a challenge to the very premises on which a large corporation operates. (1989: 360–361)

The cowboy is disruptive like the charismatic hero, but the cowboy builds a new social order on constant disruption (criticism, innovation).

The cowboy, that is, rides away or settles down, letting laissez-faire operate. The charismatic hero, however, according to Weber, generally takes control and consolidates power, stifling further disruption. The market, it seems, creates a special kind of charismatic hero, a *market* charismatic hero – the cowboy. The cowboy can be a market hero simply by being disruptive, as he is in many popular stories, because disruption is always a social necessity in a society based on individualism. Weber saw the need for a frontier as well as the end of the frontier, so he could only be pessimistic about the market. But he also saw the constant possibility of disruption by detached, 'natural' heroes, and disruption, at least, would offer the possibility of resisting oppressive control.

Marx could envision a revolutionary hero to create a good society, a rational industrial society. Weber could only envision increasing bureaucracy and thus oppression and indifference. But he could also envision, occasionally, a charismatic hero arising to disrupt the bureaucracy. Bureaucratic order would always return, so Weber, unlike Marx, could only expect social sterility, not a social utopia. Both Marx and Weber, however, envisioned an individualist hero, a hero from the outside to lead social change. Both these theorists, then, in a sense, envisioned a 'cowboy' hero to fight for social decency. Marx saw his 'cowboy' (the revolutionary) as ultimately successful, and Weber saw his 'cowboy' (the charismatic leader) as ultimately unsuccessful. Both of these theorists, then, imagined some kind of individualist hero – essentially a frontier hero – as part of their social theories. Both criticize the industrial market (the mythical urban East) as a place of class monopolies. They both imagine a social hero that fights for freedom and equality, but Weber, unlike Marx, can only imagine this hero achieving brief but doomed disruption.

The market needs the image of a cowboy. More fundamentally, the ideas of freedom and equality need the image of a cowboy, including the image of a frontier. Even if the market cannot be civil, as Marx and Weber agree, then disruption should at least be valued as a form of freedom, as Marx suggests with revolution and Weber with charisma. The image of the cowboy is basic to modern society, not only in its legitimating theory, market individualism, but also in its critical theory, including Marx and Weber. The cowboy symbolizes an open frontier, and the frontier is the implicit reference for freedom and equality, for the rational idea of a good society. The cowboy myth remembers all this while the theorists usually do not. Thus, the cowboy tends to be explicit in our culture but only implicit in our theory.

Weber recognized the frontier as the American barrier to class, a barrier that would soon be lost. Without the frontier there would be no further hope for a humane and equal society, a rational society with honor. The frontier would enable structural equality, a society of owner-workers, but market innovation (cowboy disruption) would generate industry and a structure of class monopolies. This was Weber's industrial dilemma, and communism was not a solution, at least not for him. The frontier would soon be lost and with it all hope for civility.

Perhaps, however, there is another possibility, other than communism or despair. Perhaps the industrial market could be restructured to support structural equality in the sense of real equal opportunity. The problem with the industrial market, according to Marx and Weber, is its structure of owners and workers, so perhaps it could be rearranged to prevent class monopolies and support owner-workers. This would mean, in effect, that constant substitute 'frontiers' of real equal opportunity would have to be maintained. The original frontier of free western land would have to be replaced to support structural equality, and government would have to make this possible, essentially by providing new 'frontiers'. In general, this is the perspective of our third social theorist, Emile Durkheim, the only one of these theorists who thinks the industrial market can still be civil.

Illustrative films

An image of the cowboy's honor appears in all Westerns. It is central in *High Noon*, where the hero stays to fight, because of his sense of duty, when everyone wants him to leave. In *Shane*, of course, as in most Westerns, the hero chooses to face the villains in a fair fight, while the villains are willing to lie and cheat. In *The Sheepman*, as in many Westerns, the villain remarks that he is willing to shoot someone in the back but he knows the hero will not. In *Destry Rides Again* the hero's duty to enforce the law leads him to support the villains against the citizens. In *The Professionals* the heroes turn against their employer and reject his money when they find he has lied to them. In *The Wild Bunch* the heroes enter a hopeless fight rather than abandon a member of the gang. In *The Tin Star* and *The Far Country* the hero tries to be strictly self-interested, but he finally must act with honor and join a community. In *Red River* (1948) John Wayne refuses to shoot a man who will not draw. In *Blood on the Moon* the hero arrives to help his friend, but he finds his friend is dishonest so he decides to help the citizen. In *Yellow Sky* the hero, an outlaw, keeps his promise to an old man even when his gang turns against him. In *The Tall Men* the hero refuses to take more money than he is owed, even after his employer, the villain, has tried to have him killed. In *Firecreek* (1968) and *Warlock* (1959) the heroic but weak sheriff decides to face the fast gunfighter and virtually certain death because of his sense of honor. And many cowboy heroes make the point that all women, regardless of their pasts, should be treated with equal respect – *Stagecoach, Duel at Diablo, Two Rode Together* (1961), *The Stalking Moon* (1969), *The Searchers* (1956), *The Outlaw Josey Wales*.

The cowboy organizes and leads the people, and is almost a charismatic hero, in *Shane, Destry Rides Again, El Paso, War of the Wildcats, Man Without a Star, The Violent Men, The Spoilers* (1942), *Joe Kidd, Red River, The Outlaw Josey Wales*. After achieving civility, however, he always relinquishes power, unlike the charismatic hero.

Images of oppressive bureaucracy are not common in Westerns, but such images often characterize films about official promises made to the Indians. These promises are usually made by the hero as authorized by the government, and then the promises are broken by government bureaucrats – *Broken Arrow* (1950), *Apache* (1954), *How the West Was Won* (1962), *Fort Apache* (1948), *Drum Beat* (1954).

Images of oppressive bureaucracy in modern society are shown in *Clear and Present Danger, Enemy of the State, Dirty Harry, Armageddon, The Net* (1995), *The Siege* (1998), *Rules of Engagement* (2000), *A Civil Action* (1998).

6

EMILE DURKHEIM

Endless 'Frontiers'

Durkheim was born in France in 1858 and died in 1917. He was a university professor in France all his life, the first professor to teach social science. He wanted to advance the science of sociology, and he founded the first social science journal in France. He wanted to use social science to improve social life, to make it more equal and civil. He admired industrial production just like Marx and Weber, but he was far more optimistic about the market. He agreed the industrial market would create class division if it operated by laissez-faire. But he argued that this market could be made civil and decent through government regulation and control. Government should be used to prevent structural inequality, which means to prevent class monopolies. But government should not be used to end private property as Marx recommends with communism.

Durkheim calls himself a socialist, in the sense of a regulated market, but he rejects the idea of communism, the idea of socialized property. He wants to achieve structural equality in a context of market industry. He embraces the idea of a rational society, a society with science and industry, but he agrees with Weber and not with Marx that this requires a market. A market will encourage individualism and thus criticism, innovation, change. Individualism is the basis for freedom and equality, the basis for rational order, and individualism requires a market in private property, not the socialized property of communism. Durkheim admires the market but he fears its class monopolies, so he rejects the *free* market of Adam Smith and seeks an active government.

Social solidarity

Durkheim's theoretical focus is on the issue of social solidarity. He seeks to understand what holds societies together, what makes them cohesive and stable. Without social solidarity no society can be decent and just, and social solidarity requires shared values, a sense of social unity. All societies, according to Durkheim, must share some basic values, some sense of moral commitments. Without these basic values no social order is possible Some societies, however, have more shared values than others, more cohesive morality. Durkheim analyzes different kinds of social structure and different kinds of solidarity. In one kind of society, solidarity is strong and assured, but in another kind of society solidarity is often weak and threatened. It is usually strong and assured when individualism is weak and minimal. But it is often weak and threatened when individualism is dominant and encouraged. Individualism depends on private self-interests, and self-interests always undermine a sense of shared morality.

Durkheim compares tribal societies with modern industrial society, and he finds tribal societies to be far more cohesive. Tribal societies have simple productive activities, primarily hunting and gathering. They have strong religious beliefs, strong traditional rules, and no class divisions. They are not very good at individualism, including innovation and criticism, but they are generally very good at solidarity, stability, and continuity. Modern society, however, is very good at individualism and not very good at cohesion. The market encourages self-interest and social change, disrupting traditional rigidity. But too much self-interest and too much change can weaken shared values and social stability. In particular, a free industrial market will lead to class structure, a structure of owners and workers. But the market is ruled by self-interest, with no traditional constraints, so this class structure will be excessively oppressive and social solidarity will fail.

A free industrial market, for Durkheim, will undermine shared morality and generate instability because of class division. To this extent he agrees with Marx, but he thinks the market can be rearranged rather than completely rejected. It can be rearranged to be both moral and individualistic, both cohesive and self-interested. He sees the possibility of a *moral individualism* where the private individualism of the market is constrained by public morality. This is what government should be able to achieve by regulating and controlling the market. But this moral individualism will only be possible in a context of structural equality. Individuals can only share social values if their interests are somewhat similar, not severely class divided. So government should try to reshape the market to prevent class monopolies. Government should shape the market to guarantee, in effect, real equal opportunity for all individuals. In such a context of equal opportunity, like that of the wilderness frontier, a shared morality will always be compatible with private market self-interests.

All societies, including market society, require a shared morality, but the morality of market society must be weak. The market depends on individual differences, on innovation and criticism, so the unifying social values cannot be too strong. If they are too strong, as in a common religion, then individual differences are discouraged and the social order becomes sacred. A society committed to reason, and therefore to criticism and change, must have a weak shared morality, but it must still have a sufficient and effective shared morality. If its morality is too weak, all hope for social cohesion is lost and the social order will fail. This is Durkheim's theoretical problem: how to maintain a weak but sufficient shared morality to support a civil market, a market with industrial production. For Marx and Weber this cannot be done, but Durkheim argues that it can be done if the issues of solidarity are properly understood.

Morality must be strong if there is little or no division of labor. But in a division of labor, as in market society, individualism is encouraged so morality must be weak. The division of labor means specialized production. Different individuals have very different skills and specialize in different products – shoes, plows, chairs, insurance. Individuals make money by doing or making one thing, and then they trade that money for all the others things they need, things other specialized individuals make. The market encourages a division of labor, and the division of labor depends on individualism. Individual differences must be encouraged for the division of labor to work, differences in ideas, values, interests, beliefs. The division of labor encourages innovation in the sense of new specializations. Without a division of labor, all people in a society do essentially the same things. There is no specialization and no complexity of production. Usually, there is not even money. All productive tasks are simple, everyone can do them all, and most people (or family groups) do all or most of those tasks for themselves – farming, clothing, housing, etc. Without a division of labor, individualism is not needed and indeed it is even a threat. But with a division of labor, individualism is a necessity.

Durkheim distinguishes different societies in terms of the division of labor. The market requires a division of labor and tribal society does not. He does not, however, identify the market with the division of labor, at least not the *free* market, the market of Adam Smith. He takes the idea of the division of labor directly from Smith, but he argues that individualism depends on the division of labor, not on free market relations. He endorses the division of labor because it supports individualism, but not a free market because it creates class. So he focuses on the division of labor instead of laissez-faire. He supports the individualism of the market, including a commitment to private property. But he argues that the market must be regulated and controlled in order to achieve civility. It cannot be the free market of original market theory, the market of the *invisible hand*.

Durkheim identifies two basic types of social solidarity, two ends of a solidarity continuum. Tribal societies, with little division of labor, are characterized by *mechanical solidarity*. They have the solidarity of uniform similarity, very few individual differences. Everyone tends to have the same knowledge and skills, so they have the same values and beliefs. Durkheim calls it 'mechanical' because all the people are essentially alike, as though they were mechanical reproductions of one another. This kind of society depends on strong shared values for cohesion and stability. Families are essentially self-sufficient, since everyone has all productive knowledge, but the tribe is held together by religion and tradition. Since everyone knows and does the same things, common beliefs are easy. Strong common religious beliefs generate mutual trust and understanding and this is the basis for mechanical solidarity.

Market society, in contrast, is characterized by *organic solidarity*, if it has solidarity at all. Organic solidarity means mutual interdependence, the interdependence of specialized individuals. This is the solidarity of the division of labor, the weak solidarity that must support individualism. Individuals know different things, do different things, and have different values, so they cannot share strong common beliefs. They are, however, according to Durkheim, more mutually dependent than tribal members. Everyone in a division of labor depends on the skills of others, while everyone in a tribal society knows most of the skills. All individuals in the division of labor need products other people make, so everyone has an interest in maintaining interaction – solidarity – with people who are different. This kind of solidarity emerges from social interdependence, not from strong shared values. It is 'organic', in Durkheim's terms, because it is similar to an organism. In the body, for example, the heart, lungs, and brain are all interdependent. If the body is to survive, and by analogy a society, all the different parts must work together (maintain solidarity).

The division of labor itself, however, in Durkheim's view, will not tend to generate solidarity. The mutual interdependence of specialized production will generate individualism and even class division, not necessarily social cohesion. Individuals may be mutually dependent in the division of labor, but they will still need a shared morality, a basis for social unity, to have a good society. The market can only be stable and decent in a context of trust and honesty, respect and honor. A free, unregulated market will generate class divisions and cynical private interests, encouraging abuse and exploitation. As Durkheim comments in *The Division of Labor in Society*, as translated by Giddens:

> If one class of society is obliged, in order to live, to take any price for its services, while another is absolved from such a necessity – thanks to resources it possesses, but which are not intrinsically expressive of any social superiority – the latter is able unjustly to force the former to submit to its dictates. In other words, there must be unjust contracts as long as there are rich and poor at birth. (1972: 11)

To avoid this class oppression, Durkheim recommends government controls on the market to maintain structural equality. The division of labor can make life better – more productive, more critical, more free – but only if structural inequality can be prevented so relations can be fair and just. Only with structural equality can specialized individuals with different ideas and values – individualists – share enough trust and honesty to create a civil society, that is, to have organic solidarity.

In an industrial market context of class, there cannot be sufficient shared morality. And without sufficient shared morality the market will become unstable and tend to break down. Durkheim offers two important ways the market can fail at solidarity – *egoism* and *anomie*. Egoism is excessive individualism, excessive selfishness, and it is encouraged by market self-interest. Durkheim assumes, like Marx and Weber, that individuals are inherently social, not inherently autonomous. People need social involvement in order to be human, but a free market encourages egoism and egoism undermines all social involvement. Individuals become so isolated in the pursuit of private property that life loses all meaning and value. In his famous study, *Suicide*, Durkheim uses suicide statistics to demonstrate egoistic suicide. Individuals are more likely to commit suicide, he contends, the more they are socially isolated – single, not religious, Protestant rather than Catholic, focused on market success. Suicide, he argues, is a sign of social breakdown, a sign of failed solidarity, and the excessive individualism of free market relations will increase the rate of suicide.

Anomie occurs when the social order changes too fast. People are inherently social for Durkheim. This means they can only exist as humans within a context of social stability and shared social values. The market, however, encourages individualism and change, not stability and shared values. It encourages innovation, criticism, and constant disruption for the sake of private profit. Without sufficient shared morality to constrain private interests, change will be too rapid and anomie will increase. When people become anomic, they lose all sense of social confidence, all sense of place, identity, meaning. Without a stable context of social values they begin to feel lost and confused. People who feel anomie become socially disconnected and thus are more likely to commit suicide – anomic suicide. Durkheim argues, using statistics, that rapid social change, encouraged by the market, increases the rate of suicide, and he takes this increased rate of suicide to indicate the market failure of stability and solidarity.

Egoism and anomie are dangers of a free industrial market, a market without sufficient moral cohesion. The central market problem, for Durkheim, is the emergence of class monopolies in a context of private self-interest. If owners are able to oppress and exploit workers strictly to maximize their wealth, with no moral constraints, then solidarity cannot be possible and market social order will fail. This will occur, he argues, if the market operates freely in accordance with Adam Smith. He directs his social analysis directly against original market theory and specifically against the idea of laissez-faire. No society can be stable, he argues, much less decent, if it is strictly based on private self-interests. No *invisible hand* of the market will create a good society. Some social commitment to a unifying morality is necessary, some shared moral constraints on private market individualism. So some *social* effort must be made to maintain a shared morality, and this means a social effort must be made to prevent class monopolies. In the context of industry the market must be restructured to support moral cohesion – organic solidarity. Durkheim suggests how this could be done, suggestions that follow from this theory. In general, he suggests that government should rearrange market relations, including market politics, and should put more limits on the use of private property.

Restructuring the market

Durkheim wants to use government to support greater equality, and this makes him a liberal more or less like Keynes. If Keynes is a liberal, however, Durkheim must be a super-liberal, a very radical liberal. He wants a far more active government than Keynes – he calls himself a socialist – but he still supports private property, not the fully socialized property of Marx. Keynes wants an active government to maintain equal opportunity, and his idea of equal opportunity is full employment – the chance for everyone to sell their labor and get a job. Durkheim, in contrast, wants an active government to maintain *real* equal opportunity, which means to prevent class structure. Keynes is a liberal who accepts an industrial structure of owners and workers – class inequality. But Durkheim seeks a structural equality of industrial owner-workers. A structure of class division, he argues, will undermine moral cohesion. In general, both these theorists have a liberal concern with equality. Conservatives, in contrast, as we have seen, are generally more concerned with freedom. They tend to support market freedom even if it means less equal opportunity. They worry more about government restrictions on private property than about helping workers and the unemployed.

In one sense, however, Durkheim can be seen as quite conservative. Conservatives generally resist social actions – government actions – to achieve greater equality. They tend to think that such liberal actions will do more harm than good. They assume an existing social stability and argue that it should be preserved – conserved – with minimal government interference. To support the free market, they argue that private property should be protected from more government control, even at the expense of inequality. More government control, in their view, will cause more instability than market inequality. Durkheim argues against a free market and for more market equality, more government support for equality. In this economic sense he is far more liberal than conservative. But he is also very concerned with stability, and he worries about things that disrupt stability. For some issues, then, he seems to support, at least theoretically, existing inequality for the sake of social stability, essentially a conservative position. And this is most apparent when he considers the role of women.

He tends to assume, as most theorists have until recently, that women should accept sexual inequality for the sake of social stability, specifically family stability. His deep concern with inequality tends to be focused strictly on class issues. As a result, he can often seem to endorse other forms of inequality, particularly sexual inequality, for the sake of social stability. This was probably more of an oversight than an intention on Durkheim's part, and this oversight was common in his time. But the oversight was built into his theory, and this theoretical perspective has had modern conservative implications. If some kinds of inequality are not as important as social stability, then women, for example, might need to stay in their 'proper', inferior place for the sake of social order.

With respect to class inequality, however, Durkheim is quite liberal, even radical. He wants to use government to create structural equality within an industrial market. Marx also wants structural equality but thinks it is impossible with private property. Weber wants it as well but thinks it will be forever lost with the end of the frontier. Durkheim makes specific proposals to prevent class monopolies. In particular, he proposes a new legal structure of private property and a new way to organize political participation.

Just like Marx, he is more interested in analyzing the problems than in proposing solutions, so he makes various suggestions without much elaboration. It is not clear, therefore, at least not in Durkheim, that these specific proposals can work. Nevertheless, they indicate optimism about the market and thus they remain interesting. Neither Marx nor Weber thinks the industrial market can support a good society, but we all now live within an industrial market. Only Durkheim, of these three theorists, is optimistic about the market, so his theoretical approach at least offers the possibility of improving our modern society. His particular strategies may or may not work, and other possible strategies might work better. But Durkheim thinks that strategies still exist to make the market civil, strategies based on government.

He recommends ending the private inheritance of wealth. If wealth cannot be inherited, class monopolies cannot arise and real equal opportunity can be maintained: 'let us suppose that men enter life in a state of perfect economic equality, which is to say, that riches have entirely ceased being hereditary' (Durkheim, 1964: 30). Individuals could still become rich through market competition, but they could not leave their wealth to their children. Rather, their wealth, after their death, would somehow be made available to all individuals equally through government redistribution. Durkheim essentially argues, unlike Marx, that class is an issue of private inheritance, not of private property. The class problem is not that some individuals are richer than others. The problem is, according to Durkheim, that rich individuals can create a class structure, with inherited class privileges, by leaving their wealth to their children.

Without private inheritance, he argues, market class structure cannot arise. Various other theorists have made a similar argument, including

Herbert Spencer and John Stuart Mill. Individual inequality is acceptable as long as it can never be the basis for class. This involves, in effect, a redefinition of private property. According to market theory, following Locke, individuals have a 'natural' right to own private property and use it however they wish, including leaving it to their children. This 'natural' right justifies market government, so government, in theory, has no legitimate right to take that property when they die, even for equal redistribution.

Durkheim is proposing that the right to own private property should be limited to an individual's lifetime, and this would be a fundamental change in the structure of private property. Property would only be private as long as its owner lives. This would alter, it would seem, many private market incentives. More immediate personal spending, for example, might begin to seem preferable to providing protections for descendants. All children, upon coming of age, would have the same opportunity through government redistribution. So parents with money would have less ability to protect their children's futures. Parents without money, however, would have more confidence in the prospects for their children's futures.

The social implications of this idea are vast and complex. Much would depend on how government would claim and use the property it would inherit. Fundamentally, it is not clear that the market could continue to work with this idea of private property. On the other hand, it might continue to work very well with much more equality and decency. The specific institutional structures would have to be carefully considered, but Durkheim at least offers a market strategy that is more than despair (Weber) and less than revolution (Marx). He is trying to rearrange the market for civil industrial production, and this, of course, is essentially what we have been trying to do through judicious use of government for the last century or so.

This idea of ending inheritance is suggested for structural equality – no class monopolies. Structural equality is necessary, according to Durkheim, to achieve sufficient shared morality for organic solidarity. But even structural equality in a market of private interests does not guarantee social cohesion, so government must also build institutions that assure a shared morality. Durkheim proposes that government create occupational associations – 'corporations', as he calls them. These 'corporations' would not be corporations in our modern, familiar sense – private businesses seeking private profit. Rather, they would be semi-official organizations for organizing, unifying, and supporting their members, and their members would be people with similar occupations and skills. People with jobs, Durkheim assumes, would have similar interests and values. Each occupational association, then, would consist of people with similar values, and moral unity would be easy to achieve.

These 'corporations' would be more than unions and less than businesses. They would represent the interests of their members both in work and in politics. They would also be able to own private property in the names of their members, property their members could work. The members, then, of each 'corporation' would essentially be owner-workers. Moreover, democratic participation would now take place through these occupational 'corporations'. Each individual would vote as a member of a 'corporation', and this would restructure the entire political process. Each individual, presumably, would have a greater sense of political power and influence by voting through an organized group with similar interests and values. Each 'corporation' would create an internal sense of shared morality and an external sense of political influence. As a result, this structure of different 'corporations' would create a general sense of shared morality across all 'corporations'. Support for individual differences would be maintained, through different 'corporations', in a general social context of democratic participation and civil involvement. The shared morality of organic solidarity would thus be achieved in a structurally equal industrial market.

Durkheim mentions all these ideas briefly, and all of them clearly have problems. They would need far more conceptual attention to be used as practical strategies. But they suggest various directions for rearranging the market and restructuring politics. The general lesson, however, from Durkheim and all the liberals, is that government must be used to support individual equality, enough equality to ensure stability and maintain market legitimacy. Keynes argues, with most modern liberals, that this only requires full employment, the equal opportunity to get a job. Durkheim argues, with many socialist liberals, that this requires much more, a far greater effort to achieve structural equality. In any case a government commitment to equality must be encouraged since industrial market relations create class monopolies.

Durkheim does not address the closing of the frontier, as Weber does. But Durkheim, in effect, wants government to maintain a commitment to real equal opportunity in an industrial market, that is, to maintain *frontier-like* opportunity. The market can only be civil, he argues, with no class monopolies, so government must shape market relations to support structural equality. Durkheim shares the original individualist vision, the vision of a civil society of independent owner-workers. But the original vision was agrarian owner-workers enabled by a wilderness frontier, and Durkheim wants to achieve industrial owner-workers enabled by an active government. He wants to preserve all the positive aspects of the market – freedom, equality, science, criticism, individualism, industry – and he wants to eliminate class, with its implications of egoism, anomie, oppression, instability. So he wants government to provide, under industrial conditions, what the frontier originally provided, an endless context of real equal opportunity.

The problem, of course, is that the original individualist vision, the vision of civil society, was based on limited government and a free market. Freedom was compatible with equality exactly because of the frontier. Everyone could be an owner-worker, at least in theory, without a strong, regulatory government. Under industrial conditions, however, government must become more dominant and market freedom more threatened in order to support equal opportunity. Marx, of course, argues that market government can never support equality because it will only serve the owners. For Weber, market government, like all rational organization, must rely on bureaucracy, and bureaucracy will stifle all hope for civility, including the hope for equality.

Durkheim, however, thinks government can improve the market, making it civil and just, and this general strategy of Durkheim, if not his specific suggestions, has characterized our modern market. We have generally created an active, regulatory government to try to protect equality and civility under industrial market conditions. We have tried to use government to maintain a minimum legitimating commitment to equal opportunity, a commitment originally offered by the open frontier. Government has been used to maintain new 'frontiers' as the basis for equal opportunity. Only with something like an endless 'frontier' can individualist society be civil, and this is what the cowboy myth suggests. It will always remain the market myth of origin if its frontier is interpreted symbolically.

New 'frontiers'

If the myth is interpreted literally, it suggests that the market can only be civil on an agrarian frontier, a frontier of free land. This was the assumption of the early individualists in their vision of civil society. They did not think that a free and equal society could be compatible with urban, industrial production, and neither did Turner, Marx, or Weber. But the myth can be interpreted symbolically, with the image of the frontier symbolizing real equal opportunity, not necessarily free land. From this perspective, the myth symbolically suggests that a *frontier-like* context of equal opportunity must be maintained for the market to be civil. This context may not have to be a wilderness, and individuals may not have to be agrarians. But the basic characteristics of an open frontier would still be necessary, particularly a commitment to equality of opportunity and the prevention of class monopolies.

In many ways the cowboy myth reflects elements of Durkheim's theory. On the agrarian frontier, as literally portrayed, the division of labor is not fully developed. Most people do similar kinds of things – farming, ranching – so a common commitment to shared values is easier to achieve than in the urban East. That is, there are more elements of mechanical solidarity – a strong, unifying morality – than in the industrial city, which requires organic solidarity. The frontier, however, is a market society with an emerging division of labor, so it also requires aspects of organic solidarity, in particular, a moral individualism. The frontier supports individual differences, but it also supports structural equality, and this makes a shared morality possible, a morality for equal individuals. This is the cowboy's sense of honor, an honor derived from the wilderness, an honor that is open and inclusive, not traditional and exclusive. The cowboy's sense of honor is Durkheim's moral individualism. It is the moral assumption of Locke and Smith, a universal morality for rational individuals.

The urban East, in contrast, has a developed division of labor. People from the East, according to the myth, are egoistic and anomic. They are egoistic because they only think of private self-interests, not social decency. They only want to maximize wealth, not to achieve civility. They lie, cheat, betray their friends, become quite isolated, and usually get killed because they are so egoistic. The mythical East also generates anomie. Many eastern disruptions – rapid social changes – have torn people from their homes and left them lost and confused. The Civil War is one such disruption, the one most commonly portrayed in the myth, but other eastern disruptions are also portrayed – market failure, class oppression, racial intolerance, religious persecution. Many mythical characters, often including the cowboy hero, leave the eastern cities with no social roots or identity. But they lose their sense of anomie in the civil communities of the West.

The myth agrees with Durkheim about the dangers of class monopolies. The frontier West can be moral and cohesive because of structural equality. The urban East, however, is corrupt and oppressive, egoistic and anomic, because of class monopolies. This is the classic individualist imagery, the imagery of Smith and Jefferson as well as Turner and Weber. All these theorists, however, and Marx as well, are deeply pessimistic about the prospects for market industry. Only Durkheim thinks the industrial market can still be civil and decent. He does not refer to the American West as Weber does, but his image of a good society is similar to that of the frontier myth – market relations, structural equality, and moral individualism. He thinks the industrial market can inhibit class monopolies and enable moral cohesion if government is used properly. Government must provide endless equalizing opportunity, and this means, in effect, in terms of mythical symbolism, that government must provide endless, equalizing 'frontiers' to replace the original frontier. Such new 'frontiers' of equal opportunity can continue to make the market civil, just as it was imagined in the original agrarian vision. From the theoretical perspective of Durkheim, the frontier imagery of the cowboy myth should not be seen as simply a wilderness but rather as a symbol of an endless 'frontier', a symbol of real equal opportunity.

Durkheim was writing at the end of the nineteenth century, about the same time as Weber and Turner and a little later than Marx. Like these theorists he saw market industry as leading to class inequality and thus to increasing oppression and indifference. Many commentators of the time, including Weber, Turner, and Theodore Roosevelt, worried about the closing of the American frontier. The frontier had provided, at least in theory, the basis for equal opportunity. Without the frontier, or something like the frontier, American democracy would probably fail. Something would have to replace the lost frontier so individuals would still have new 'frontiers' of opportunity. In this sense, the image of the wilderness frontier soon became symbolic, an image of opportunity that would have to be sustained for the sake of civil society.

As the American frontier closed, one obvious source of a new 'frontier' was colonial invasion and conquest – claiming foreign lands through military action for the sake of American profit. If western wilderness land could be taken from the Indians for American equal opportunity, then foreign wilderness land could also be seen as providing 'frontier' opportunity. The market needs constant expansion to maintain equal opportunity, so some kind of 'frontier' expansion – foreign 'frontier' expansion – had to be continued after the western frontier closed. Many American businessmen, according to William Appleman Williams:

> vigorously reasserted the axioms of the free marketplace and on that basis moved ... to find a new frontier ... the end of one frontier implied the need for a new frontier ... the frontier would have to be moved from the continent to the world. (1969: 276–278)

Turner's frontier thesis was used to justify colonial expansion. That thesis essentially reflected Adam Smith's analysis of the market. The market could only be civil if it could constantly expand to provide equal opportunity. Freedom and democracy required new 'frontiers', and those 'frontiers' had to be found in Mexico, Cuba, Latin America, Hawaii, the Philippines, Japan, China:

> Turner eloquently expressed an idea that had permeated American thinking from the beginning of the eighteenth century. The frontier-expansionist conception and explanation of American reality was an idiomatic (and romantic) statement of Adam Smith's marketplace-expansionist model of the world. (1969: 360)

This colonial idea of new 'frontiers' shaped American foreign policy. Government had to be active and involved – sending an army, establishing control, arranging treaties – to enable colonial adventures. Later in the twentieth century government efforts to support colonialism became government efforts to support imperialism. This meant less direct military control and more indirect economic control, control through local puppet leaders as well as loans, banks, trading rules, and currency exchange. Throughout the twentieth century government supported global expansion, first primarily militarily and later primarily economically. Now at the beginning of the twenty-first century one of the new 'frontiers' that government helps provide is the 'frontier' of the global economy, where many market opportunities are seen as awaiting entrepreneurs.

In the late 1920s, however, these new colonial 'frontiers' could not sustain the market, and America and the world entered the Great Depression. For many, this meant the market would no longer work without an open frontier, just as Turner predicted. To others, like Franklin Roosevelt and John Maynard Keynes, it meant that the market would no longer work according to market theory. It would need an active, regulating government because free market theory had assumed an agrarian frontier. Roosevelt used government to constrain the rich and help the poor, trying to maintain at least a legitimating semblance of the market commitment to equality. Keynes developed a new market theory to justify government controls to support equal opportunity in the sense of full employment. Both these efforts, political and economic, recognized the industrial failure of free market theory. But the Depression only ended when government became more dominant than either of these men had imagined, by taking over the economy during World War II.

The economic recovery that accompanied the War seemed to support the earlier efforts of Roosevelt and the earlier ideas of Keynes. Industrial market relations could only be made stable and prosperous through active government controls. The wilderness frontier had supported the free market by providing constant expansion, constant opportunity. But without the wilderness frontier, free market expansion would quickly lead to collapse, so government would have to regulate the market to sustain growth and expansion. Government, in effect, would have to support constant new possibilities of equalizing opportunity, constant new 'frontiers'. At a minimum, it would have to constrain market freedom and redistribute wealth to maintain market stability and legitimacy.

After World War II, then, American government generally became much more active in supporting and regulating the market. In the middle of the 1950s America entered the Cold War, justifying massive government spending and involvement to sustain a prosperous market. Also, in the years after World War II government began to spend much more money and create more controls in various efforts to minimize blatant market inequality. Support for social welfare dramatically increased, as did support for public education. Workers were given more protections in the form of legalized unions, better health care, improved working conditions, minimum wage guarantees, and laws against discrimination. Unions, of course, were legalized just prior to World War II, but worker benefits from legal unions only began to be fully realized after the end of the war. Government generally became more active in support of market equality, and by the 1960s most market governments, including American government, had begun to adopt Keynesian policies for regulating market relations. The ideas of laissez-faire were no longer convincing. Government now had to be active to maintain full employment and market stability, that is, to maintain minimum equal opportunity.

All these new government efforts in the market context of industry were directed toward greater equality. The close of the frontier had certified class inequality, as Turner and Weber feared, and the Great Depression had certified the failure of free market relations and intensified class inequality. The market could not work if class became too oppressive, particularly with high structural unemployment. So government had to mitigate inequality for the sake of market stability, and that meant, symbolically, it had to maintain the assumption of equality that was based on an open frontier. Keynes thought this meant, minimally, a commitment to full employment, but Durkheim thought it meant a commitment to real equal opportunity, the structural equality of the open frontier. In general, though, government increasingly became responsible for maintaining legitimating equality, which meant among other things maintaining market expansion. These were the original market contributions of the wilderness frontier, so government somehow had to replace that lost frontier.

In our modern industrial context, new 'frontiers' of opportunity have often been announced. First, there were the colonial 'frontiers', and then there were the technological 'frontiers', the 'frontiers' of science, space, medicine, genetics, information, global business, and the internet. In 1961 President Kennedy offered the policies of his 'New Frontier', essentially applying Keynesian economics to industrial market relations, and *Star Trek*, also in the 1960s, began exploring 'Space, the final frontier'. More recently, in the new twenty-first century, the Business Editor of the *Denver Post*, Don Knox, has written about the 'frontier' of the internet: 'Like the Wild West, there's still a lawless aspect of the Internet that's yet to be reined in' (2000: 1I).

Perhaps the most important of these various new 'frontiers' has been the effort for public education. As the wilderness frontier closed in America, public education began to be seen as offering a possible replacement, a new basis for equal opportunity. Government should provide free education for all citizens as a substitute for the lost frontier. Turner made this argument, as did James Bryant Conant, according to Nicholas Lemann:

> What could replace the frontier? To Turner, and also to Conant, the obvious and only answer was public education. Like the frontier, this distinctive American institution could give every citizen the opportunity to rise in the world. (1999b: 48)

Conant was deeply influenced by Turner's frontier thesis. He became President of Harvard in 1933; he helped build the atomic bomb; he influenced national and international policies; and he helped design and legitimate the modern American system of public education. In the early 1940s he wrote, in a book never published:

> We have before us a new type of social instrument whose proper use may be the means of salvation of the classlessness of the nation ... Through public education we can in this country hope in no small measure to regain that

great gift to each succeeding generation, opportunity, a gift that once was the promise of the frontier. (Lemann, 1999b: 54)

Conant also, along with Durkheim and others, recommended ending the inheritance of wealth to prevent the development of a structure of class.

The stock market has also sometimes been seen as offering a kind of replacement 'frontier', an equalizing source of opportunity. Warren Buffet, the most successful investor in American history, has made this comparison, as Lemann points out: 'What the frontier was to Frederick Jackson Turner, what public education was to James Bryant Conant, the stock market was to Buffet, an open arena of opportunity where the deserving could count on being rewarded' (1999a: 256). In recent years, indeed, the classic market distinction between owners and workers has become somewhat blurred as more and more 'workers' have managed to invest in stocks, essentially becoming modern versions of individual owner-workers. To some degree the stock market indeed provided some equalizing opportunity for some workers, workers who were able to save some money and buy stocks.

These substitute 'frontiers', like the original frontier, are asserted as versions of equal opportunity. The wilderness frontier, however, provided more of a myth of equal opportunity than a reality, as many Western historians have recently pointed out. These new 'frontiers', like the wilderness frontier, generally offer little opportunity for the poor and desperate. Nevertheless, they are important, like the wilderness frontier, as a legitimating image of equal opportunity. The idea of a civil market depends on such an image, which means it depends on at least a mythical assertion of endless equal opportunity.

One modern source of opportunity is specifically open to the poor and desperate. It offers the possibility of high profits, but it is also dangerous and lawless, like the original frontier. This is the trade in illegal drugs, a trade that provides well-paid jobs in many poor neighborhoods. It works very much like the original State of Nature. Opportunities exist, but violence is necessary to claim and own property. This modern 'frontier' of illegal drugs is similar to the earlier 'frontier' of illegal alcohol during the time of Prohibition. Strength and daring can be rewarded, just as on the mythical frontier, but risks are always high when no social contract exists.

The 'frontier' of illegal drugs provides economic opportunity, often great opportunity, for people in America with few if any other economic options. In this sense it helps legitimate the market – a source of equal opportunity – but this 'frontier' is not compatible with market law and order, that is, with the social contract. If drugs are ever legalized, as alcohol was, then profits from the trade in drugs will go to privileged owners, not to the poor and desperate. This was the consequence of repealing Prohibition: profits from alcohol went to corporations, not to the otherwise unemployed. If drugs are legalized, it would remove a source, perhaps the only source, of employment and opportunity for many poor people. As Alexander Cockburn has written:

> In today's inner cities, there are no realistic economic alternatives to substitute for the drug commerce that is often the only rational career option for urban youth ... Legalization would mean government licensing of monopolies to large corporations, which would swiftly wipe out these small producers and vendors. (1993: C3)

This could intensify poverty and anger to the point of class violence, the violence of riots and burning.

It may be, therefore, that the legitimacy of our modern market society, in the sense of equal opportunity, depends upon illegal drugs. Drugs provide a crucial, even a legitimating source of opportunity for people who tend to have no legal market opportunities. From this perspective, modern market stability may depend on a 'frontier' of opportunity that cannot be legalized. This version of the 'frontier', a version that contributes legitimacy, would have to remain outside the social contract. The people benefiting from that 'frontier' would have to remain in the State of Nature – defiant, violent, uncivil. If this is right, our modern market is built on a contradiction, and it can only be damaging, if not fatal, to the prospects for a civil society.

All the legal substitute 'frontiers' that government has supported – science, education, the internet, Keynesian policies, even the proliferation of lotteries – have tried to mitigate inequality but have not tried to achieve structural equality. They have offered possible sources of new opportunity for some individuals but not the constant real equal opportunity envisioned in individualist theory and the cowboy myth. What we have tried to do in industrial America since the frontier closed is maintain some sort of delicate compromise between original free market principles and the original legitimating assumption of structural equality, the vision of a civil society of independent owner-workers. Government has tried to maintain a legitimating commitment to equality in the minimum sense of opportunity to get a job, but not in the maximum sense of structural equality, the sense Locke and Smith assume and Durkheim requires as the basis for a good society.

The problem, of course, is that all these government efforts restrict market freedom. The tension between freedom and equality remains. Government can only mitigate inequality in an industrial market by restricting the legitimating freedoms – the 'natural' freedoms – of private property. Government must try to maintain substitute, equalizing 'frontiers', but none of these 'frontiers' can have the original individualist quality of the vision of a wilderness frontier, the vision of endless free land. Only through a vision of endless free land can the necessary market freedoms of private property be theoretically combined with the real equal opportunity for everyone to be an owner-worker. This was the original individualist idea, the idea of civil freedom and equality, the idea

Jefferson understood and Turner lamented. And this is what the cowboy myth reflects, as the market myth of origin. The myth also suggests, symbolically, that some kind of substitute 'frontiers' must be maintained if the industrial market is to be stable and possibly civil. But the original wilderness frontier is the definitive market frontier, the frontier of limited government, the frontier of freedom *and* equality.

Illustrative films

Many Westerns show the communal need for a shared morality – *The Westerner, My Darling Clementine, Shane, The Magnificent Seven, The Outlaw Josey Wales, Silverado*. They also show that this shared morality is easier for frontier agrarians than for people from the East (or the city) with its greater division of labor and thus of class and rank – *Stagecoach, Fort Apache, Vera Cruz, Man Without a Star, The Professionals, The Wild Bunch*. Villains from the East are shown with a disruptive sense of egoism – pure self-interest: the banker in *Stagecoach*, the lawyer in *Tall Man Riding*, the lawyer in *Tall in the Saddle*, the new ranch owner in *Man Without a Star*, the judge in *The Spoilers*, the oilman in *War of the Wildcats*, the railroad owners in *The Professionals* and *The Wild Bunch*. Many characters, including many heroes, are shown with a sense of anomie, a sense of loss and meaninglessness derived from the disrupted East: the gambler in *Stagecoach*, Doc Holiday in *My Darling Clementine*, the heroes in *Run of the Arrow* (1957), *Dances With Wolves* (1990), *Vera Cruz, The Outlaw Josey Wales, The Searchers*. In all these films the frontier West offers a chance to end anomie through new social involvement.

The constant need to escape urban encroachment and find a new frontier as the basis for individual freedom is shown in *Dodge City, Man Without a Star, The Magnificent Seven, Run of the Arrow, Shalako, Butch Cassidy and the Sundance Kid, The Professionals, The Wild Bunch, Dances with Wolves*.

Part 3

MYTHICAL INSIGHTS

Preface

Hidden issues

As a fictional story, not a theoretical argument, the cowboy myth has to be more culturally *convincing* than socially *accurate*. The characters, the situations, the emotions and dilemmas must all seem familiar and believable. The specific social setting may be remote or imaginary – ancient Rome, other galaxies, the mythical West – but the problems and actions must resonate with the experiences of the audience. Popular stories are always instructive as well as entertaining. They offer basic cultural strategies – self-confidence, individualism, love, paranoia – for standard social conflicts. In general, these cultural stories support established institutional structures, providing dramatic, reinforcing models of appropriate behavior and values. In the cowboy myth the characters and actions reflect the legitimating concerns of individualist theory, not the historical reality of the American West. So the general cultural message concerns the proper social behavior for a rational market society.

The myth offers images of success and happiness, risk and failure, and through these images it tells us how to think and act in a market individualist context. The theoretical issues of individualism – rationality, autonomy, self-interest – become dramatic images of characters – heroes, villains, citizens, agrarians. These characters, however, unlike theoretical concepts, have specific human qualities, including age, sex, race, friends, family, a past. All mythical stories provide entertaining support for their social institutions. In the process, they expose and humanize the organizing principles of those institutions. In market society the mythical stories complete and reinforce market theory, turning abstract discussions of rational individuals into dramatic images of human people, people who are male, female, black, white, old, young, confident, afraid, passionate, ill, brave, dishonest, and so forth. The myth shows how the theory should work in ordinary social relations, so it often reveals dimensions of the abstract theory that were hidden behind the abstractions.

The following three chapters raise three such hidden dimensions – sex, race, and the environment. The issue of sex is the issue of sexual relations and gender identities, particularly the image of women. The issue of race is the issue of white superiority and racial inferiority, the issue of savagery versus civilization. And the issue of the environment is the issue of constant market expansion for the sake of equal opportunity. If the market can no longer expand across an endless frontier because of environmental limits, then freedom and equality no longer make sense and the individualist promise is broken. All these issues are central to market relations, and they are all apparent in the images of the myth though not in the concepts of the theories.

7

SEPARATING THE WOMEN

An image of women and sexual relations was always implied in individualist theory but never made explicit. The theory was about rational individuals, and rational individuals were assumed to be men. But the theory also contained, in the abstract idea of rational individuals, many hidden assumptions about the 'proper' market roles of men and women. In general, men were assumed to be dominant over women and women subservient to men. These assumptions were implicit in market theory, but they were always explicit in market culture and particularly in the cowboy myth. The theory only talked about abstract individuals, but the myth told social stories, stories about men, women, and sexual relations.

Separate spheres

The implicit assumption of individualist theory was that rational individuals could only be men, specifically white men. The individualist idea of the rational individual, the idea of individual equality, was never about all individuals. Only white men, essentially European men, were assumed to be rational, so the entire attack on class inequality assumed sexual and racial inequality. In the seventeenth and eighteenth centuries this assumption could be taken as obvious and not explicitly discussed. Men were rational and women were not, so women, it was assumed, should stay in the family and out of the market. Women were not so much forgotten by the theory as set aside and ignored. The early individualists certainly understood that market society would include women, children, and families. Women, however, and thus children and families, were not relevant to the *theory* of the market, a theory about rational individuals, a theory of freedom, equality, democracy, and private property. As Stephanie Coontz has commented, '... the powerful legal, political, and economic principles of liberal theory – liberty, equality, fraternity, and the rights of man – could claim universality only by ignoring women and the family' (1992: 59).

But if women were not in individualist theory, they were always in individualist culture. The market myth of origin dramatized market relations, so women had to be shown playing their 'proper' role, the role assumed by the theory. Explicit individualist ideas – freedom, equality, private property – had to be portrayed in terms of women, which meant in terms of sexual issues – love, passion, families, children. These sexual issues were implicit in the theory but had to be explicit in the culture. The cultural stories explained the abstract theory for daily social life, and women only appeared in the cultural stories, not in the abstract theory. So the cultural stories, and particularly the frontier myth, explained the issues of women and sex for the new market society. The stories explained all the issues of individualism at the visceral level of culture, and they were the only source of social understanding for the issues of gender and sex. These issues are important for social life, but they were not explained in the concepts of the abstract theory.

Just like the theory, the myth is primarily about men. It shows, just like the theory, that men should be rational, autonomous, and self-interested. The mythical contribution, then, in terms of sex, is how to interpret this idea of men in an explicit context of women. What the myth shows, of course, is that men should be dominant, aggressive, confident, and strong, while women should be dependent, subservient, weak, and passive. In particular, men should be competitive and self-interested while women should be compassionate and moral. Women, in effect, should be the opposite of rational men. Women should provide what a good society needs in addition to rational, competitive self-interest. They should provide, that is, a tempering context of morality, generosity, and support. Women are 'naturally' suited for love, emotion, and obedience, just as men are 'naturally' suited for dominance, aggression, and independence. In particular, women should not be competitive with men. Rather, they should provide a loving, supportive refuge for men, that is, the family.

This familiar cultural image reflects individualist theory, the implicit assumptions of the theory. But it also *revises* that theory in an interesting way, because the abstract theory never included women. According to the myth, women are important to rational men. Women provide a necessary place of refuge and renewal and a necessary moral constraint. Women, as a result, become a necessary component of the idea of a civil society, and this is not true in the theory, at least not explicitly. If rational men need loving women to build a civil society, then these rational men – rational individuals – are not as autonomous as the theory suggests. According to the theory, rational, autonomous individuals should simply pursue private profit, and civil society will emerge. According to the myth, however, women must love rational men and temper their autonomy for the sake of civil society.

Men in the myth need a safe, loving refuge, the family, and this makes them less autonomous and self-interested than the theory asserts. Women, in effect, according to the myth, mitigate male autonomy for the sake of civil society. The culture, then, makes clear, in contrast to the theory, that women and families are necessary for a civil society. Men and women together create a civil society, so the cultural problem, then, ignored by the theory, is how to explain the role of women so that men are still autonomous and self-interested.

The solution is an image of *separate spheres*. Men and women have separate sexual spheres, and each sphere requires specific sexual roles. Both women and men should stay in their respective spheres for the sake of a good society. Men should stay in the rational sphere of the market and women should stay in the emotional sphere of the family. The male sphere must dominate the female sphere, and the female sphere must be defined in terms of serving the male sphere. Men are 'naturally' dominant and competitive while women are 'naturally' subservient and moral. Therefore, the 'natural' morality of women must constrain through love the 'natural' self-interest of men, as E. Anthony Rotundo describes:

> The doctrine of separate spheres entrusted women with the care and nurture of communal values – of personal morality, social bonds, and, ultimately, the level of virtue in the community. Men were left free to pursue their own interests, to clash and compete, to behave ... selfishly. Women now stood for traditional social values, men for dynamic individualism ... It gave men the freedom to be aggressive, greedy, ambitious, competitive, and self-interested, then it left women with the duty of curbing this behavior. (1993: 24–25)

The image of separate spheres was implicit in individualist theory, and the culture made it explicit. Women could be seen as socially important but only in their separate sphere, the sphere of the family. Men had to be autonomous and self-interested, as rational individuals, but they also had to be civil and honorable. Their private self-interests had to be tempered somehow by a commitment to trust and honesty, a commitment to shared morality. Both Locke and Smith recognized this moral need when they made their moral assumption, and Durkheim recognized this need in his idea of organic solidarity. The culture also recognizes this need but if offers a different solution. The culture suggests, through its image of women, that women will provide the necessary morality to make rational men civil. Men will create the rational market based on private self-interests, and women will temper those private self-interests by offering love and the family.

The idea of separate spheres meant women had to be unequal to contribute to market civility. In theory, of course, market society was committed to legal equality – equal market opportunity for rational individuals. But women could not be rational individuals and offer the necessary morality, the refuge of love and the family. Women could only contribute to civility if they had no market equality, no equality as market competitors, and that meant they could have no legal equality. As a result, the market idea of legal equality for men depended on legal inequality for women. The theory never made this clear, but the laws and institutions of early America made it clear, and America was built on individualist theory.

In the laws of early America, women were essentially considered the property of their fathers or husbands. They had few legal rights and little legal recourse from dependence or abuse. They could not own property, could not enter universities, could not serve on juries, and could not vote. They were, however, legally required to stay in their 'proper' sphere, that is, to serve and obey their husbands. This pervasive legal inequality seemed perfectly compatible with the market commitment to equality because of the idea of separate spheres. Over the following centuries in America, women asserted an equal legal status as rational individuals, and most of these legal inequalities have now been removed. The culture of separate spheres, however, is still quite prominent. Our modern society, according to Mona Harrington, continues to struggle with 'the tortuous implications of moving women from the separate sphere of the home to a position of full, meaningful equality' (1999: 7).

The early individualists lived in feudal society, and feudal society also saw women as inferior and made them legally unequal. But feudal society was based on family commitments, not on individual autonomy. Also, feudal society was based on legal inequality – class inequality – while market society, at least in theory, was based on legal equality. Women were always legally inferior to their husbands or fathers, but many men were legally inferior to other men and some men, in a lower class, were legally inferior to some women. In market society, in contrast, all women were initially legally inferior to all men, so market ideas, in a sense, initially seemed to endorse even greater inequality for women. In feudal society a woman would be head of the family in the absence of any men, and then she would have the legal rights of men, rights usually denied to women. In the market, however, at least initially, women could never have the legal rights of men regardless of family issues because women could never be seen as rational individuals.

The market, of course, was based on rational equality, so women could make a claim for legal equality, a claim they have used effectively. They could not make such a claim under feudalism because feudalism saw inequality as sacred. Market society offered an argument for equality even to those it denied equality, and in this important sense individualism improved the status of women, at least potentially. But the idea of a *civil* market always depended on the inequality of women, since women have to stay in the family. If women become market equals, where will the tempering morality come from, the necessary honesty and trust, and who will take care of the children? Women may assert their rational equality and achieve legal equality, but the underlying assumption of their secondary sphere remains a market necessity. The market can only be legitimate if it is civil, and the idea of civil society assumes the inequality of women. This is why the equality of women has always been contentious, and why a culture of female subservience remains so pervasive today.

In feudal society, women always had an important productive role despite their legal inequality. The family was the productive unit, not the individual, and women were integral to the family. Thus, if a family lost all its men, the family would still have legal rights so a woman could claim those legal rights, normally the rights of men. In market society, however, the individual became the productive unit and individuals (rational individuals) could only be men. The market, as a consequence, took women out of any productive role, a role they had always had when the family was the productive unit. Without a productive role, women could have no legal rights – they could not be owners of property.

This meant, to the early individualists and to market culture, that women should maintain the family as their only important role. The family would remain compatible with an individualist market because of the inferiority of women. When women assert equality, however, they assert a productive role, a role as rational individuals, potential owners of property. This means the equality of women must threaten the stability of the family according to market assumptions. When the family was the productive unit, the family was always compatible with production. But when the individual is the productive unit, the family is only compatible with production if women are 'naturally' unequal and therefore socially relegated, culturally if not legally, to the family.

The feminine hand

According to Adam Smith, the *invisible hand* could only work in a context of trust and honor. Like Locke, he assumed innate morality to justify laissez-faire. But this moral assumption was always incompatible with the other assumptions of individualism – rationality, autonomy, self-interest. The market could only be civil if pure self-interest was morally constrained, but the source of that morality, of altruism mitigating egoism, became a difficult problem. Both Locke and Smith just assumed the necessary morality, but they also assumed the structural equality of independent owner-workers on an endless agrarian frontier. Market theorists generally agreed that some morality was necessary, but few could assume it was simply innate, and the market was clearly more complicated than equal independent farmers.

The market problem of morality was difficult to solve in terms of theory, but it was easy to solve in terms of culture. Cultural stories, but not the theory, distinguished men and women, so women could be seen in the culture as providing social morality. Men could be competitive since women were compassionate. The culture could solve the market problem by designating gender roles, as Stephanie Coontz has remarked:

> Self-reliance and independence worked for *men* because *women* took care of dependence and obligation. In other words, the liberal theory of human nature and political citizenship did not merely leave women out: it worked precisely because it was applied exclusively to half the population. Emotion and compassion could be disregarded in the political and economic realm only if women were assigned those traits in the personal realm ... The cult of the Self-Made Man required the cult of the True Woman. (1992: 53)

This cultural perspective essentially revises market theory. The market needs women as much as it needs men, because women provide the morality. The *invisible hand* will only work – the market will only be civil – if there is also a feminine hand. Strong competitive men need loving, moral women, and then these men can create a good society. Men must stay in their 'proper' sphere to make the market work, and women must stay in their 'proper' sphere to make the market civil. Not only must they stay in their 'proper' spheres, but they must be attracted across the spheres, like opposite magnetic poles. The sexual attraction is the basis for a good society, and the culture has made it a central image, the image of romantic love.

From the cultural perspective of separate spheres, love makes civil society possible. Love combines the different spheres into one family unit with a rational, independent man and a moral, dependent woman. Because of love rational men will make the market civil, and also because of love moral women will support and obey their men and take care of the children. This is what the idea of love requires as the basic sexual glue for market social relations. The cultural image of romantic love depends on separate spheres, and the cultural image of separate spheres solves the market problem of morality. Love is a popular image because it is seen as fulfilling, and it can only be seen as fulfilling if it supports a stable family and a stable social order. So the cultural image of romantic love assumes the dependence of women. Women must provide a safe, loving refuge for rational, competitive men, a family haven of renewal for further market struggles. When women fall in love, according to this image, they surrender to dominant men, and when men fall in love, they accept family dominance together with civil morality.

This cultural image of love is clearly successful and appealing. It offers personal happiness together with sexual passion. It is probably the most familiar and pervasive image in our culture, and it always explains market relations. It always explains, that is, the 'proper' market roles of men and women, the roles that offer personal happiness as well as a civil society. While the idea of romantic love has been around for centuries, a social commitment to romantic love arose with market society, as a solution to market problems. As the role of the family declined in the face of individualism, the idea of romantic love developed as the basis for marriage and children. In feudal society marriages had to be based on family needs and duties. But marriages in market society had to be based on private individual choices, so love became the individualist basis for marriage. It could solve the problem of morality because it combined a concern with private self-interest (personal happiness) with a strong concern for another person (a moral commitment). The idea of romantic love was ideally suited for the market issue of sexual difference as long as sexual difference is understood through separate spheres.

Love is important for men because it offers support and renewal. But men are 'naturally' rational and autonomous, so they cannot take love too seriously. Women, however, are defined by love according to the cultural imagery. Their 'proper' social role is to love and serve men, and this is their social contribution. Men contribute rationality to a civil market society, and love must temper that rationality. Women, however, contribute love and love must only support, never dominate, reason. Men must judge their social success primarily in terms of the market and somewhat in terms of love. But women must judge their social success primarily in terms of love, which means marriage and the family. According to the cultural imagery, love must be crucial to women and far less important to men. Both men and women need love for the sake of personal happiness. But men must resist love while women must embrace it, since men must be autonomous and women must be dependent. They should stay in the family, hidden and obedient, providing love from their 'proper' sphere. They should only be appendages of rational men, and this view of women, implicit in the theory, was written into the laws of early America.

Male identity

The romantic idea of love validates male superiority. When a woman loves a man, according to the image, she surrenders to his strength. Her love reinforces his masculine identity, his masculine confidence and control. She reinforces the man's identity as strong, dominant, and independent, an identity derived from market theory. Through this image of love, women validate the individualist qualities needed for market society.

As a consequence the idea of love becomes crucially important for men but only in a subtle way. They do not need love as much as women to fulfill their market destiny, because men must be rational and autonomous. But men, then, in terms of the image, need a woman's love to validate their market identity as strong, dominant individualists. In our popular, mythical stories, the hero not only wins the fight, he also wins the woman. His success in the battle, fighting for law and justice, is validated and completed by his further success in love. According to this cultural image, then, the love of a beautiful woman is necessary for masculine success. Simply winning the fight and saving the citizens can never be sufficient reward. If a man wins the fight but not the woman, his strength and dominance must be questioned and he cannot be a true hero. Our cultural imagery of masculine success depends on the imagery of love. The hero must win the battle and also the woman he loves. He may, however, lose the battle and still be a hero but not if he loses at love.

Part of our cultural image of success, then, of heroism, is the associated image of romantic love, the love that always follows for heroic, strong individualists. According to our culture, market success (winning at competition) is not by itself sufficient to establish social success – true heroism. The heroes in our stories succeed at competition, and they also succeed at love. If a man fails at love in one of our stories, no matter how many fights he wins, he cannot be seen as a hero or the story will not be popular.

According to our cultural imagery, the love of a beautiful woman validates male success. Women essentially become rewards for strong men. Winning a woman's love, then, according to the imagery, can validate a man's identity, his sense of himself as a dominant individualist. In market society, all men need to see themselves as dominant individualists. Few men, however, can see themselves this way in terms of market competition. Most men work for others, take orders, worry about money, and feel unsuccessful. Few men succeed in the market, but all men can try to succeed at love. Our cultural image of love offers the possibility that all men can feel strong and heroic by winning a woman's love even when they are not so successful at market competition.

A woman's love, however, according to the imagery, can only validate a man's success if she stays in her secondary sphere. Romantic love must take place across separate spheres. A woman must lovingly surrender to male dominance to find her true happiness. A man must feel like a hero so he can compete in the market, and a woman must provide a safe, supportive refuge – the family – to make him feel like a hero. Her social task, in terms of romance, is to accept his control and authority while also constraining, simply through love, his rational, autonomous self-interest. This is what a woman must do to validate her individualist man, so this is also what a woman must do to sustain a civil society.

When men and women fall in love across their separate spheres, just as portrayed in our popular stories, they always feel happy and fulfilled. Men feel strong and capable, women feel soft and loving, families seem happy and promising, and social order seems decent and just. This romantic ideal tells men and women how to interact sexually to maintain a civil market. The problem, of course, is that very few women can stay in their 'proper' place and play their 'proper' role. This romantic ideal assumes that women are inferior and justifies social inequality. It also suggests that women who try to leave their 'proper' sphere are threats to a decent social order. Women have an important job to do, a dependent, subservient job, and if they refuse to do that job they threaten civil society. If a woman begins to compete with a man as a rational, equal individual, she undermines his strength and dominance, his market masculine identity. She also removes her moral constraints, the constraints that enable civility. If a woman strays from her 'proper' sphere, she endangers the good society. So she needs to be returned to that sphere, according to the image, forcefully if necessary, or she needs to be punished.

In our popular cultural stories women are always being returned to their 'proper', dependent place through the dominant control of men. This is particularly clear in the cowboy myth and in its urban, action variation. Sometimes the men gently rebuke the women, and sometimes they are forceful and physical. The women generally accept the rebuke and admire the men even more, finding true happiness as loving wives. Sometimes, however, a woman resists her 'proper' sphere with too much defiance, and then she has to be killed as a threat to social order. Sometimes she is simply a villain, not only an 'improper' woman but also dishonest and calculating. And sometimes she recognizes the error of her ways and dies in the hero's arms, wishing things had been different. Our popular culture reflects market assumptions, even in the image of love, and market assumptions require women to admire and obey men, not to threaten them.

In our modern market society, and particularly in modern America, women have long been asserting their rights as market equals. Legitimating market theory asserts the equality of all individuals, but market institutions and market culture have put up great resistance to the idea of women as equals. In many important ways, both legal and cultural, women have been successful, but they have also succeeded in threatening many men and generating much hostility. Even in modern society, the problem is still the original problem, the problem of morality and the family. The idea of a civil market depends on separate spheres with women subservient and unequal. In modern America many cultural commentators have been stressing the need for 'family values' in the face of declining morality. They see the market as increasingly uncivil because the family has been weakened as the source of social morality. The family has been weakened, they argue, because women have tried to be equals. Women should stay in the family, in their view, while men compete in the market, so the family can be stable and the market can be civil.

The romantic image of love implies this role for women in the 'proper' market family. Women were always tacit in original individualist theory, but our popular cultural stories exposed the idea of women, the idea of separate spheres. According to these stories, the market can only be civil if women are unequal. Individualist theory could assert individual equality and ignore the issue of women, but individualist culture had to portray both men and women so it had to confront the assumption of inequality. As a result, the individualist implications for women have generally been worked out in our popular, entertaining stories. These stories offer an instructive guide to market sexual relations, and the most definitive stories generally take place in the mythical Wild West.

Love and the cowboy

The cowboy typically helps the community because of romantic love. He is alone and independent with no social involvement. The frontier community is threatened, and only he can help. Initially, he is only interested in a woman, not in helping the community. The woman, however – a teacher, a reporter, an entertainer – has independent moral strength, a commitment to the community. She finds the hero attractive but initially rejects his interest because of his social indifference. His 'natural' honor, however, is influenced by her love, and he decides to fight the good fight, accepting her social commitments. He also tells her of his dream to start a ranch someday 'down by the bend of the river'. He becomes more moral in order to win her love, and she becomes more dependent because she falls in love. For him, falling in love tempers his individualism and makes it civil – a moral individualism. For her, falling in love enables true fulfillment in her 'proper', inferior sphere. He is a wilderness stranger and she is a social participant, and love binds them together to build a civil society.

Usually they marry and settle down after the community is safe. Sometimes, however, he rides away, winning the fight but leaving the woman and her love. In either case the community is saved by his strength combined with morality. Love creates the necessary civil balance between wilderness and society. He must surrender some autonomy and she must surrender initial independence for the sake of social order. He becomes a strong market individual, not a strong wilderness individual, and she becomes a dependent moral wife, not an independent moral woman. Love always requires compromise across the separate spheres, and both the man and the woman are changed. But the woman is changed more because she must surrender all her independence. He remains strong with slightly less autonomy, but she becomes weak and dependent despite her original strength.

She is initially strong and confident, committed to a moral community. She is initially attracted to the hero because of his strength and honor, but she is also initially resistant because of her moral strength. She is repulsed by his wilderness autonomy, that is, by his moral detachment, and he must become committed to civil honor before she can fall in love. His wilderness sense of fairness, respect, and equality must become a civil sense of law, order, and property. Her strength and independence attract the hero and shape his social actions. She has a moral strength and independence and it matches his wilderness strength and independence.

In this sense they initially meet as equals and both represent social necessities. Their different strengths must be combined for civil society to emerge, and the way these strengths are combined is through the idea of romantic love.

When she falls in love, however, she must lose her strength and independence. Love means she accepts male dominance in order to be fulfilled. She specifically loses her moral convictions, caring more about love than the safety of the community. As a moral, independent woman, she first convinces the hero to fight; then, as a loving, dependent woman, she begs him to run away so he will not be killed. She loses her moral strength, in effect, surrendering to true love, just as he becomes the true individualist, the savior of civil society. He resists her pleas and fights the good fight, since 'a man's gotta do what a man's gotta do'. She becomes weak through love and he becomes moral through love, but he remains strong. She often becomes angry and emotional, even threatening to leave him if he fights the good fight. Sometimes she is so upset he has to calm her down physically, grabbing her, shaking her, slapping her – controlling her with his strength. Only he knows what is best, what honor and duty demand, and she has become weak through love, taking her 'proper' role. Finally she loves him even more, after the villains are gone, accepting and admiring his masculine strength and dominance.

In most cowboy stories there is only one attractive woman, one contender for the hero's love. In some stories, however, there are two women, and the second woman is *too* independent. This woman is socially tainted because of her independence: she is too cavalier about sex, she acts like a market competitor, she associates with questionable men, she seeks wealth and property. Both women are attractive, but one is respectable, concerned with morality, and the other is shady, concerned with self-interest. All men desire the tainted woman and all women are jealous of her, but only the cowboy can win her love. He is always initially interested because of her fiery independence, but he typically chooses the respectable woman who accepts her 'proper' sphere.

The tainted woman is not an appropriate choice to build a civil society. Indeed, she usually has to be killed or at least humiliated and driven away. She is often involved with the villain, but then she betrays the villain because she loves the hero, and she dies saving the hero. She finally accepts, as she dies in his arms, that love is more important than independence. She tries to be an equal and becomes a civil threat, sacrificing what women 'truly' want and need. She must be killed for the sake of decency, but she is also redeemed by falling in love and realizing her mistake. According to this image, independent women are attractive to men, but too much independence is dangerous. Society can only be civil if love makes women dependent, so decent women must want love more than independence. This image of separate spheres appears in many Westerns, and also in many popular films over many years – *Gone With the Wind*

(1939), *Boom Town* (1940), *Leave her to Heaven* (1945), *The Graduate* (1967), *Fatal Attraction* (1987), *Dick Tracy* (1990).

Conquest and violence

The image of love in popular stories shapes our cultural attitudes toward love and marriage. Men are attracted to independent women, and women are attracted to dominant men. If romantic love succeeds, the man must stay dominant and the woman must become dependent. Much of a man's self-respect can depend on a woman's love. She can validate his masculine dominance, his market individualism, if she surrenders to his strength. According to the image of love, a man must conquer and tame an independent woman to prove his masculinity. She must become submissive to demonstrate her love, but her initial independence was what made her attractive. The hope for civil society depends on separate spheres, so weak, dependent women must love strong men. But men need to retain their self-respect in the face of market pressures, and conquering an independent woman can reinforce self-respect.

This means, following the image, that a woman who already loves a man can no longer validate his strength. Once she has surrendered to validate that strength she can no longer serve that purpose. Romance is about conquest, not daily life, so men need new conquests, not simply a woman's submission. This is why our films usually end just as the romantic conquest succeeds. The image offers continued happiness, but the story of romance is over. The masculine star of the film may play a character who has found true love, but the star himself will soon appear in another film making another conquest.

According to our image of love, men need successive conquests of independent women to maintain their masculine identity. A woman may follow the cultural image and surrender to a dominant man. But when she does, according to that image, she is making herself less attractive to a man who needs a new conquest. Marriages in modern society tend to rest on romantic love, and marriages, as we all know, have not been very stable. One possible reason is the image of romantic love. According to this image, love must begin to fail as soon as it succeeds. A woman must become less independent, and thus less attractive, in order to prove her love.

The cowboy hero, as the model individualist, always conquers an independent woman. The woman is beautiful and desirable, the most desirable in town, and she only falls for the hero. The cowboy also defeats the villains and saves the social order, but he cannot be seen as hero unless he wins the woman. If she rejects him, for example, and decides to marry a barber, the cowboy cannot be seen as heroic. The cowboy must win the woman as well as his fight. The woman must love him from her 'proper' sphere, admiring and obedient, and she must provide a safe family haven. In a positive sense, this image of love promises happiness, validates individualism, and enables civil society.

In a negative sense, however, this image can mean something else. It can mean that men who are rejected by women are somehow diminished as men. A man cannot appear heroic – strong, masculine, dominant – if he fails to win a woman's love. If he were truly a man – a real man – he would not take 'no' for an answer. When a hero in a story is rejected by a woman, he does not take 'no' for an answer. Rather, he becomes more aggressive, and then she falls in love. This is what the image suggests, that women often do not know what they really want. They may say 'no', but they do not really mean it. A woman really wants to fall in love and accept her family sphere, but only if a man is strong enough to conquer her resistance. A woman always wants to be conquered, according to the romantic image, so a woman's apparent resistance is basically a test of a man's masculinity.

According to the image, if a woman rejects a man, he must become more dominant and aggressive in order to win her love. As many people have pointed out, this cultural imagery can easily lead to violence, even to rape. If a man is influenced by the image, he could easily believe that a woman will gladly submit if he takes more control and acts with more force. Many popular stories support this idea. Many heroes in films have forced their attentions on resisting women – essentially an image of rape – and the women have fallen in love. Sometimes a man captures or kidnaps a woman, and sometimes he hits her, kicks her, and humiliates her in public. Each time the woman falls in love, abandoning her resistance. Westerns with this imagery include *Duel in the Sun* (1946), *Waterhole #3* (1967), *Red Mountain* (1951), *The Man Who Loved Cat Dancing* (1973), *McLintock* (1963), *Yellow Sky*, *Tall in the Saddle*. Other popular films with this image of romance include *Gone With the Wind*, *On the Waterfront* (1954), *Rocky* (1976), *The Quiet Man* (1952).

Violence, of course, is a crucial individualist image, an image associated with freedom. As a true individualist, the cowboy often needs to be violent to create and protect civil society. One requirement for civil society is a structure of separate spheres, and violence may sometimes be necessary to create and protect this structure, according to the image of romance. The image often tells us that appropriate male violence toward reluctant women can lead to true love and thus to a good society. This may help explain, again following the image, why incidents of domestic violence – violence toward women – have reached epidemic scale. If a man feels rejected, his identity may be threatened, and according to the cultural image he needs to be more aggressive, perhaps more violent. Women are seen in popular stories as responding with love to masculine force, and this popular imagery must encourage to some degree male violence toward women.

In another aspect of the cultural image a man must be forceful, even perhaps violent, to control a woman's emotions. The strong, rational hero is often seen grabbing or slapping a woman to try to calm her hysteria. She is only concerned with love and wants him to run away. He must fight against the villains to save civil society, but first he must constrain the woman, also for civil society. The villains may pose a social threat, but so does a woman who is too emotional and doubts her man's authority. The hero must use his strength to keep her in her 'proper' place, and this use of force serves civil order, according to the image of love, just like his gunfight with the villains.

When a woman is too independent in the cultural stories, she is seen as a threat to social order, and she also tends to suffer violence. She defies the 'proper' role for women, she is usually killed, and the woman who lives to marry the hero accepts her 'proper' sphere. This is the other side of the romantic image that women do not really mean 'no' and they want men to be more forceful, more aggressive. If a woman really means 'no', if she really wants to be independent, to be an equal, then she must be punished according to the imagery, even killed. From this imagery a man may learn that he needs to be more insistent with a woman who resists, more force-ful. If she still resists, then he can see her as a threat to social decency and begin to feel that violence and punishment are justified. Our cultural image of love can encourage male violence for the sake of 'proper' order. Women must stay in their separate sphere, and romance may turn into dominant control, even into violence, when women try to leave that sphere. Romance pervades our market culture as does domestic violence, and romance implies a need for violence whenever male dominance is threatened.

The individualist problem of sexual difference is how to create stable families in a context of market self-interests. Individualist theory offered little help because the issue of sexual difference remained tacit. But individualist culture interpreted the theory, and as it did it interpreted the implicit ideas of sexual difference and sexual relations. It asserted the idea of separate spheres and the idea of romantic love to combine the separate spheres. If women stay in their 'proper' sphere, the family will be stable and happy and the market will operate with rational individu-als, individuals who can only be men. Our culture explains our sexual relations, and that explanation modifies and completes market theory. Women should stay in the market background, lovingly supporting autonomous men, and then a market in private property can become a civil society.

The cowboy myth makes all this clear, as the market myth of origin. The cowboy conquers and tames the wild frontier, and also in the process he conquers and tames the women. The market idea of freedom and equal-ity depends on male superiority, as the myth always shows. This sexual image was implicit in individualist theory, and a similar racial image was also implicit, an image of white superiority. As the cowboy conquers the wilderness and the women, he also conquers all non-whites, and those non-whites, the theory implies, have even less claim on freedom and equality than weak, dependent women.

Illustrative films

An image of a strong woman influencing an independent hero to become more moral is seen in *Stagecoach, Dodge City, The Westerner, Vera Cruz, El Paso, The Naked Spur* (1953), *A Man Alone* (1955), *The Violent Men, Arrowhead, Blood on the Moon.* The good woman pleads with the hero to avoid the fight in *Dodge City, Shane, High Noon, Arrowhead, Gun Glory* (1957), *Warlock, Firecreek.* In *Destry Rides Again* and *The Far Country*, the tainted woman pleads with the hero not to fight and run away with her. A woman falls in love with a man who abuses her, forces her, captures her, or constrains her in *Duel in the Sun, Yellow Sky, The Man Who Loved Cat Dancing* (1973), *Valdez Is Coming* (1971), *McLintock, Tall in the Saddle, Waterhole #3, Red Mountain, A Man Alone.* An aggressive but tainted woman, who dies or is rejected, appears in *Destry Rides Again, The Far Country, The Violent Men, Johnny Guitar* (1954), *Jubal* (1956), *Tall Man Riding, Ramrod, Rancho Notorious* (1952), *Flaming Feather* (1951).

8

REMOVING THE INDIANS

Racial inequality

The original individualist conception was strictly concerned with class inequality, not racial or sexual inequality. All individuals were assumed to be 'naturally' equal, but they were also assumed to be white males. Women and non-whites were implicitly assumed to be 'naturally' unequal, and much of the individualist conception depended on this assumption. In the new American nation this assumption was used to endorse racial as well as sexual discrimination. One American version of racial discrimination was slavery for blacks, but slavery was always contentious in a society based on equality, so it was bitterly debated. Other forms of racial discrimination, however, were much more easily accepted. Some early Americans thought humans should not be owned, but most early Americans thought only whites could be rational, in the sense of civil society. Early individualist ideas created American institutions, including racial and sexual inequality. But early individualist ideas asserted individual equality, so many racial and sexual struggles followed. In America these struggles have included the Civil War, women's suffrage, and the civil rights movement. Because of these struggles and many others, most of the early structure of legal inequality has been removed. Much practical, cultural inequality, however, still remains. The market still rests on individualist ideas, and individualist ideas assumed a contradiction: individual equality with racial and sexual inequality.

Only white men were assumed to be rational in the sense of civil society, and not even all white men. In Locke's political theory, and also in early America, men who did not own property – workers – were not considered rational. Locke argued that they should not vote and America usually denied them the vote, along with women and non-whites. Workers who were white males, however, could potentially own property and thus be seen as rational. As a result, workers soon had the vote and this structure of legal inequality changed. Women and non-whites, in contrast, could not be seen as rational according to market ideas, so their legal inequality was much harder to change.

Women could not be seen as rational since they were needed in the family. The market could only work, that is, as the basis for civil society, if women had no rights. Non-whites could not be seen as rational since whites needed to take their land. The market could only work, that is, if non-whites had no rights. Blacks, of course, were enslaved in early America, but whites in early America were also often enslaved through indentured servitude. Slavery in America was essentially a remnant of the feudal class structure where serfs had sometimes been bound to the lords who controlled the feudal estates. America, however, was never very comfortable with traditional feudal structures and this made slavery a problem. Feudal structures inhibited the market, so slavery inhibited the market, and slavery was finally rejected. Racial inequality, however, was perfectly compatible with the market and indeed was a market necessity. The market could only work in America if land were free and available, and this meant the non-white inhabitants of the land could have no rights of ownership.

If non-whites were assumed to be rational, then they would have to be seen as legitimate owners of property. In particular, the native inhabitants of America – the Indians – would have to be seen as legitimate owners of wilderness land, not as savage barriers to progress. America needed the idea of free land as the basis for equal opportunity, so it had to see an empty wilderness full of savage interlopers. Legitimating individualist theory assumed an open frontier, and America was the model for this open frontier, so Indians could not be rational. The idea of rational destiny implied the conquest of savages, so Indians had to be seen as infesting the land. The individualist market required a frontier, and the need for a frontier, in turn, required racial inequality.

Like sexual inequality, racial inequality was taken for granted by the early individualists. Feudal society was based on inequality, sacred class inequality, and the individualists asserted a radical idea of equality. Their idea of equality, though, was to end class privilege, and they still took other forms of inequality for granted. They wrote, abstractly, about individual equality, and now we understand that idea much more broadly than they did. They only meant that all white males should be able to own property, and only white male property owners should have political equality. This was the idea of the market, and this market idea of equality still required an assumption of racial and sexual inequality.

Individualist culture portrayed market theory, so the implicit theoretical assumptions became explicit cultural images. The theoretical individual became the image of a white male. American popular stories have generally portrayed white male superiority for more than two centuries. Non-white characters – blacks, Hispanics, Asians, Indians – have either not been portrayed at all, or they have usually been portrayed as inferior, primarily suitable for servitude, removal, or pity. Many of our stories have simply left them out, essentially asserting by dramatic default that only white people are important and interesting. But many other stories, particularly Westerns, have commonly included non-white characters, and these characters have typically been shown as dangerously irrational – savage barriers to civilized (white) society.

Savagery

The cowboy must often defeat the Indians in order to civilize the wilderness. The Western is the market myth of origin, so Indians in the myth have always symbolized the market version of racial difference. Many popular stories, of course, have included non-white characters and images of white superiority. But the frontier myth portrays the market vision, including the vision of race. So Indians are market cultural symbols, symbols for thinking about race. What they symbolize is that whites can transcend the original State of Nature because they are 'naturally' rational. But non-whites (Indians) never can because they are 'naturally' savage.

For the early individualists, the American wilderness was the dangerous State of Nature and Indians in America were part of the dangers. Rational (white) individuals had a rational destiny to tame the State of Nature, so the Indians had to be conquered and removed. The image of the State of Nature was central to individualist theory, to the ideas of freedom and equality. And the image of the State of Nature was that no legitimate social order, no legitimate government, existed. Everyone in the State of Nature was savage and dangerous; it was a war of all against all. Implicit in this image, however, was the idea that some individuals – white males – were capable of rationality. These individuals could transcend the State of Nature and create a civil society. The State of Nature was available wilderness land, so it could be used as a source of private property, the basis for equal opportunity. This was the individualist vision, and this vision required that Indians had no rights to their land. Indians were racially different, and they needed to be seen as savage, not rational, so they could have no legitimate property rights. Thus, they were seen as racially inferior, racially incapable of rationality, and this made market theory work.

Market theory needed a distinction between savagery and civilization. The State of Nature was a condition of savagery and the social contract enabled civilization. This distinction was inherent in social contract theory, and a racial distinction was then added. Whites, it was assumed, could make the transition from savagery to civilization, the State of Nature to the social contract, but non-whites could not. With this added racial assumption, America became an empty wilderness, a land of rational destiny. The Indians were racially savage, categorically non-rational.

As a result, they could be seen as a symbolic threat, a threat to civil society. The Indians remained in the violent State of Nature, a danger to decent people, and this idea of 'savage Indians' helped shape American culture, as Vine Deloria, Jr, remarks: 'The stereotypical image of American Indians as childlike, superstitious, creatures ... a subhuman species that really has no feelings, values, or inherent worth ... permeates American Society ...' (1995: 20).

The political uses of this image of 'savage Indians' has been documented by Richard Slotkin, Richard Drinnon, and Frances FitzGerald, among others. It is intended to suggest that disruptive groups, when characterized as 'savage Indians' (angry Blacks, stricking workers, protesting students), are so uncivilized they deserve no legal respect. It justifies violence and conquest in the name of rational destiny, and it always suggests racial inferiority. It has justified American colonial actions against Indians in the West and also against Mexico, the Philippines, Cuba, China, Vietnam, and many other countries. As Vine Deloria, Jr, comments

> The Indian wars of the past should rightly be regarded as the first foreign wars of American history ... When the frontier was declared officially closed in 1890 it was only a short time before American imperialistic impulses drove this country into the Spanish-American War ... the acquisition of America's Pacific island empire ... [and] numerous banana wars in Central and South America. (1989: 51)

The image of 'savage Indians' has justified many American actions. It typically suggests that certain groups of people, usually non-white people, are so irrational and inferior that the laws and rights for rational individuals simply do not apply. Violence is therefore justified against such savagery for the sake of rational individuals.

In early America the image of savage Indians was used to justify expansion. Indians on the frontier always seemed strange and primitive, and they were sometimes dangerous to settlers. But all American relations with the Indians, all the wars and treaties, were based on individualist theory. America was seen as providing civilization but the savage Indians stood in the way, still in the State of Nature. These Indians, therefore, could not be rational and could have no legitimate property rights. American expansion was therefore just and Indians were barriers to reason. Individualism required an open frontier so Indians had to be seen as inferior. And they also had to be seen as *racially* inferior, that is, as racially irrational, so they could never claim legitimate property rights. America was committed to individualist ideas, so Indians had to be dismissed. But individualism was far less important in Canada, for example, and the Indians were treated much better.

The image of the frontier is an image of market expansion, and that image has always implied a racial distinction between savagery and civilization. When Jefferson wrote that democracy depended on free land, he assumed this racial distinction. When Turner wrote the same thing, a century later, he assumed the same distinction. When Locke saw America, a century before Jefferson, as the original State of Nature, he envisioned a rational individual working free land to own that land. This required the same racial assumption that Indians were inferior and savage and thus had no claim to the land. When Smith assumed constant market expansion as the basis for the *invisible hand*, he made this racial assumption. As William Appleman Williams has commented, 'According to Smith's logic … market expansion was the necessary condition for the realization of individual freedom and liberty' (1969: 61), and market expansion in early America required contempt for the Indians.

Turner, in particular, instilled this racial assumption into American thinking about its frontier and its history. Turner's frontier thesis influenced American history for much of the twentieth century, and he saw American democracy as dependent on free western land: 'These free lands promoted individualism, economic equality, freedom to rise, democracy … the West gave, not only to the American, but to the unhappy and oppressed of all lands, a vision of hope' (1949: 33). This meant, in effect, that white Europeans and Americans had a more legitimate claim to land in the West than the Indian inhabitants of that land. This frontier perspective implied white superiority and justified conquest and exploitation. Turner's historical perspective, as we have seen, has been severely criticized, by Richard Drinnon among others:

> Turner partook in the perennial revoicing of the national creation myth … It made dispossession of the Native Americans … the defining and enabling experience of the republic. From it flowed ineluctably the inference that the European immigrants had built their economy of possessive individualism and their relatively open policy of Lockean liberalism (popular sovereignty, representative government) on the red man's unfree grave and had fenced their gardens with his bones. (1980: 461)

The Turner thesis stated for American history what Locke and Smith assumed in individualist theory and what the cowboy myth portrays in individualist culture. Savage (non-white) Indians infest the enabling wilderness, and they must be conquered and removed for the sake of (white) civilization. The savage/civilized distinction is central to individualist thought, and the discovery of Indians in America helped to stimulate this distinction. As Margaret Hodgen has argued, the early encounters with Indians in America contradicted Christian ideas, the ideas that supported feudal society. According to Christianity, all people were descended from Adam and Eve, but this Christian version of 'all people' only tended to include white Europeans, since few other kinds of people were known. Encountering the Indians in America made Europeans begin to feel:

> aching doubts and anxieties seeping into the very Holy of Holies of theological security … Whence came these creatures, whether human or sub-human,

virtuous or bestial? Were the Red Indians and the Black Africans, with all their fantastic, horrid ways, descendants of Adam?

...as a new image of the universe began gradually to take shape, and the old one withered away, mankind itself no longer appeared to be a single homogeneous species or unit. It was cleft to the core into at least two cultural categories, the civil and the barbarous, the polished and the savage.

...the heart of the difficulty ... lay in the settled and unshakable belief that the native tribes of the New World were ... a breed apart; that their cultures, if indeed they were the cultures of true men, had departed so far from the accustomed canons of European diversity as to seem polygenetic in origin, or anomalous, aberrant, and intellectually intractable.

It followed therefore that .... if mankind was ever again to be understood ... these aberrant men had to be brought conceptually into the framework of European thought. (Hodgen, 1964: 375, 376, 386, 387)

The effort to bring these 'aberrant men' into European thought encouraged individualist theory. The Indians stimulated the savage/civilized distinction, a distinction central to individualism. In this sense, the Indians were crucial to individualist ideas, just as America was crucial to those ideas. The Indians were also racially different, so the distinction between savagery and civilization became a racial distinction. This racial perspective on different kinds of people, including racial inequality, was not very compatible with the Christian tradition. It was quite compatible, however, with the new ideas of market individualism, and particularly with the individualist vision of *empty* wilderness land. The wilderness had to be available and free, so the people in it had to be discounted. The idea of racial inferiority could easily make that possible. As a result, the savage/civilized distinction was also a non-white/white distinction, and this distinction was used to justify market expansion into new lands and the killing or enslaving of the natives:

Over the years, the theory of the degeneracy of the savage races ... or its close relation, the concept of the unimprovability of savagery, was often employed in response to the problems of colonization, or in defense of Negro slavery. (Hodgen, 1964: 379–380)

To Europeans and then to European-Americans, Indians became symbolic concepts much more than human beings. They symbolized the savage threat as well as racial inferiority. They also symbolized the State of Nature, free wilderness land, rational destiny, and the civil (white) goal of freedom and equality. As a result, they could virtually never be seen as having viable cultures or social institutions. Americans generally dealt with the Indians in terms of individualist ideas, which meant the Indians could only be symbols. As W. Jackson Rushing has commented: 'Euro-Americans were forever prevented from seeing the first Americans as real people. Calculated or not, this was the specific function of the Indian as idea or concept, as opposed to Indian as human' (1995: 2). As individualist symbols, however, the Indians not only represented their own western presence on land the Americans wanted, they also came to represent the American idea of race, the 'natural', threatening savagery of all the non-white races.

The cowboy and the Indians

The Indians symbolize racial savagery whenever they appear in the cowboy myth, but they do not always appear. Conflicts in the myth are typically between whites and whites, citizens and villains, not between whites and Indians. In many Westerns, Indians do not appear, and in other stories when they do appear, they are usually a background issue, not the central threat. The wild frontier is always dangerous and Indians can be part of that danger, but the danger is not always Indians. Jane Tompkins, for example, writes in her book on Westerns, *West of Everything*: 'When I sat down to watch Western movies ... I expected to see a great many Indians ... But the Indians I expected did not appear. The ones I saw functioned as props, bits of local color, textural effects. As people they had no existence' (1992: 7–8). So she left them out of her book:

> After the Indians had been decimated by disease, removal, and conquest, and after they had been caricatured and degraded in Western movies, I had ignored them too. The human beings who populated this continent before the Europeans came and who still live here, whose image the Western traded on – where are they? Not in Western films. And not in this book, either. (1992: 10)

Richard Slotkin, on the other hand, in his book *Gunfighter Nation*, argues that Indians are central to Westerns, even to Westerns without Indians. Indians define the wild frontier, the frontier of American myth, so they are always present in mythical stories, even if only implicitly:

> The Myth of the Frontier is our oldest and most characteristic myth ... According to this myth-historiography, the conquest of the wilderness and the subjugation of the Native Americans who originally inhabited it have been the means to our achievement of a national identity, a democratic polity, an ever-expanding economy, and a phenomenally dynamic and 'progressive' civilization ... At the core ... is the symbol of 'savage war.'... The Frontier Myth is divided by significant borders, of which the wilderness/civilization, Indian/White border is the most basic. (1992b: 8, 12, 14)

Westerns, for Slotkin, tell the myth of a 'savage war'. Indians are the central issue because the myth is about conquest and race. Tompkins, however, finds Westerns to be about many social issues – men, women, animals, the land – but not about Indians and race. This is an interesting critical difference about the social meaning of the myth, and both perspectives offer insights. As Tompkins suggests, many other issues are apparent in the myth, issues other than Indians and race. But the issues of Indians and race are also in the myth and always symbolically present as Slotkin suggests, even when Indians are not. The frontier myth portrays the individualist promise, the promise of rational destiny. Rational individuals must tame the wilderness, the violent State of Nature, and the State of Nature always contains a savage, racial threat.

Noble or vicious?

The cowboy in the myth emerges from the wilderness to leave the State of Nature. As a 'natural' individual he knows about the wilderness, and Indians in the myth represent the wilderness, the original State of Nature. The cowboy has lived with the Indians and fought the Indians. He knows their language, he knows their values, he knows their strategies. Unlike the Indians, however, he is white and rational, so he can leave the wilderness and create a civil society. The Indians are non-white and savage, so they can only remain in the State of Nature and oppose rational destiny.

The Indians are always savage but not always cruel and vicious. The savage/civilized distinction is important to individualism, but there are two versions within individualism of what savagery means. One version has been the most common, where savages are bestial, sub-human. But the other version has always been influential and has been more prominent recently. This is the version of the noble savage, of 'natural' innocence and purity. In neither version of savagery can the savages be seen as rational or compatible with civil society. Otherwise, however, they are quite different versions. One, the bestial version, always serves to endorse rational market relations. This is the version implied in social contract theory, the version of Locke and Hobbes. The State of Nature, full of savages, is a constant state of war, so rational market relations – the social contract – can only be an improvement, a vision of civil society. The other version, the noble version, always serves to criticize the rational market. Savages in the State of Nature were originally kind and generous, and rational market relations corrupt and degrade that innocence.

Indians always symbolize both versions of savagery. Sometimes they are seen as mindless social threats, intractably violent. Other times they are seen as impeccably honest and honorable, and they are always betrayed by lying, corrupt whites. These two kinds of Indians regularly appear in stories of the cowboy myth, and both are derived from the assumptions of individualism. The bestial Indian is derived from Locke and the noble Indian is derived from Rousseau. Both these theorists accepted the new idea of Nature, the idea that enabled the development of individualism. Both theorists asserted a vision of the State of Nature to support their social arguments, with Locke asserting a vision that justified the market and Rousseau asserting a vision that criticized the market. Both these theorists, in addition, based their visions of the State of Nature on assumptions about American Indians, explicitly using the Indians to support their social claims.

The discovery of America changed European thought, and encounters with the Indians shaped that change. These two versions of savagery developed with individualism, and the Indians of America were seen as validating both. According to Ray Allen Billington, Europeans began to think about Indians when America was still a 'little known ... mystery-shrouded land'.

> Yet an image of that distant frontier was already shaping in the minds of Europeans, based not on what they knew but on what they hoped to be there. They saw America as a slightly improved version of the Garden of Eden, overflowing with Nature's bounties, and peopled by a race of superior beings who lived in a perfect state of equality, without want and without masters ... Then, as colonists brought back word of the realities of pioneer life, that image changed, to picture first a land of savagery where barbarous Indians tortured and murdered, then once more an idyllic wonderland where Noble Savages sported in forest bowers, a wonderland rooted not in reality but in the spirit of romanticism that swept Europe in the eighteenth century. (1981: 1)

These two versions of the Indians were always about European issues, particularly the individualist market. Savagery could be seen as a threat or criticism, and Indians became part of arguments about the market. Indians helped shape the individualist conception as well as the romantic reaction, since they could support various positions, as W. Jackson Rushing notes:

> The dichotomous trope of the good/bad Indian has been ubiquitous ... The bad Indian – naked, treacherous, violent, unlearned, sexually licentious, lazy, filthy, and godless – represented a negative standard against which Euro-American peoples could judge themselves ... The other half of the Janus conception, the good Indian, often existed in parallel to the negative image and served an opposite purpose. Heroically nude, trustworthy, peaceful, dignified, communal, industrious, as well as a pantheistic worshiper and an instinctual child of nature, the good Indian symbolized humankind's Arcadian past. (1995: 2)

The Romantic reaction against the market was articulated by Rousseau in the middle of the eighteenth century. He appealed to an idea of Nature, just like the individualists, and he talked about 'natural' individuals, individuals in the State of Nature. But the individualists appealed to the Nature of Newton, the Nature of mathematics and physics. Their 'natural' individuals, as a result, were rational, autonomous, and self-interested. But Rousseau appealed to a different Nature and envisioned different individuals. His was a Nature of beauty and passion, a Nature of wilderness purity. His 'natural' individuals, then, were innocent and pure, kind and decent. They were more concerned with emotional experience than rational calculation, as Lewis Mumford has described:

> Rousseau's Nature was not Newton's Nature – a system of matter and motion ... established in ... mathematical calculations. By Nature Rousseau meant the mountains ... the mantle of vegetation ... the fields ... where a simple peasantry practiced the elementary routine of living ... What made the authority of Rousseau's doctrine so immense was the fact that there awaited the European in America a Nature that was primitive and undefiled. In the purely mythical continent that arose in the European mind, the landscape was untainted by blood and tears, and the Red Indian ... led a life of physical dignity and spiritual austerity. (1953: 22–23)

Indians and social theory

Rousseau saw American Indians as 'naturally' simple and childlike, and he used them for his market critique. They were pastoral beings uncorrupted by greed, and they embodied the noble savage. They were not only honest and trusting, they were also 'naturally' wise, in a way superior to science. 'It is entirely evident,' he wrote, 'that the learned companies of Europe are only public schools of lies. And there are certainly more errors in the Academy of Sciences than in a whole nation of Hurons' (1979: 204). Rousseau used the Indians to suggest an earlier purity, a time of 'natural' innocence among simple, tribal people. He used this Romantic image to criticize the market, and later social theorists adapted this image to the idea of traditional society. Marx, Weber, Durkheim, as we have seen, all used an image of tradition, as constraints on pure self-interest, to criticize market relations. Marx saw tribal society as essentially communal, Weber saw traditional society as more humane, and Durkheim saw tribal society as more cohesive. For all these theorists the idea of tradition suggested what the market lacked, a sense of shared commitments, and they derived their idea of tradition from Rousseau's Romantic imagery, an imagery based on the Indians.

Rousseau envisioned 'natural' individuals who were social and generous, not autonomous and self-interested. These individuals, in his view, were made selfish and greedy by the market, they were not 'naturally' selfish and greedy. He saw the market as corrupting an earlier innocence, and this idea was incorporated into later social theory as the distinction between tradition and reason. Rousseau envisioned this earlier innocence based on what he knew and imagined about American Indians, so the Indians, through Rousseau, influenced the ideas in social theory of traditional cohesion and community. The Indians also influenced the development of a savage/civilized distinction, and through that distinction the development of individualist ideas and market institutions. European encounters with Indians and European ideas about Indians have stimulated and shaped many of our modern social concepts and practices. The symbolic image of the Indians has been instrumental in generating the idea of the social contract, the ideas of Romanticism, the image of the frontier, and the development of social theory. Their conceptual presence is not always obvious and indeed is often well hidden. But the image of Indians, as a symbol of savagery, has shaped our modern world in ways we seldom realize.

It is important, then, to remember that the image of Indian savagery is also an image of racial inferiority. In either version of savagery, noble or bestial, the savages symbolized by the Indians are seen as less than civilized, incapable of rationality. They may be vicious threats or they may be simple critics, but they cannot participate as equals in a rational civil society. They are failures at rationality, and in terms of the Indian as symbol, that failure is based on race. This racial aspect of the idea of savagery was in many ways its central point. If the savages were capable of becoming rational, then they could potentially become owners and equal like all other individuals. But the savage/civilized distinction, as symbolized by the Indians, asserted that the savages were categorically unequal, forever unequal, because they were racially inferior. The savage/civilized distinction, then, could be used to justify conquering and killing non-whites for the sake of market expansion (rational destiny). And it could also be used, to some degree, to justify enslaving non-whites. This was the conceptual message of the savage/civilized distinction, the image of the Indians, and it served a market necessity.

In this sense most of our modern ideas and practices, including social theory, contain this racial assumption. Our modern market ideas and institutions rest on the savage/civilized distinction, the image of the Indians, so they rest on an implicit image of white superiority. This image used to be much more explicit, in American laws, culture, and institutions, and much progress has been made in changing the laws and institutions. But the idea of white superiority is deeply ingrained in the individualist market, a market that has always required an assumption of racial savagery. In many ways the legitimating idea of a civil market rests on racial inequality, just as it rests on sexual inequality. As a result, many aspects of racial discrimination still remain in modern society, and they may be more difficult to purge than we may hope.

In terms of social theory, the image of Indians helped to generate, through Rousseau and the Romantics, the idea of traditional community as opposed to market cynicism. Much of social theory employs an assumption of traditional values to criticize rational self-interest. This traditional-rational distinction is usually intended to suggest that traditional societies are less unequal and oppressive, but it also tends to suggest that traditional societies are incapable of rationality, no matter how humane and decent they may be. In our modern world this traditional-rational distinction has essentially become a Third World-First World distinction, where First World countries have market industry and dominate the planet and Third World countries remain extractive (agriculture, mining) and serve the industry of the First World. The First World-Third World relationship is often exploitative, and First World countries are generally white, while Third World countries are generally non-white. In this sense the traditional-rational distinction, while intended to be critical, may still carry with it the savage/civilized implications, the implications of white exploitation of non-white land in the name of rational destiny.

Slavery versus savagery

America was built on the idea of individual equality as well as on the assumption of racial inequality. Slavery in America was the most obvious and extreme form of racial inequality, but slavery was always contentious, even in the writing of the Constitution, and it finally led to the Civil War. Slavery then ended but severe racial inequality continued in America. Non-whites continued to be denied many legal rights and most political access. Slavery, in effect, was much less compatible with the needs of the market than were other forms of white superiority. Slavery could be dramatically ended and the market would work better, but other forms of racial inequality have supported market relations and still continue today. Slavery was certainly difficult to end – it took a brutal war – but that was a war between new market industry and old traditional agriculture, essentially the feudal South. The Civil War ended the racial inequality that supported feudal agriculture. It did little, however, to end the racial inequality that supported market relations.

Slavery on southern farms meant aristocratic power and privilege. The market was compatible with many forms of inequality – racial, sexual, class – but it could not be compatible with a feudal form of agriculture that generated class privilege. The market needed workers and it could not use slaves. Workers could be hired and fired based on market competition. Owners could have little investment in workers beyond their daily wage. But slaves were a long-term investment and would have to be fed and protected. Slave owners, then, would have to be committed to a stable agrarian economy, a feudal class structure. They could not experiment with new ideas or develop new machines, machines that would require fewer slaves. Moreover, slave owners could never be 'dirtied' by physical work, because physical work was done by slaves. The market, however, needed to glorify work, as an honorable, noble effort – the path to success and salvation, the Protestant ethic. The market needed the idea that workers could become owners, but slavery could not abide the idea that slaves could become owners. The market needed private property, not aristocratic privilege. Slavery was only a problem in America because it contradicted the market, not because it contradicted equality.

The market needs workers that can be dismissed, replaced, and ignored, not workers that need to be housed, fed, and protected. The market can benefit from racial inequality only with workers hired for wages, not with workers owned as slaves. Racial inequality must make it easier to use and discard workers, to use machines to replace workers, to move a business and find new workers. The market needs wage labor, not slave labor. Racial inferiority, then, has to be seen in terms of savagery, not in terms of slavery. If non-white workers are seen as savages, they have no necessary place in market society. They can be used and exploited as workers, but they are seen as less rational so they deserve less pay. They can easily be fired and ignored, even killed, since the issues of equality do not apply. If non-white workers are slaves, however, they become necessary, even crucial, to a slave economy. A rigid class structure must arise, not rational market relations. The market idea of racial inequality had to be based on the Indians as symbols of racial savagery. For the market to work, the racial inequality of slavery had to be replaced by the racial inequality of savagery, the racial inequality of the Indians.

The image of 'savage Indians', as Slotkin argues, has always defined the American idea of race. Indians were a symbolic (non-white) barrier to rational (white) progress. This was the cultural message of the frontier myth, the market myth of origin:

> At the core of the Myth is the belief that economic, moral, and spiritual progress are achieved by the heroic foray of civilized society into the virgin wilderness, and by the conquest and subjugation of wild nature and savage mankind. According to this Myth, the meaning and direction of American history – perhaps of Western history as a whole – is found in the metaphoric representation of history as an extended Indian war. (Slotkin, 1992b: 531)

The image of savage inferiority always had racial overtones. It was never, however, only about race. It was also, and perhaps more importantly, always about class. The savage/civilized distinction could also be used, and was often used, to endorse rational owners over savage workers. The image of 'savage Indians' could be applied to striking workers, and this could justify strong police actions against crazed, irrational savages, savages who could also be seen, through this image, as racially contaminated:

> Behind the mystique of the Indian War lay a concept of social relations that insisted on the racial basis of class difference, and insisted that in a society so divided, strife was unavoidable until the more savage race was wholly exterminated or subjugated. This was a doctrine applied first of all to social relations in industry and the new cities of ... America; and it could also apply to the governance of nonwhite populations beyond the seas, when an imperial America went in search of those new lands and virgin markets. (Slotkin, 1992b: 531)

An assumption of white superiority arose with individualist theory and shaped market institutions. The image of the Indians stimulated and helped define market racial ideas. The underlying distinction between savagery and civilization has influenced many aspects of market social relations, from the idea of the social contract to class conflicts and foreign relations. The issue of race and the issue of savagery are still important today, but they tend to remain hidden in both market and social theory. They are always made clear, however, in the cultural images of the cowboy myth. In particular, the myth always reminds us, as little else does, of the central importance of the image of the Indians to the development of modern society.

The mythical cowboy tames the frontier including the savage Indians. He fulfills the individualist destiny of rational (white) individuals. He creates a civil society by knowing and killing Indians so the wilderness can be seen as empty and equal opportunity as endless. The individualist vision depends on an open frontier, and this is what the cowboy offers as he takes Indian land.

Illustrative films

Images of Indians as bestial savages, simply another wilderness threat, appear in *Drums Along the Mohawk* (1939), *Stagecoach, Winchester '73, Red River, The Searchers, Arrowhead, The Last Wagon, Shalako, The Unforgiven* (1960). Images of Indians as noble savages, but still a barrier to progress, appear in *Broken Arrow, Run of the Arrow, Apache, White Feather* (1955), *A Man Called Horse* (1970), *Dances With Wolves*.

9

SUSTAINING THE WILDERNESS

Abundant Nature

The individualist idea of the market is based on rational Nature. If Nature is rational then individuals are rational and they can build a rational order, a market society. If the universe is sacred, everything is controlled by God or the gods. All natural processes – rain, the seasons, fertility, the crops – may be affected by human social actions because the gods are always watching and judging. If the universe is rational, however, everything works like a mathematical machine. All natural processes follow rational laws, and human social actions can never influence those laws. In a world of rational Nature, no sacred morality can be required. People can change their social order and pursue their private interests with no fear of offending the gods.

The idea of rational Nature, then, encouraged science and technology, innovation and industry. If Nature as an explanatory concept (capital N) is rational and mathematical, then nature as the physical world (small n) can be endlessly manipulated and developed. Respect for sacred tradition can no longer restrict productive innovation. In a sacred universe the gods could impose sacred limits, including limits on production and technology. In a rational universe, however, nothing in the idea of Nature, the legitimating social reference, could impose limits on production and technology. In a rational universe, rational individuals were free of sacred limits, free to maximize their own self-interests. So the rational idea of Nature implicitly assumed an infinite physical nature, an abundant physical environment that individuals could endlessly exploit to maximize their private interests (Wright, 1992).

This vision of infinite Nature was asserted by Isaac Newton in the crowning, defining achievement of the new scientific knowledge. Prior to Newton, Europeans generally believed, as taught by Christianity, that the realm of heaven surrounded and limited the earth and the realm of heaven, including the stars and the planets, was the domain of God.

Humans could study and understand natural events on earth because earth had been made by God to support human life. But humans could never hope to understand the events of the stars and the heavens because that was the realm of God. Humans, then, lived in a limited world. Earth was surrounded by the heavens, and the heavens (the universe) were beyond all human knowledge. The universe, that is, had to be accepted on faith. Newton changed this idea of the universe and defined rational Nature. He argued that the same rational laws, the laws of motion, apply to the heavens and the earth, to stars in the skies just like apples in the trees. This argument removed all sense of limits from the new idea of Nature. Humans could now understand, according to Newton, the infinite reaches of the universe. As a result, at least by implication, they could also conquer and exploit the infinite resources of nature.

The idea of rational Nature justified individualist thought, and it also implied endless natural resources. All of individualist thought, then, all of market theory, assumed a context of abundant nature, an endlessly productive environment. If God was no longer watching, then all the resources of the planet – water, air, land, minerals – were available for productive development with no sacred limits on technology. Further, all rational individuals should have an equal opportunity to exploit those resources as much as possible (market freedom) for their own private interests. These ideas of freedom and equality legitimated market society, and these ideas assume an endlessly abundant environment as implied by rational Nature.

The individualist assumption of abundant nature was supported by the image of America. Just as Newton validated rational Nature in the middle of the seventeenth century, the image of wilderness America validated the individualist ideas derived from rational Nature. America was mysterious, bountiful, abundant – the land of rational destiny, the original State of Nature. America was only a wilderness vision to the Europeans who developed individualism. But they could see it through their concepts as empty and available, offering endless equal opportunity. It was the bountiful gift of rational Nature, the confirmation of individualism, the promise of freedom and equality. The American wilderness seemed to prove exactly what Newton was suggesting: Nature is infinitely rational, and nature is infinitely productive.

In the seventeenth and eighteenth centuries, America indeed seemed infinite, as did the rest of the planet. Most of the world was unknown to Europeans, so it could easily be seen as vast beyond all human knowledge and impervious to all human efforts. After centuries of sacred limits, the individualist euphoria was the removal of all limits. From our modern perspective, however, the individualist market has created a new concern for limits, a concern for environmental limits. When the idea of rational Nature removed the threat of the gods, it created an impetus to industrial production that may now be threatening a viable environment and thus our social future. The vision of a civil market arose when the planet seemed infinite, and that market vision is not very compatible with the idea of a limited planet.

According to market theory, the market can only be civil if it can constantly expand. Smith's idea of the *invisible hand* assumes constant expansion – an endless frontier. The rational idea of Nature assumes an endless frontier, a frontier of rational knowledge. Similarly, the market idea of civility assumes an endless frontier, a frontier of abundant nature. The endless scientific frontier implies an endless productive frontier, so if the productive frontier closes because of environmental limits, all our market ideas as well as our scientific ideas may begin to be threatened.

The modern concern for environmental limits is both familiar and growing. The market has encouraged industrial expansion, and the planet no longer seems impervious. Issues of environmental pollution, resource exhaustion, and species depletion plague our modern world. If the environmental damage continues, it could threaten stability and prosperity as well as human health. The market can only be civil, and any social order can only be viable, if the people in it can live healthy lives. The water and air must be clean and the natural environment must support sufficient production. In our modern world, however, many environmental problems exist. Pollution is damaging the air, the water, the oceans, the soil, the ozone layer, the climate. Forests and wilderness are being destroyed, genetic diversity is being lost, and many productive resources are being depleted. The market requires constant expansion as individuals maximize their private interests. But constant market expansion can damage the supportive environment and thus human health.

In a context of environmental limits, the market cannot endlessly expand. Individuals cannot use their property – the resources of the environment – strictly for their own private interests. Constraints must be put on the use of private property, which means property must become less private. In a context of market relations, government must act to preserve a supportive environment, which means to preserve the hope for a good society. Environmental limits, then, threaten private property by increasing the need for government controls.

The existence of environmental limits must also raise questions about the idea of rational Nature, including scientific knowledge. This idea of Nature encourages scientific technology and technological manipulation. If the universe is a great mathematical machine, then humans can manipulate nature using rational, technical knowledge. This idea implies, however, that none of these human manipulations can threaten human life. If the idea of rational Nature leads humans to damage their environment and threaten their own survival, then the idea of rational Nature must be questioned. The idea of Nature removed all traditional limits and suggested that no rational limits exist. But if the environment is limited, then unconstrained technical manipulation can no longer be seen as rational. Environmental limits imply that market individuals can no longer freely pursue their private self-interests. And such limits also mean that humans must begin to understand their world – their natural environment – in terms of necessary limits. They must begin to question the idea of an infinite mathematical universe and begin to think in terms of sustainable ecological processes.

The problem, of course, is that the market values of freedom and equality depend on the idea of rational Nature, that is, on the idea of a universe without necessary limits and social constraints. In particular, these values of freedom and equality depend upon private property, abundant nature, and constant expansion. The values of freedom and equality presume a good society, a decent, civil society. But this means they also always presume, tacitly, a healthy society with a supportive environment, a society where freedom and equality do not contradict a sustainable, prosperous future. If the environment is limited, then market freedom and equality – industrial expansion – will damage the environment, undermine health, and degrade the future. Our modern market society is justified by individualist ideas, but individualist ideas assume abundant nature – an open frontier on an endless wilderness.

Ecological nature

In cultural imagery, the implicit assumption of abundant nature became a wild frontier. The cowboy myth made this explicit just as it did other implicit assumptions. The market could be civil on a wilderness frontier because of free land, just as Jefferson hoped. The image of the wilderness in the cowboy myth represents rational Nature and also abundant nature. The idea of rational Nature implies abundant nature – an infinite, manipulable universe. But the idea of rational Nature – scientific, technical knowledge – also undermines abundant nature if the planetary environment is limited. This is the dilemma of rational Nature in a context of environmental limits, and the cowboy myth portrays this as the need for endless wilderness.

In social contract theory and the cowboy myth, rational Nature is the original State of Nature, the source of 'natural' freedom and equality and 'natural' private property. But freedom and equality must contradict private property unless the wilderness is endless. The wilderness must always be available to provide private property so the market can be civil through equal opportunity. But the wilderness must also always be pure and unspoiled as an original 'natural' condition, the source of freedom and equality. If the wilderness is endless, 'natural' freedom and equality – the cowboy emerging from the wilderness – will always be compatible with 'natural' private property – the wilderness as endless opportunity. But if the environment is limited, then nature is not abundant, and the social implications of rational Nature – the idea of a civil market – become deeply confused.

For the market to be civil, there must always be an empty, untouched wilderness, a wilderness across the frontier. The wilderness represents original Nature, Nature as the basis of individualism, Nature in its pure condition. Nature is the source of universal truths, the source of rational knowledge, and pure, unspoiled Nature generates freedom and equality. The cowboy myth always makes this clear, but individualist theory seldom does. The wilderness must always be settled to build a civil society, but the wilderness must always remain beyond the open frontier. When the wilderness is gone, as in the urban East, the market becomes corrupt and oppressive and freedom contradicts equality. The wilderness must always exist, pure and unspoiled, so freedom can be compatible with equality and both can be compatible with endless private property.

This image for wilderness purity was always inherent in individualist ideas – the original State of Nature. This image could also be interpreted in two different ways. For Hobbes and Locke this original wilderness was violent and dangerous, so civil society always looked good. Rousseau, however, took this idea of original wilderness and saw it as uncorrupted, a source of original purity. Rousseau's idea of unspoiled Nature offered a market critique, not a market endorsement. The image of original wilderness could serve to correct the market, to condemn its greed and selfishness. Honest, honorable people lived in this wilderness – noble savages – and no society could claim to be civil by despoiling this original condition.

Rousseau adapted the individualist idea of Nature and used it against the market. His romantic critique was effective because the idea of unspoiled Nature was always inherent in market ideas. He essentially turned those ideas against themselves by seeing unspoiled Nature as a source of social decency, not a source of violence. He used his idea of Nature to make a social critique: a good society requires uncorrupted people, people with original community. But his idea of Nature could easily be adapted, and has been adapted, to make an environmental critique: a good society requires uncorrupted nature, nature with original ecology. Rousseau asserted a critical idea of Nature – the market corrupts 'natural' purity (the purity of people) and social decay must follow. Modern environmentalists assert a similar idea – the market corrupts natural purity (the purity of ecology) and social decay must follow.

When environmentalists assert this idea, they are using, just like Rousseau, the idea of the market against itself. The hope for a civil market depends on unspoiled wilderness just as much as it depends on spoiling that wilderness by turning it into private property. On an endless wilderness frontier an unspoiled wilderness is always compatible with private property. But if the environment is limited, unspoiled wilderness cannot survive an endless market quest for private property. This is a tension within market theory, a tension of limited nature. Environmentalists then add a further concern, a concern with health and sustainability.

The image of the wilderness for environmentalists is an image of ecological purity, an image of environmental necessity. The wilderness represents the natural ecological processes needed for a good society. These are the processes needed for clean air, clean water, renewable resources, a chain of life – that is, for sustainable social relations. The wilderness for environmentalists is not just a legitimating market image – the original State of Nature. It is also an image of what must be protected from the onslaught of private property, an image of ecological sanity. It is also, however, a legitimating market image, the image of unspoiled Nature. So the image of the wilderness always offers an effective market critique, a critique from within, just as Rousseau understood. Environmentalists can use the wilderness as an image of ecological necessity, and they can also use the wilderness, from within market concepts, to question the idea of private property.

The cowboy and the wilderness

The cowboy myth portrays all this in its image of endless wilderness. The cowboy represents the civil freedom of private property, but he also represents the 'natural' freedom of unspoiled wilderness. As long as the frontier is open, these two aspects of the cowboy are compatible. When the frontier is closed, however, and the environment is limited, the cowboy begins to contradict himself. More exactly, the cowboy begins to contradict the wilderness, with the cowboy representing freedom and private property and the wilderness representing health and social coherence. From the perspective of the wilderness no society can be civil and decent, free and equal, unless it protects its environment. And from the perspective of the cowboy, no society can be civil and decent, free and equal, unless it protects private property.

The cowboy myth is the market myth of origin, so its images in modern society are resonant and potent. Two of its most potent images are the cowboy and the wilderness, and they have been used against one another in modern environmental politics. Environmentalists use the image of the wilderness to support environmental controls. Government must become more dominant and more restrictive of private property in order to maintain a sustainable ecology. In particular, government must protect, as a symbolic commitment to the environment, what little wilderness remains – the forests, the wetlands, the beaches, the wildlife. The defenders of private property, in turn, use the image of the cowboy to support market freedom and resist government controls. Government must remain limited and nature must remain available for private individual use. Wilderness for its own sake is not as important as the freedom of private property, the freedom symbolized by the cowboy. And environmental dangers, from this perspective, are minimal compared to the dangers of government control.

The early individualists and also the social theorists feared the class inequality of an urban, industrial market. In effect, they feared the loss of free land, a wilderness frontier, as Jefferson, Turner, and Weber all observed. These theorists worried about the social consequences of greed, selfishness, oppression, exploitation, and this theoretical concern has been portrayed in the cowboy myth as the cynical, corrupt East, as well as the modern city of the urban action film. This concern with class led to a mythical contrast between the West and the East, the western possibility of civility and the eastern certainty of despair. All these class concerns still make sense today, but now we have added a new market concern, a concern these earlier theorists missed. We now have to worry about exhausting the environment and damaging our health and our future. This is another social consequence of industrial production and it supports the bleak mythical image of the East. But this new concern also creates a new division in the imagery of the myth, a division in the West itself. Now the cowboy contradicts the wilderness, and the entire market conception begins to collapse. The market can only work with both a cowboy and a wilderness, and the end of abundant nature means they are bitterly opposed.

An image of wilderness purity is built into market legitimacy. As a result, when the market threatens the wilderness, it threatens its own legitimacy. The idea of a good society legitimates market relations, and an image of wilderness purity defines that good society. Rousseau made this point in the name of community, and environmentalists make this point in the name of sustainability. If people cannot be kind and decent, the market cannot be civil. Also, if people cannot be healthy and the future is not secure, the market cannot be civil. The market needs abundant nature, a frontier on the wilderness. Without a wilderness frontier, as Jefferson comments, the market cannot be civil. Environmentalists follow Rousseau and simply extend this argument. Without a wilderness ecology – pristine nature – no society can be civil, and the market destroys the wilderness.

In a context of environmental limits, the market promise of civility contradicts the market commitment to expansion. Private property must be restricted and laissez-faire must end. Government must impose controls to protect human health, but the market idea of a good society requires limited government. Liberals have always endorsed more government, more constraints on market freedom, in the name of market equality. So environmentalists generally join the liberals in support of active government.

Environmentalists, however, often endorse a more active and controlling government than liberals would endorse. The liberal argument supports the market vision, including the market ideas of freedom and equality. Liberals always support private property and do not want government to end market freedom. They only want government to balance freedom and equality in a context of industrial production, a context of owners and workers. The environmental argument, in contrast, supports sustainability, a commitment to health and the future. From the environmental perspective, this commitment could easily require the end of private property, the end, that is, of the market versions of freedom and equality. If a market in private property will degrade health and the future, then the market values of freedom and equality are destructive and must be rejected.

Liberals accept the original market vision and want to adjust it for industry. Environmentalists accept an ecological vision and that vision may contradict the market. Private property is always compatible with the liberal idea of government, but it may not be compatible with the environmental idea of government. This is the implication of environmental limits, the end of abundant nature. If the market destroys the wilderness, and the wilderness, as pristine nature, represents sustainable ecology, then the market cannot create a good society even with liberal adjustments. If private property threatens the environment, and thus human health, then issues of equality and freedom are not our primary concern. The issue of environmental limits makes market institutions suspect, and those institutions must be questioned in the name of wilderness purity.

Marx, of course, wanted to end private property for the sake of social decency. But communist countries have generally been more destructive of the environment than capitalist countries, and capitalist countries have been quite destructive. Communist countries, just like capitalist countries, are committed to a scientific idea of Nature and require constant expansion. Communist countries, however, must follow central plans, and government must create and maintain those plans. As a result, communist governments generally maintained commitments to their central plans even when those plans damaged the environment. In capitalist countries, government can try to protect the environment through constraints on private property. But in communist countries government tends to ignore environmental damage in order to maintain the plan.

The environmental critique of the market, then, is not a communist critique. If private property threatens the environment, socialized property seems to threaten it even more. Both capitalism and communism assume abundant nature. That is, they both assume that no natural limits exist to constrain industrial production. Communism is primarily concerned with issues of equality, and it is just as unconcerned as capitalism with the issue of sustainability. Communism assumes that Nature is rational, just as capitalism does. Thus, both assume an infinite universe and endless resources that science and technology can exploit. The environmental critique is basically a critique of the idea of rational Nature, the idea of a technical, indifferent universe. In this sense, the critique applies to communism as well as capitalism. From the environmental perspective, we must begin to think about our natural world as limited and fragile, not as infinite and impervious. We must think in terms of living in nature, not in terms of manipulating nature. We are not outside an indifferent, mathematical system – rational Nature. Rather, we are inside a delicate ecological system – our environment. From this perspective, however, nature is not abundant, and market freedom and equality cannot make much sense.

Some people concerned with environmental issues have suggested that the entire idea of rationality should be rejected. Rather than rationality we should respect and admire tradition and return if possible to simpler, traditional relations. According to this perspective, the traditions of a traditional society tend to protect the environment, while the science of a rational society tends to destroy the environment. This is a version of the romanticism of tradition and it does not offer much environmental hope. Traditional societies are simply traditional, not ecological, and their traditions may sustain or damage their environment. We tend to know about sustainable traditions because these are societies that may still exist. Societies whose traditions damaged their environment tend to have disappeared, as the Rapa-Nui of Easter Island did when the island became unlivable.

The environmental critique is a critique of tradition as well as of science. It suggests that the universe is neither sacred nor technical. The universe, rather, is ecological, so we must begin to think ecologically. We must develop an ecological idea of reason and build social institutions accordingly. It is not very clear, however, what this would mean. There is not much consensus from the environmental perspective on how to build ecological institutions. What is clear, however, is that the environmental critique is a fundamental threat to the market, to the idea of private property. If the environment is limited, market institutions must be drastically changed, even dismantled, because the market requires expansion into abundant nature. In this modern context deep political tensions must arise, tensions much greater than those between liberals and conservatives. If the environment is limited, the entire market vision becomes incoherent, and legitimating market images – freedom and decency, the cowboy and the wilderness – begin to turn against themselves.

Environmental tensions

The social tensions of environmental limits can often become quite bitter, even violent. Liberals and conservatives always have some common ground – the legitimating market vision – but defenders of the environment and defenders of private property often have no common ground, only mutual hostility. Many issues of environmental protection – clean water, clean air, endangered species, wilderness preservation – conflict with issues of market necessity – jobs, property rights, resource development, limited government. Factories may be closed, forests may not be cut, minerals may not be mined, fish may not be caught, and rivers may not be dammed. Many people support environmental regulation and limits on private property. Many others, however, support limits on government and the freedom of private property.

In America environmentalists have often been threatened and attacked, as David Helvarg reports in *The War Against the Greens* (1994):

> The last six years have seen a startling increase in intimidation, vandalism, and violence directed toward grassroots environmental activists ... ranging from vandalism, assaults, arsons, and shootings to torture, rape, and possibly murder, much of it occurring in rural and low-income communities ... much of the rhetoric and anger springs from a common fount of explosive rage that blames greens for everything from the contracting of resource industries to the closing of the American frontier. (1994: 13–14)

Also, government officials have sometimes been attacked, officials who try to enforce environmental controls. In the West various government agencies are responsible for public lands, and many western ranchers have depended on these lands. Many of these ranchers, then, resent government controls and resist environmental restrictions, particularly wilderness restrictions. As a consequence, many government officials – forest rangers, range managers, wildlife managers – have been threatened, and many government offices have been bombed. Also, active environmentalists have opposed and sabotaged many private efforts to develop public lands. Private interests have used public lands – forests and wilderness – not only for grazing cattle but also for cutting forests, mining minerals, developing recreation, and dumping wastes. To stop these efforts, some private buildings have been burned, some bombs have been sent to corporate officials, and some loggers and other workers have been hurt.

Environmental issues, particularly in the West, are seen as directly threatening to freedom and private property. As government regulations have increased, various anti-government organizations have emerged. Many of these organizations specifically oppose environmental controls – Sagebrush Rebellion, Wise Use, People of the West, and others. These organizations defend private property and they all see themselves as part of a broad 'property rights movement'. They are stridently opposed to the federal government, some much more than others, and their position has been summarized by William Perry Pendley in *War on the West: Government Tyranny on America's Great Frontier*:

> Today the American West is a battleground. The men and women whose families settled the West, who have lived on the land for generations, find themselves besieged by environmental extremists ... The War on the West is about whether Westerners will have an economy, or property rights ... It is about laws and culture and whether the freedoms guaranteed by the Constitution will survive ... They have declared war on the most enduring

symbol of the American West – the cowboy ... Many are starting to realize that the War on the West is, in fact, a war on Western civilization ... For what is at stake is not simply the right of one landowner to his or her property, but the viability of the Fifth Amendment to the Constitution. If, under the rubric of an 'environmental crisis,' environmental extremists can demand that we ignore such a fundamental right, and if the federal government carries out those demands, then not one of us is safe; no freedom is secure. (1995: xvii–xviii, 7, 18–19)

In general, the 'property rights movement' sees environmental controls as undermining freedom, the Constitution, and the cowboy. 'Environmental protection, when taken to extremes, threatens the entire concept of private property' (Pendley, 1995: xv–xvi), as US Senator Kay Bailey Hutchison asserts in a preface to Pendley's book.

Some of these anti-government groups have become virulently hostile and endorse violent resistance. These are the paramilitary groups, groups that call themselves Militias, Patriots, Sovereigns, Nazis. These groups hate other races as well as government, and they generally endorse white male supremacy. They oppose many types of government activity – taxes, gun laws, farm policy, affirmative action, the United Nations – but they started to attract more members and achieve more political legitimacy when they began to include in their anti-government rhetoric attacks on environmental controls. The issue of the environment seems to polarize anger toward government as little else does, probably because it threatens so deeply the basic idea of the market – market freedom and equality. In general, environmental issues tend to give some credibility to anti-government groups, groups that see government as the enemy of freedom. Environmental issues, that is, have given the legitimacy of property rights to otherwise fringe groups – white supremacists, militias, paramilitary groups. These groups have always preached violence against government in defense of individual freedom, and when they shift their rhetoric to support property rights and condemn environmentalists, they tend to attract more members and have more political access. As Helvarg comments, 'a new force on the political Right ... sees environmental change as an imminent threat to free enterprise, private property, and industrial civilization' (1994: 126).

The violence can be considerable, as the *Washington Post* reported in 1995 from a forum in Washington, a forum sponsored by members of Congress:

A county employee in California was beaten and lashed with a knife. A murder contract has been put out on a Montana judge. And a federal wildlife worker received a threat that his wife and children would be bound in barbed wire and stuffed down a well.

These people say they were targets of terror by citizen militias and other right-wing extremist groups that viewed them as part of a sinister government conspiracy to wipe out individual rights and liberties ... law enforcement authorities, government workers, environmentalists ... described incidents of harassment, intimidation, and violence carried out by paramilitary groups. (Kovaleski, 1995: 8A)

These groups endorse violence, white supremacy, and anti-semitism, and their anti-government rhetoric led to the bombing of the federal building in Oklahoma City in 1995 where 168 people died.

The cowboy is a cultural symbol of individual freedom, a symbol of limited government. The cowboy, then, can symbolize resistance to government in the name of freedom and property. The mythical cowboy often breaks the law and fights against government when government becomes corrupt and oppressive. The cowboy can symbolize property rights, the right to develop the wilderness. He can also symbolize other market assumptions, assumptions that generally remain implicit – the assumption of white supremacy, the assumption of male supremacy, and the assumption of necessary violence, violence as an aspect of freedom. The cowboy is the individualist hero, and individualism endorsed racial and sexual inequality as well as deep suspicion of government. The cowboy, then, can be used to support the 'property rights movement' and government resistance generally. He can also be used, as Abby L. Ferber has argued, to support white supremacists:

> Within both Westerns and white supremacist discourse, white heroes are allowed to dispense with the law in obedience to a supposedly higher good which only they are in touch with ... White supremacist discourse ... promises a future of happy white nuclear families, safe, economically secure, and strong, if only white men would stand up and play the part of the traditional Western hero – reclaiming white women, claiming Western territory, and eliminating the non-white threat to white civilization. (1996: 306, 309)

The necessary wilderness

The cowboy image of freedom always depended on the wilderness. The wilderness was the source of freedom and equality as well as the source of strength and honor. The wilderness enabled civil society, a society of private property, and the cowboy had to respect the wilderness as much as private property. The market could only be civil if the wilderness was compatible with private property, and that required an endless frontier, a frontier of equal opportunity. The American version of civility was particularly dependent on the wilderness because wilderness defined the American promise, as Roderick Nash has commented:

> In the early nineteenth century American nationalists began to understand that it was in the *wildness* of its nature that their country was unmatched ... And if, as many suspected, wilderness was the medium though which God spoke most clearly, then America had a distinct moral advantage

over Europe ... In the proportion that civilization disappointed, wilderness appealed. It was the bedrock on which American culture rested (1967: 69, 261)

If wilderness defined the American promise, the West defined the American wilderness. The West was validating grandeur, the bountiful gift of Nature, the vision of freedom and equality. The beauty of the western wilderness symbolized American destiny, so parts of that symbolic wilderness had to be protected. National parks began to be established as the frontier started to close just to protect the legitimating American image of wilderness beauty. America needed the wilderness as a source of private property, but it also needed the wilderness as an image of validating Nature, an image of unspoiled purity. All the early national parks were in the American West, and later national forests and wilderness areas began to be set aside. When wilderness was clearly threatened by constant market expansion, symbolic areas of American wilderness had to be protected, as William Cronon has observed:

> For the Americans who first celebrated it, wilderness was tied to the myth of the frontier ... It is no accident that the movement to set aside national parks and wilderness areas gained real momentum just as laments about the vanishing frontier reached their peak. To protect wilderness was to protect the nation's most sacred myth of origin ... wilderness came to embody the frontier myth, standing for the wild freedom of America's past and seeming to represent a highly attractive natural alternative to the ugly artificiality of modern civilization. (1995: 42)

America needs the cowboy and it also needs the wilderness. The market needs private property but it also needs an open frontier. If nature is not abundant, then the idea of rational Nature may destroy our environment, civility will contradict private property, and the cowboy will turn against the wilderness. Market expansion cannot be sustained, so government must become dominant and curtail market freedom. Individuals must be encouraged to act ecologically, as opposed to strictly privately, and this would require new ideas of nature and freedom as well as new structures of property and government.

Industrial class inequality has always been a serious threat to the market idea of equality and thus to market civility. But the prospect of environmental limits may even be a greater threat because it threatens health and the future. Government can always be used, as Keynes and Durkheim recommend, to negotiate freedom and equality in a context of private property. But government cannot be used to negotiate freedom and ecology in a context of private property. If property is private, the market must expand, but if expansion threatens health and the future, property cannot be private. If the environment is limited, the market cannot be stable or civil and the cowboy cannot be a hero. The cowboy needs a wild frontier to endorse market individualism. If all frontiers are gone, however, and the vision of wilderness is ended, then nature as ecology may be lost. If the market destroys a fragile environment, then the cowboy's individualist freedom can only degrade the future.

Illustrative films

The image of an endless wilderness, where all new people (homesteaders, small ranchers) can and should have an equal chance, appears in most Westerns, including *The Westerner, Destry Rides Again, Shane, The Violent Men, Jubal, Silverado, Heaven's Gate*. The image of a closing wilderness, where the hero must search for a new wilderness in order to remain free, appears in *Man Without a Star, The Magnificent Seven, The Professionals, Butch Cassidy and the Sundance Kid, The Wild Bunch, Lonely Are the Brave*.

CONCLUSION

The Wild Individualist West

Individualism and tradition

The practices of market individualism dominate our modern world –
science, technology, industry, innovation, competition, the rule of law,
private property. Most of the nations of the world today trade in a global
market. The assumptions of individualism characterize this market,
assumptions that tend to undermine lingering traditional values. The
basic assumptions are that individuals are rational, autonomous, and self-
interested. They should have equality before the law and the freedom to
maximize their private property. Innovation in the pursuit of profit
should be encouraged even if it disrupts established social relations and
authority. Social standing and respect should be based strictly on market
success (individual merit), not on sacred tradition, government protection, or class privilege. A commitment to individualism should replace a
commitment to tradition, and the more a nation accepts the market, the
better it will be at industry. Market relations will tend to sweep away a
traditional sense of unity, but they will also tend to lead to industrial prosperity and thus to greater economic independence in the new global
market.

Japan, however, might seem to be a counterexample. It is often seen as
a market success and also as quite traditional. Japan's market success,
however, is also often seen as threatened by its traditions. Those traditions, in the view of many Japanese, discourage competition and innovation and harm the Japanese economy. Many executives and officials, then,
seek to stimulate the Japanese economy by encouraging individualism
and discouraging tradition. They want to direct Japanese workers more
toward private self-interest and less toward group acceptance. Hitachi
is one of many Japanese corporations that are trying to promote individualism, according to Ginny Parker of the Associated Press: 'The major
Japanese appliance maker Hitachi is doing away with three staples
of Japan's straitlaced corporate world. The goal? To promote individual-
ity.' Hitachi is no longer requiring 'somber suits and ties', 'addressing

superiors by their formal titles' ('use personal names instead'), or 'morning calisthenics'.

> Hitachi reasons that allowing its employees to wear casual clothes will bring out their personality and stimulate creativity. And that, the thinking goes, will lead to new ideas about how to improve the company. 'The emphasis is on respect for the individual,' [a company representative] said. 'We want to give employees ... freedom to make their own judgments.' ... It's a big change in a corporate culture that long has preferred – and often demanded – a docile, faceless conformity from its workers. (Parker, 1999: 3C)

According to this article, Hitachi has suffered economically because of its inflexible structure, its commitment to tradition. Other companies have had similar problems, and all are trying similar strategies to encourage individualism.

America is the most successful and dominant market nation at the beginning of the twenty-first century. It is also the market nation most committed to individualism. More than any other market nation, America was constructed on individualist ideas. America had no traditional past, and most of the people who built America were escaping from a traditional past. The market nations of Europe and Asia, in contrast, have all had long traditional pasts. In general, then, these market nations still have some commitments to traditional values that temper their market individualism. Many of these nations, like Japan, seek to become more individualistic for the sake of market success. Most, however, are happy to remain less individualistic than America. They want to retain some traditional concerns for the general social welfare. They do not want to emulate America's commitment to pure private self-interest.

This means that most market nations in the modern world have a stronger traditional sense than America of shared social values and mutual responsibilities. Most market nations, as a result, provide stronger social protections than America for workers, the sick, the elderly, and the unemployed. These nations – France, Germany, England, Japan, Sweden, among others – are more willing to constrain individualism to provide a social safety net, while America is more willing to embrace individualism and provide less social help. America, however, tends to remain the most successful market nation.

America may be more successful because it is more individualistic. But America also tends to be more callous, divided, violent. America is far less supportive than other market nations of unions, health care, and welfare and far more characterized by crime, distrust, and indifference. This is a problem for American society, and it reflects a problem in market theory. Market relations must be based on private self-interests, but those relations also need, in order to be civil, a unifying sense of social morality, a shared commitment to honor. The original market vision, the vision of Locke and Smith, assumed that private self-interests would support a shared morality. This civil market vision, however, assumed agrarian equality, and the market soon led to industrial class inequality. In this industrial context, as the early individualists and the social theorists agreed, private self-interests will tend to lead to oppression and division, not to decency and unity. America is the market nation most committed to individualism, in the sense of private self-interests, and it also seems to be the most uncivil.

Some market nations encourage more individualism as a way to increase success, while America, the most successful market nation, often tries to encourage tradition to temper excessive individualism. Many politicians and commentators in America worry about a loss of morality, and they often recommend more government efforts to enforce more traditional values. They want, for example, more official support for religion in schools as well as for family values (less legal support for gays, lesbians, and abortions). There has also been in recent years a general corporate effort in America to reduce individualism in the workplace by organizing workers in teams. The point of this effort, borrowed from Japan, has been to decrease worker self-interest and encourage more corporate loyalty. According to the theory of team organization, efficiency and quality will be improved and corporate culture will be enhanced. In effect, some American companies have tried to reduce individualism while some Japanese companies have tried to increase individualism. Individualism, however, is deeply entrenched in America, and most of America's effort at teams has been more style than substance. As *The New York Times* reported in 1998, using a Wild West metaphor:

> One can forgive many employees if they don't buy the teamwork pitch ... for all the talk of the need for team players, ... this is the age of the celebrity C.E.O. – the lone ranger who can ride into any troubled company and turn things around, reaping outsized rewards compared with the 'team' that helps him. (Bryant, 1998: 6 (4))

America represents the individualistic side of a basic market tension, a tension between morality and individualism. The unity of the group is always in conflict with the freedom of the individual. In the above *New York Times* article, historian James T. Kloppenberg comments on American society: 'There is a central tension, of hardy individualism and the sense that we're all in it together ... And it can't be resolved' (Bryant, 1998: 6 (4)).

The market myth of origin

The cowboy is the symbol of market individualism in America and around the world. He represents freedom and equality, but he also represents the idea that market freedom and equality can lead to a good society, a civil society. The cowboy, then, also represents a commitment to honor and decency, a commitment to honesty and trust. He emerges from the wilderness to create market society, and his vision of civility is defined by an open frontier. This is the mythical frontier between wilderness and community, and it reflects a theoretical frontier between Nature and society, between the State of Nature and the social contract. It is the frontier between complete 'natural' freedom and rational market freedom, between wilderness purity and private property, between savagery and civilization. The cowboy is a wandering stranger with no traditional rank or lineage. He is the equal of everyone and respectful of everyone, but he is also a 'natural' aristocrat because of his individual ability. He crosses the frontier to build the market, but his honor and freedom depend on the frontier and civility requires his honor and freedom.

The image of the cowboy permeates market culture and particularly American culture. This image is obvious in Westerns, but it also permeates major American novels as Leslie Fiedler has shown. Fiedler analyzes famous novels – *Moby Dick*, *The Sun Also Rises*, *Huckleberry Finn*, among others – and none of these novels, apparently, are about the Wild West. However:

> It is possible to regard these classic works ... as Westerns. Despite certain superficial differences, they are, indeed, all closely related to the pulp stories, the comic-books, movies, and TV shows, in which the cowhand and his sidekick ride in silent communion through a wilderness of sagebrush, rocks, and tumbleweed. (1966: 355)

Robert B. Ray makes a similar point about classic American films, including *The Philadelphia Story*, *Gone With the Wind*, *Casablanca*, *On the Waterfront*, *The Godfather*: 'Many of Classic Hollywood's genre movies, like many of the most important American novels, were thinly camouflaged Westerns' (1985: 75). According to Ray, virtually all American popular films revolve around the 'the traditional American mythology' of the open frontier. In this mythology, the frontier reconciles 'the opposition of natural man versus civilized man' (1985: 59), the values of individualism and the values of social order.

> Grounded in a frontier mythology ... the pure Western reassured its audience about the permanent availability of both sets of values ... It had once been possible to have either the wilderness and its freedom or the community and its security, but, except for a brief moment that had really existed only in American mythology, it had never been possible to have both. (1985: 75, 243)

The Western is the market myth of origin and its imagery pervades market culture, the imagery of the lonesome cowboy and the wild frontier. It endorses market freedom, equal opportunity, private property, limited government, and constant expansion. It also endorses violence as a necessity of freedom, legitimate resistance to government, the need for an endless frontier, the need for wilderness purity, and white male superiority. It assumes that market freedom (maximizing property) is compatible with market equality (equal opportunity). It also assumes that individual inequality (some are richer than others) is compatible with market equality as long as that inequality does not become class privilege. Further, it assumes that constant expansion will always be compatible with wilderness purity, and that a commitment to individual equality is compatible with racial and sexual inequality.

All of these assumptions and endorsements are inherent in market theory, and all of them require the image of an open frontier. In particular, these assumptions and endorsements are based on a market of independent agrarians. This is implicit in legitimating market theory and it is simply made explicit in the market myth of origin. On an open frontier all market individuals can become owner-workers. Class monopolies cannot exist, so everyone can be structurally equal. The *invisible hand* will work, so government can remain limited. Freedom is compatible with equality, and morality is compatible with self-interest. Nature is endlessly abundant, so expansion is compatible with wilderness. Sexual inequality is necessary, so morality will temper self-interest, men can always feel successful, and children will be protected. Racial inequality is necessary, so whites can see wilderness everywhere, land infested only by savages.

When the frontier closes, however, this cowboy market vision begins to collapse. Real equal opportunity will no longer exist, so class monopolies will arise. Freedom will not be compatible with equality, and morality will not be compatible with self-interest. Cynicism and indifference will result, oppression and corruption – the mythical urban East. This is what Smith, Jefferson, and Turner feared and what Marx, Weber, and Durkheim saw. Marx recommended revolution and Weber simply despaired. Durkheim argued, along with Keynes and the liberals, that government could maintain the best aspects of the market – individualism, innovation, criticism – by restricting market freedom and supporting equal opportunity. This would mean that government would have to encourage constant new 'frontiers', 'frontiers' of equal opportunity, and if this were possible the market might be civil even in a context of industry. One aspect of the original frontier, however, might be irreplaceable, the aspect of abundant nature. If the environment is limited, then market expansion will degrade the future. The market can only work and hope to be civil if 'frontiers' of opportunity are available. If all 'frontiers' must come to an end because of a fragile environment, the legitimating market vision can no longer make much sense.

The disruptive cowboy

The image of the frontier is crucial to market individualism. It offers relief from tradition and government, that is, it offers freedom and equality. This market version of the frontier, however, is not the only version. Another version of the frontier is described by Tom R. Sullivan in *Cowboys and Caudillos: Frontier Ideology of the Americas.* Sullivan analyzes Westerns written in Mexico and Latin America. These Latin Westerns are immensely popular in their own countries, but they are set in North America, the American Wild West. They tell stories of frontier heroism, just like American Westerns, but they portray a different kind of frontier and a different kind of hero.

They focus on the image of a caudillo, 'a local or regional strong man', as opposed to the image of a cowboy. The caudillo is a dominant authority on a threatening, disruptive frontier. The cowboy, in contrast, is an equal individual on a promising, enabling frontier. The equal cowboy sees the frontier as a place of social hope, while the dominant caudillo sees the frontier as a place of social danger. From the Latin perspective the frontier should be avoided and fenced off; the community or the hacienda should be enclosed in walls. The frontier is 'a brutal place where the weak are devoured by the strong, and where justice must be imposed (and reimposed) through forceful action by representatives of legal and traditional authority from far off centers of power' (Sullivan, 1990: 31). In these stories the social focus is inward toward family, duty, and stability, not outward toward profit, opportunity, and change. The caudillo represents traditional order and the frontier represents a threat to that order. The cowboy, in contrast, rejects traditional order. He seeks to build civil freedom and equality from wild frontier opportunity:

> Latin Americans like popular narratives that inculcate a sense of distrust concerning frontiers ... [They] look toward the center, not toward the hinterlands, for civilizing power ... In Anglo America ... they imagined a frontiersman, later to become a cowboy, as a nomadic man of violence ... venturing ever into land which he would pacify in order to make way for liberty, democracy, and the colonies. (1990: 159–160)

As Sullivan suggests, the concept of the 'frontier' does not necessarily imply individualist values. It may imply, as it does in Latin America, values that oppose individualism. The market version of the frontier, however, reflects individualist values. Indeed, it is probably the central cultural image that captures and symbolizes individualism. The discovery of the American wilderness supported the ideas of individualism, but the experience of the American frontier did not generate individualism. The ideas of individualism, rather, generated the market idea of an open frontier, the idea of the American frontier. The market needed a promising image of a 'natural' but civil society. This society had to stay close to Nature, the Nature of freedom and equality, so it would not become too organized, too committed to privilege and duty. This was the frontier required by individualism, the frontier that resisted authority. The cowboy always had to ride away or settle down. He could never become a powerful, dominant authority, a caudillo.

The cowboy must defy authority as an autonomous individual. He represents the market need for entrepreneurs, for innovation, criticism, change. He endorses limited government on the open frontier. Government should only provide order and otherwise maximize market freedom. The cowboy can be free with honor on the open frontier, but he can only be defiant and disruptive in the modern industrial city. Our urban action hero must always resist established authority, the rigidity and injustice of bureaucracy. He breaks the rules and ignores orders, but only his defiant individualism can defeat the villains or save the world. He is usually denounced as a 'cowboy' by his bureaucratic superiors. Clint Eastwood's character, Dirty Harry, is condemned for his 'cowboy' tactics, and so is Bruce Willis, who plays a policeman in *Die Hard*. The pilot in *Top Gun* (1986), played by Tom Cruise, constantly breaks the rules and has the call sign 'Maverick'. In *Armageddon*, Bruce Willis and his drilling crew are dismissed as 'space cowboys' by soldiers, astronauts, and bureaucrats. In each case, however, only these 'cowboy' heroes can defeat the villains or save the world.

The image of the defiant 'cowboy' is also common in business and journalism. It is used to suggest an anti-bureaucrat, someone who breaks the rules, takes risks, and gets things done regardless of proper procedures. In the context of business, this is an innovator or entrepreneur. Such a 'cowboy' individualist can sometimes be quite successful in the market and sometimes quite destructive. The market always needs innovators and entrepreneurs, but it also always needs bureaucracy and stability. Innovation always leads to disruption and instability while bureaucracy always leads to certainty and accountability. In an article in *The Economist* the image of the 'cowboy' suggests market change:

> Timeshare-holiday operators have a cowboy image. But life on the wild frontier has produced the most innovative marketing in the travel industry ... The future of the whole travel industry may lie with quick-on-the-draw market-makers on what used to be cowboy territory. ('Timeshare holidays...' 1996: 53–54)

However, when John Scully was brought in to rescue Apple Computers, he made the company more bureaucratic: 'The heroic style – the lone cowboy on horseback – is not the figure we worship at Apple anymore' (Kanter, 1989: 51).

As Rosabeth Moss Kanter has said, 'The cowboy strains limits, but the corporation manager has to establish limits' (1989, 360). The 'cowboy' disrupts bureaucracy, and the industrial market runs on bureaucracy. The 'cowboy' is individualist freedom and equality, and bureaucracy is rules and hierarchy. Bureaucracy increases industrial efficiency but it degrades the civil vision. The bureaucrat is a necessary market character, necessary for industrial organization. And the 'cowboy' is also a necessary character, necessary for industrial vitality, necessary for freedom.

The bureaucrat runs the industrial market, but the 'cowboy' legitimates that market, even as he often disrupts it. The market needs rules and hierarchy, acceptance and submission, but it also needs criticism and innovation, disruption and change. It needs bureaucratic obedience but also private self-interest. Before the rational market, virtually all societies – traditional societies – *only* needed acceptance and submission, rules and obedience. The market still needs these as all societies do, but the market also needs, more uniquely, criticism, innovation, and self-interest. In other words, the market always needs a 'cowboy' just as it always needs a bureaucrat. The 'cowboy' is the individual who makes industry possible and bureaucracy necessary, but he hates cities and bureaucracy. The 'cowboy' built the industrial city, but he built it with individualist freedom, and that vision of freedom requires an open frontier.

Market culture developed frontier stories to reflect individualist values, and these stories became the market myth of origin, the myth of the Wild West. The cowboy in the mythical West is a central market character, but he has always appeared more clearly in culture than he ever has in theory. The image of the cowboy reflects the market need for an open frontier, and this need for a frontier has also appeared much more clearly in culture than it ever has in theory. The cowboy myth illustrates most individualist assumptions, and many of those assumptions were always left out of the theory. So the myth can help us to understand the ideas of individualism and the problems of market society. The original vision of the market, the vision the myth portrays, was not a vision of urban industry, and many of the original values of the market are threatened by urban industry. Our theories can help us understand the issues of market industry, but the cowboy myth can help us understand legitimating market values. The assumptions of the market may no longer make much sense, but the image of the mythical West can still seem to make sense, as Joyce Carol Oates has remarked:

> As the actual lived lives of most Americans become even more complex and fractured and, in a sense, more generic and impersonal, we yearn for 'authentic' experiences, if only in fantasy. The West still beckons seductively as our region of myth and the testing ground of what remains of the American spirit. (1999: 32)

The 'cowboy' embodies the proud individualism of civil market society, the individualism of freedom and equality. He also embodies the sordid individualism of violence as freedom, white male superiority, and environmental abuse. He dramatizes market individualism in all its various dimensions, and some of those dimensions, he suggests, imply oppression and injustice. He tells us what we want to hear about a free and equal life, life on the open frontier. And he also tells us, particularly in the urban action film, that the modern industrial market is incompatible with a free and equal life. He always rides tall in the saddle across the wilderness frontier, and as he does he explains individualism in terms of the Wild West.

REFERENCES

Arieli, Yehoshua (1964) *Individualism and Nationalism in American Ideology.* Cambridge: Harvard University Press.

Astor, Michael (1997) 'Brazilians riding rough 'n'tough – American-style rodeos stampeding nation', *Chicago Tribune*, 7 February: 8.

Billington, Ray Allen (1981) *Land of Savagery, Land of Promise: The European Image of the American Frontier in the Nineteenth Century.* New York: Norton.

Bryant, Adam (1998) 'All for one, one for all and every man for himself', *New York Times*, 22 February: 1, 6 (4).

Buscombe, Edward (ed.) (1988) *The BFI Companion to the Western.* New York: Atheneum.

Cockburn, Alexander (1993) 'Time to admit we've lost the drug war', *Arizona Republic*, 31 October: 3C.

Coontz, Stephanie (1992) *The Way We Never Were: American Families and the Nostalgia Trap.* New York: Basic Books.

'Cowboy in the Black Forest: Daimler chief's tough style isn't business as usual for Europe', (1996) *New York Times*, 16 January: 1C.

Cronon, William (1995) 'The trouble with wilderness', *New York Times Magazine*, 13 August: 42.

Deloria, Vine, Jr (1989) *Custer Died for Your Sins: An Indian Manifesto* (originally published 1969). Norman, Oklahoma: University of Oklahoma Press.

Deloria, Vine, Jr (1995) *Red Earth, White Lies: Native Americans and the Myth of Scientific Fact.* New York, NY: Scribner.

Drinnon, Richard (1980) *Facing West: The Metaphysics of Indian-Hating and Empire Building.* Minneapolis: University of Minnesota Press.

Dunn, John (1969) *The Political Thought of John Locke: An Historical Account of the Argument of the 'Two Treatises of Government'.* New York: Cambridge University Press.

Durkheim, Emile (1964) *The Division of Labor in Society* (George Simpson, trans.). New York: Free Press (first published 1893).

Durkheim, Emile (1951) *Suicide: A Study in Sociology.* New York: The Free Press.

Durkheim, Emile (1972) *Selected Writings* (Anthony Giddens, ed., trans., Introduction). New York: Cambridge University Press.

Fallaci, Oriana (1972) 'Kissinger: An Interview with Oriana Fallaci'. *New Republic*, 167 (23): 17–22.

Ferber, Abby L. (1996) '"The White Bastion": the western myth in contemporary white supremacist discourse', in Will Wright and Steven Kaplan (eds), *The Image of the American West: Selected Papers of the 1996 Conference of Society for the Interdisciplinary Study of Social Imagery.* Pueblo, CO: University of Southern Colorado, pp. 302–311.

Fiedler, Leslie A. (1966) *Love and Death in the American Novel.* New York: Stein and Day.

FitzGerald, Frances (1972) *Fire in the Lake: The Vietnamese and the Americans in Vietnam*. Boston: Little, Brown.

Gaddis, John Lewis (1999) 'Living in Candlestick Park'. *Atlantic Monthly*, April: 65–74.

Gerth, H.H. and C. Wright Mills (1958) 'Introduction: the man and his work', in H.H. Gerth and C. Wright Mills (eds), *From Max Weber: Essays in Sociology*. New York: Oxford University Press.

Griswold, A. Whitney (1948) *Farming and Democracy*. New Haven: Yale University Press.

Halevy, Elie (1966) *The Growth of Philosophic Radicalism*. Boston: Beacon Press.

Harrington, Mona (1999) *Care and Equality: Inventing a New Family Politics*. New York: Alfred A. Knopf.

Heilbroner, Robert L. (1980) *The Worldly Philosophers: The Lives, Times, and Ideas of the Great Economic Thinkers*. New York: Touchstone.

Helvarg, David (1994) *The War Against the Greens: The 'Wise-Use' Movement, the New Right, and Anti-environmental Violence*. San Francisco: Sierra Club Books.

Hobbes, Thomas (1958) *Leviathan*. Indianapolis: Liberal Arts Press (first published 1651).

Hodgen, Margaret (1964) *Early Anthropology in the Sixteenth and Seventeenth Centuries*. Philadelphia: University of Pennsylvania Press.

Jefferson, Thomas (1903) 'To James Madison – Dec. 20, 1787', in Andrew A. Lipscomb and Albert Bergh (eds), *The Writings of Thomas Jefferson*, vol. VI. Washington, DC: Thomas Jefferson Memorial Association, pp. 385–392.

Kanter, Rosabeth Moss (1989) *When Giants Learn to Dance*. New York: Touchstone.

Karp, Jonathan (1996) 'Indians and cowboys: businessmen query India's free-market reforms', *Far Eastern Economic Review*, 159: 78–79.

Kluger, Richard (1996) *Ashes to Ashes: America's Hundred-Year Cigarette War, the Public Health, and the Unabashed Triumph of Philip Morris*. New York: Alfred A. Knopf.

Knox, Don (2000) 'Internet still ripe for lawlessness', *Denver Post*, 11 February: 1I.

Kovaleski, Serge F. (1995) 'Officials at forum describe alleged militia threat', *Washington Post*, 12 July: 8A.

Lachmann, Richard (1987) *From Manor to Market: Structural Change in England, 1536–1640*. Madison: University of Wisconsin Press.

Larson, Elizabeth (1993) 'Cowboys (and cowgirls) are our weakness', *Utne Reader*, September/October: 26–27, 30.

Laslett, Peter (1960) 'Introduction', in John Locke, *Two Treatises of Government* (Peter Laslett, ed.), New York: Cambridge University Press.

Lemann, Nicholas (1999a) *The Big Test: The Secret History of the American Meritocracy*. New York: Farrar, Strauss, and Giroux.

Lemann, Nicholas (1999b) 'Behind the SAT', *Newsweek*, 134: 52–57.

Lemos, Ramon M. (1978) *Hobbes and Locke: Power and Consent*. Athens, GA: University of Georgia Press.

Locke, John (1966) *Two Treatises on Government* (Peter Laslett, ed. and Introduction). New York: Cambridge University Press (first published 1690).

Marsden, Michael T. (1974) 'Savior in the Saddle: the sagebrush testament', in Jack Nachbar (ed.), *Focus on the Western*. Englewood Cliffs, NJ: Prentice Hall, pp. 101–112.

Miller, John C. (1960) *The Federalist Era*. New York: Harper and Brothers.

Miniclier, Kit (1998) 'Sky's not the limit', *Denver Post*, 2 August: 1B.

Mumford, Lewis (1953) *The Golden Day: A Study in American Literature and Culture.* New York: Dover Publications.

Nash, Roderick (1967) *Wilderness and the American Mind.* New Haven: Yale University Press.

Oates, Joyce Carol (1999) 'Wearing out the West', *New York Review of Books*, 46: 30–32.

Parker, Ginny (1999) 'Hitachi relaxes dress code as part of makeover', *Denver Post*, 17 April: 3C.

Pendley, William Perry (1995) *War on the West: Government Tyranny on America's Great Frontier.* Washington, DC: Regnery Publications.

Petty, Terrence (1996) 'Rootin' Tootin' Teutons Still Thrill to Old West in Modern Germany', *Los Angeles Times*, 21 July: 9A (Bulldog edition).

Pletsch, Carl (1990) 'Restoration, ideology, and revolution', in *Proceedings of the Folger Institute, Center for the History of British Political Thought*, vol. 4. The Folger Shakespeare Library, pp. 105–147.

Ray, Robert (1985) *A Certain Tendency of the Hollywood Cinema, 1930–1980.* Princeton: Princeton University Press.

Rogers, John (1997) '"Star Wars" redux: may the force be with you once again', *Pueblo Chieftain*, 24 January: 4D.

Rotundo, E. Anthony (1993) *American Manhood: Transformations in Masculinity from the Revolution to the Modern Era.* New York: Basic Books.

Rousseau, Jean-Jacques (1979) *Emile: or On Education* (Allan Bloom, trans.). New York: Basic Books (first published 1762).

Rushing, W. Jackson (1995) *Native American Art and the New York Avant-Garde: A History of Cultural Primitivism.* Austin: University of Texas Press.

Seligman, Adam B. (1992) *The Idea of Civil Society.* New York: Free Press.

Slotkin, Richard (1992a) *The Fatal Environment: The Myth of the Frontier in the Age of Industrialization 1800–1890.* New York: Harper Collins.

Slotkin, Richard (1992b) *Gunfighter Nation: The Myth of the Frontier in Twentieth-Century America.* New York: Atheneum.

Smith, Adam (1911) *The Theory of Moral Sentiments* (Dugald Stewart, ed.). London: G. Bell and Sons (first published 1759).

Smith, Adam (1977) *An Inquiry into the Nature and Causes of The Wealth of Nations.* London: J.M. Dent & Sons (first published 1776).

Soule, George (1952) *Ideas of the Great Economists.* New York: New American Library.

Sullivan, Tom R. (1990) *Cowboys and Caudillos: Frontier Ideology of the Americas.* Bowling Green, OH: Bowling Green State University Popular Press.

Taylor, Overton H. (1960) *A History of Economic Thought: Social Ideals and Economic Theories from Quesnay to Keynes.* New York: McGraw-Hill.

Techi, Cecelia (1994) *High Lonesome: The American Culture of Country Music.* Chapel Hill: University of North Carolina Press.

'Timeshare holidays: the $5 billion swapshops' (1996), *Economist*, 340: 53–54.

Tompkins, Jane (1992) *West of Everything: The Inner Life of Westerns.* Oxford: Oxford University Press.

Turner, Fredrick Jackson (1949) 'The significance of the frontier in American history' (first published in 1893), in George Rogers Taylor (ed.), *The Turner Thesis Concerning the Role of the Frontier in American History.* Boston: D. C. Heath and Co., pp. 1–18.

'US Brings to Bosnia Tactics that Tamed Wild West' (1995), *Wall Street Journal*, 27 December: 7.

Warshow, Robert (1962) *The Immediate Experience: Movies, Comics, Theatre and Other Aspects of Popular Culture*. Garden City, NY: Doubleday.

Weber, Max (1951) *The Religion of China: Confucianism and Taoism* (H. H. Gerth, trans. and ed.). Glencoe, IL: Free Press.

Weber, Max (1952) *Ancient Judaism* (H. H. Gerth and D. Martindale, trans. and eds). Glencoe, IL: Free Press.

Weber, Max (1958a) *From Max Weber: Essays in Sociology* (H. H. Gerth and C. Wright Mills, eds). New York: Oxford University Press.

Weber, Max (1958b) *The Protestant Ethic and the Spirit of Capitalism* (Talcott Parsons, trans.). New York: Charles Scribner's Sons.

Weber, Max (1958c) *The Religion of India: The Sociology of Hinduism and Buddhism* (H. H. Gerth and D. Martindale, trans. and eds). Glencoe, IL: Free Press.

Williams, William Appleman (1969) *The Roots of the Modern American Empire: A Study of the Growth and Shaping of Social Consciousness in a Marketplace Society*. New York: Vintage Books.

Williamson, Chilton (1960) *American Suffrage from Property to Democracy 1760–1860*. Princeton: Princeton University Press.

Wood, Gordon S. (1992) *The Radicalism of the American Revolution*. New York: Alfred A. Knopf.

Wright, Will (1975) *Sixguns and Society: A Structural Study of the Western*. Berkeley: University of California Press.

Wright, Will (1992) *Wild Knowledge: Science, Language, and Social Life in a Fragile Environment*. Minneapolis: University of Minnesota Press.

INDEX

FILM AND TELEVISION INDEX